Competitive Comrades

Competitive Comrades

Career Incentives and Student
Strategies in China

SUSAN L. SHIRK

UNIVERSITY OF CALIFORNIA PRESS
Berkeley   Los Angeles   London

University of California Press
Berkeley and Los Angeles, California

University of California Press, Ltd.
London, England

© 1982 by
The Regents of the University of California
Printed in the United States of America

1   2   3   4   5   6   7   8   9

Library of Congress Cataloging in Publication Data

Shirk, Susan L.
Competitive comrades.

Bibliography: p.
Includes index.
1. Students—China—Political activity.
2. Socialism and youth—China.   I. Title.
LA1133.7.S553   371.8′1′091   81-2772
   ISBN 0-520-04299-9   AACR2

For my mother and my father

Contents

Preface

I began my research on China during the Cultural Revolution, when the fervor of the young Red Guards and the boldness of Mao Zedong's attack on bureaucratism and privilege offered the prospect of a socialist society without the autocracy of the Soviet Union. I chose to study schools because they played a crucial role in the Maoist revolutionary experiment, and because at a distance it appeared that the schools had been successful in promoting social equality and replacing competition with cooperation. I wanted to learn how the Chinese revolutionary regime was able to change human ideals and behavior through the schools.

When I took a closer look at Chinese schools—through refugee interviews in 1971 and 1978, and visits to China in 1971, the spring and fall of 1978, and 1980—I found a mixed picture. On one side, students had assimilated revolutionary values; even the young people who had chosen to abandon China for Hong Kong were imbued with the ethics of egalitarianism and collectivism. On the other side, however, student behavior had not been transformed in the way the leadership had intended. To be sure, high school students participated in political activities and strove for political as well as intellectual achievement. But beneath the surface of compliance was an informal student society that did not conform with the Maoist vision. Instead of cooperation there was intense individual competition. Students tended to avoid activists rather than confide in them. Private friendships, which were officially discouraged as detracting from public commitments, were strengthened rather than weakened. Public criticism had become a mutually protective ritual or an arena for personal competition.

Confronted by these perplexing findings, my analysis shifted focus. I tried to discover why these patterns of behavior prevailed in schools by tracing their logic back to the principle of educational selection and job promotion employed by the revolutionary regime. The Chinese communists, like the leaders of revolutionary movements elsewhere, have tried to transform society by controlling the distribution of career opportunities and by awarding the best opportunities to those who exemplify the moral virtues of the movement. I developed the concept of "virtuocracy" to describe such revolutionary movements and regimes. Thus what began as a research project to study how the Chinese regime succeeded in using schools to transform student motivations and social relations in the end became a book about the unintended consequences of virtuocracy.

Is there a moral in this story? Do the inadvertent negative consequences of the efforts of Chinese communist revolutionaries to transform society mean that all such efforts are doomed to failure? Of course, there are many different dimensions on which revolutions could be evaluated, and their impact on human relations is only one. But even if we consider only this one dimension of change, I do not view this book as an argument against all political efforts at social reform. Its moral is not that people will always act the same, no matter what political leaders do. Quite the opposite: The example of Chinese students demonstrates how people adapt to an environment structured by government policies. The lesson is not that all political attempts to change behavior will inevitably flounder on the intransigence of human nature, but rather that political designs for social change must continually take into account the way individuals pursue their own objectives. These designs should take account of people's real-life concerns rather than stubbornly denying them. People's motivations are always mixed; no one is purely selfish or totally altruistic. The failures of revolutionary regimes like that in China should teach us more about the complicated relationship between individual action and collective goals, rather than promote self-congratulation about the current state of human affairs in our own societies or cynicism about the possibilities for changing it. Cynicism, like dogmatism, can be an excuse for intellectual laziness. We err as much in expecting too little of people as in expecting too much of them.

I cannot begin to name all the friends, colleagues, and teachers who have read parts of this work and helped me clarify my thinking on various subjects. They will recognize their contributions and know how much I appreciate their help.

The following persons sacrificed many valuable hours reading the entire manuscript (some of them reading it several times over) and offering me their criticism and encouragement: Lucian Pye, Nathaniel Beck, Ellen Comisso, Bruce Cumings, Ronald Dore, Victor Falkenheim, Norman Frohlich, Peter Gourevitch, Alex Inkeles, Gary

Jacobson, Kenneth Jowitt, David Laitin, Kristin Luker, Thomas Metzger, John Meyer, Andrew Nathan, Joe Oppenheimer, Martin Shapiro, Arthur Stinchcombe, Ezra Vogel, Martin Whyte, and Aaron Wildavsky. I am deeply grateful to them.

My research assistant, Leung Kei-kit, helped with interviewing and offered sensitive insights into the nature of Chinese society. Gene Tanke gave me valuable editorial assistance. The manuscript was typed by Michele Wenzel, Susan Ehlinger, Judy Lyman, and Barbara Ziering. Blu Jacobs and Susan Watts helped me care for my daughter Lucy so that I was able to write.

Earlier versions of parts of the book were given as papers or talks at the Annual Meeting of the Association for Asian Studies (1975), The Workshop on the Pursuit of Political Interest in the PRC at the University of Michigan (1977), and the California Seminar on Contemporary China at the University of California, Berkeley (1977). I am grateful for the comments I received on these occasions.

I wish to thank the Foreign Area Fellowship Program, the Joint Committee on Contemporary China of the Social Science Research Council and American Council of Learned Societies, the Hoover Institution, the Institute for the Study of World Politics, the Universities Service Centre, and the Committee on Research of the University of California, San Diego, for financial and institutional support.

Most of all, I wish to thank my husband, Samuel Popkin, who gave me clear-headed criticism and the support I needed to complete this project.

ABBREVIATIONS

Full publication data for the following sources, and for all books and articles cited in short form in the notes to the text, are given in the Bibliography, pp. 209-217.

TRANSLATION AND NEWS SERVICE SERIALS

CB   *Current Background.* Hong Kong: United States Consulate General.

FBIS   *Foreign Broadcast Information Service, Daily Report, People's Republic of China.* Springfield, Va.: National Technical Information Service, United States Department of Commerce.

JPRS   *Joint Publications Research Service, Translations on Communist China: Political and Sociological.* Springfield, Va.: National Technical Information Service, United States Department of Commerce.

NCNA   *New China News Agency.* Beijing.

SCMM   *Selections from China Mainland Magazines.* (Renamed in 1973 as *Selections from People's Republic of China Magazines.*) Hong Kong: United States Consulate General.

SCMP   *Survey of the China Mainland Press.* (Renamed in 1973 as *Survey of the People's Republic of China Press.*) Hong Kong: United States Consulate General.

URS   *Union Research Service.* Hong Kong: Union Research Institute.

Xinhua   *Xinhua News Service.* Beijing.

CHINESE PERIODICALS

BR   *Beijing Review.* Beijing.

GRRB   *Gongren ribao.* (Worker's Daily). Beijing.

GMRB   *Guangming ribao.* (Bright Daily). Beijing.

HQ   *Hong qi.* (Red Flag). Beijing.

JFRB   *Jiefang ribao.* (Liberation Daily). Shanghai.

RMJY   *Renmin jiaoyu.* (People's Education). Beijing.

RMRB   *Renmin ribao.* (People's Daily). Beijing.

ZGQN   *Zhongguo qingnian.* (Chinese Youth). Beijing.

ZGQNB   *Zhongguo qingnian bao.* (Chinese Youth Journal.) Beijing.

ZXS   *Zhongxuesheng.* (High School Student). Beijing.

1

INTRODUCTION

When Mao Zedong led the People's Liberation Army into Peking in 1949, he came with ambitious plans for rebuilding a new state structure, for modernizing the economy, and for promoting national self-reliance. These plans were not narrowly political; they embodied a moral vision of Chinese society transformed. Everyone, down to the illiterate peasant, would be given equal respect; individuals would co-operate rather than compete, abandoning self-interest for a desire to serve the people and the nation. The scope and boldness of Mao's vision was awesome; it captured the imagination of people around the world. In contrast to most governments and politicians, Mao wanted not merely to manage people but to transform them: to make them more virtuous in their motivations, commitments, and relationships. And he believed that it was the responsibility of the Communist Party and the socialist state to bring about this transformation.[1]

Of course, Mao was not the first political thinker to view the moral reform of citizens as the province of political leadership. Philosophers from Plato and Mencius to Lenin and Gramsci have concerned themselves with moral progress as a political goal. Benjamin Schwartz has pointed out that Mao's political moralism resembled the moral viewpoint of Rousseau, who asserted that the state should be "the moralizing agency of human society."[2] Mao's political moralism also was rooted in ancient Chinese tradition. A fundamental tenet of Confucian philosophy was that government officials should be responsible for establishing

1. On the distinction between transformative and accommodative political philosphies in China, see Metzger, *Escape from Predicament.* On Mao's vision, see Schwartz, "Modernization and the Maoist Vision," pp. 3-19; Schurmann, *Ideology and Organization in Communist China,* esp. pp. 17-104; Munro, *The Concept of Man in Contemporary China;* Watson, "A Revolution to Touch Men's Souls," pp. 291-330; and Solomon, *Mao's Revolution,* esp. pp. 160-242.
2. Schwartz, "The Reign of Virtue," p. 160.

virtue (*de*) throughout the realm. Leaders of other revolutionary movements—such as Puritanism, Fascism, the *satyagraha* movement in India, the Islamic revival movement in Iran, as well as Marxist movements in Russia and elsewhere—have advocated total ethical transformations. Mao's effort in China attracted particular interest because it was a moral crusade that had succeeded in winning power and was pursuing revolutionary virtue in an explicit and determined manner.

Since the death of Mao and the defeat of his radical allies in 1976, talk about moral transformation is seldom heard in China, and political pessimism and cynicism are more pervasive than most observers would have believed possible. For example, when students in one college class were asked on a Young Communist League questionnaire whether they believed in socialism, capitalism, religion, atheism, or fatalism, 85 percent chose fatalism; no one chose socialism.[3] Newspaper articles with titles like "On Some Understanding of the Superiority of the Socialist System" and "Marching into the 1980s Full of Confidence" try to defend socialism and the Communist Party to those who have fundamental doubts about them.[4] Other articles describe shocking examples of cynicism. For example, when a youth fell through the ice while skating, bystanders taunted the soldiers who tried to save him by shouting, "Big soldiers, run fast, it's time to win a medal," and an old worker who joined in the rescue was ridiculed with the statement, "He just wants to join the Party."[5] Poignant short stories portray estrangement between friends, parents and children, and husbands and wives as being caused by the requirement that people keep watch over one another and criticize one another.[6]

Thirty years after Liberation we must conclude that Mao's crusade to transform social consciousness has left people more rather than less alienated from one another and from the state. Why? What happened to the dream? How can we explain the failure of the attempts to realize the Maoist vision?

This book seeks an answer to these questions by looking at the city high school as a microcosm of Chinese society.[7] My research on student

3. Personal interview, Chongqing, March 1980.
4. *Jiefang ribao* (JFRB), January 12, 1980, *Summary of World Broadcasts—Far East* (BBC: Reading, Eng.), BII, 1-3, January 17, 1980; *Gongren ribao* (GRRB), January 19, 1980, *Foreign Broadcast Information Service* (FBIS), February 4, 1980, L8-10. Also see Linda Matthew's report in *The Los Angeles Times*, May 5, 1980.
5. *Renmin ribao* (RMRB), January 19, 1980; and GRRB, January 31, 1980.
6. Lu Xinhua, and others, *The Wounded.*
7. The direct translation of the Chinese term for secondary school, *zhongxue*, is "middle school," but I shall use the use the more familiar American term "high school" instead.

behavior in urban high schools between 1960 and 1966 can help us discover the roots of the alienation, pessimism, and cynicism so pervasive today. My interviews with former high school students show that although the communist government was effective in motivating students to strive for political as well as intellectual achievement, to participate in political activities, and to accept many political goals as legitimate, beneath the surface of compliance lay an informal society which did not conform with the Maoist vision. Instead of cooperation there was intense individual competition, both academic and political. Students did not admire and confide in political activists, they avoided them. The regime's political demands on individuals strengthened rather than weakened friendship ties. Students kept their public criticism on a superficial level in order to protect their friends. Mutual criticism deteriorated into a superficial ritual or an arena for political competition. The effort to purify students' motivations and reform their relations with their classmates produced not the "revolutionary successors" Mao had hoped for, but wary adapters concerned with protecting their own futures.[8]

These discrepancies between ideal and actual behavior ought not to be explained away with facile conclusions about the intractability of human nature or the universal imperatives of economic growth. Rather we must seek an explanation in the nature of revolutionary regimes, such as that which Mao founded, which attempt to purify society. A fundamental contradiction between moral transformation and the tactics devised to realize it has plagued China and other revolutionary regimes.

A revolutionary movement coming to power (whether as a communist state as in China, a fascist one as in Germany, or a theocratic one as in Iran) tries to transform society by taking control of the distribution of opportunities and awarding the best opportunities to those who exemplify the moral virtues of the movement.[9] But as Michael Walzer says, by using state power in this way, the leaders "freeze" the revolution.[10] The noble endeavor is stymied not just by the practicalities of political rule and economic development or by the gradual erosion of

8. Lifton, *Thought Reform*, p. 401.
9. On Iran's decision to admit students to institutions of higher learning according to their political and religious beliefs, see *Le Monde*, May 2, 1980, p. 3.
10. "Revolutionaries do seize state power and use it against their opponents and also against those passive, withdrawn or simply fearful people whom the Puritans called 'neuters.' They use the state, or try to use it, to short-cut those long and difficult processes by which men are brought to pledge themselves to collective repression; they use it to reinforce

revolutionary enthusiasm, but by the social ramifications of the pursuit of virtue.[11]

A revolutionary regime that attempts to bring about the moral transformation of society by awarding life chances to the virtuous may be called a "virtuocracy." The contrast is with "meritocracies," which select according to professional or intellectual ability, and "feodocracies," which select according to ascriptive status such as caste, class origin, race, native region, sex, or religious origin. In a virtuocracy, merit and ascriptive status sometimes enter into occupational selection and promotion, but a person's moral worth remains a major criterion. No one who is not judged morally acceptable is allowed to succeed. As the Chinese put it, everyone must be "red" as well as expert (politically correct as well as skilled in work).

On the basis of evidence drawn from Chinese high schools, this book argues that *much behavior in communist systems is the result of government policies which attempt to transform behavior by awarding opportunities in part on the basis of political virtue. Virtuocracy generates acrimonious political competition, avoidance of activists, retreat into the private world of friends and family, and disaffection from the regime.*

Although this book focuses on the behavioral consequences of virtuocratic selection and promotion policies in China, it suggests that there are certain basic features of virtuocratic policies which shape behavior in all communist states and perhaps in fascist and theocratic states as well. These policies establish the incentives and rules of the game in institutions, and this policy-generated structure shapes the behavior of the people within them.[12] From this perspective, the political culture of different organizations represents the informal, adaptive

---

the new and generally underdeveloped mechanisms of mutual surveillance. But when revolutionaries do this, they 'freeze' the revolution, as St. Just realized too late. They themselves deny the possibilities of genuine self-government; they reestablish an older pattern of public conformity and private vice, and then the committed conscience of the saint and the virtuous will of the citizen become once again the 'neutral and inwardly divided mind' of the subject." Walzer, "The Revolutionary Uses of Repression," p. 129.

11. Other approaches to understanding the decline of post-revolutionary systems are the decay of "movement regimes," discused in Tucker, "Toward a Comparative Politics of Movement Regimes," 281-289; and the movement of policy cycles impelled by popular response to normative, coercive, and remunerative policies, discussed in Skinner and Winckler, "Compliance Succession in Rural Communist China." Also see the essays in Chalmers Johnson, ed., *Change in Communist Systems*.

12. Other scholars of contemporary Chinese society have analyzed the effect on behavior of organizational incentive systems. The best examples are Martin King Whyte, *Small*

postures that emerge in response to the formal policies and structures of the regime.[13] I focus on adaptive behavior and analyze the ways in which students pursued their objectives in the school setting.[14] At the core of the "neo-rationalist" or "economic" approach to understanding political culture, which this book employs, is the assumption of maximizing behavior. As articulated by John Zysman, "In its simplest form the neo-rationalistic logic states that within the limits of his knowledge, his habits, and his skill, the individual will adjust his behavior to maximize his utility in whatever currency the organization deals."[15] It is important to emphasize that *this approach does not assume that people are conscious of their efforts to maximize or that they can articulate the reasons for the patterns in their behavior.*[16] I claim only that the systematic patterns of Chinese individual behavior *are explicable* as personal attempts to increase benefits and reduce costs in an environment where the rewards and penalties associated with various actions are established by regime policies.

Groups and Political Rituals in China; Parish and Whyte, *Village and Family in Rural China;* and Oksenberg, "Getting Ahead and Along in Communist China," pp. 304-347. Andrew Nathan has suggested to me in correspondence that the study of structural effects on behavior seems particularly productive in the Chinese setting because Chinese society has so many organizations consciously designed by the government.

13. I adopt Kenneth Jowitt's definition of political culture: "The set of informal, adaptive postures—behavioral and attitudinal—that emerge in response to and interact with the set of formal definitions—ideological, policy, and institutional—that characterize a given level of society." Jowitt, "An Organizational Approach to the Study of Political Culture," p. 1173. Also see Pateman, "Political Culture, Political Structure, and Political Change," p. 292.

14. Kenneth Prewitt has criticized political socialization research for its concentration on general orientations (diffuse support, political efficacy, etc.), because such research "cannot deal adequately with such critical factors as social setting, institutional opportunities for political expression, and the perception of the concrete (though ever shifting) political agenda as it affects individual lives." Prewitt argues that since "the political behavior of the adult is largely a function of how he copes with the opportunities and constraints of these situations," political socialization research should focus on what he calls "choice behavior in educational settings." Prewitt, "Some Doubts about Political Socialization Research," pp. 111-113. John Zysman argues that it is possible to study changes in behavior without collecting data on whether there were accompanying changes in underlying attitudes, or whether "a wide variety of behaviors can be supported by any collection of attitudes." *Political Strategies for Industrial Order,* p. 172. Also critical of the focus on attitudes and the exclusion of overt behavior in political culture research are Fagen, *The Transformation of Political Culture in Cuba,* pp. 5-6, and Levine, "Issues in the Study of Culture and Politics," p. 95.

15. For the neo-rationalist approach, see Zysman, *Political Strategies,* p. 167. On the economic approach, see Barry, *Sociologists, Economists, and Democracy;* Becker, *The Economic Approach to Human Behavior;* Downs, *An Economic Theory of Democracy;* Hirschman, *Exit, Voice, and Loyalty;* and Popkin, *The Rational Peasant.*

16. Becker, *The Economic Approach,* p. 7.

This focus on virtuocratic structures contrasts with the cultural approach to understanding contemporary behavior in China. In that view, deviations from ideal behavior are explained by the persistence of traditional cultural orientations, "feudal remnants" which in time will disappear. Lenin complained about the constant struggle against "the forces and traditions of the old society." "The force of habit of millions and tens of millions is a most terrible force," he wrote. Mao shared Lenin's frustration at the strong hold of tradition on popular beliefs and behavior. He predicted that "the influence of the bourgeoisie and of the intellectuals who come from the old society will remain in our country for a long time."[17]

The Western social scientists who employ cultural explanations focus on what is unique about China and emphasize the influence on contemporary political outcomes of psychological orientations passed down from generation to generation.[18] From this perspective, if the communist leadership has not been successful in using schools to create new social patterns, it is because traditional orientations continue to be taught through family socialization.[19]

Although the influence of traditional modes of thought on modern Chinese life is undeniable, I believe that policy-generated structure is a better starting point for understanding behavior. For one thing, studying traditional values does not help us understand why people behave differently in different institutional settings in China; it does not help explain, for example, why political competition is more intense at public schools than at private schools. Analyzing the opportunity structures and incentives that characterize different institutions can explain such variations in behavior. For another, a focus on tradition does not explain why behavioral tendencies that the communist leadership views

17. Lenin, "Left-Wing Communism, An Infantile Disorder," and Mao Zedong, "On the Correct Handling of Contradictions Among the People," quoted in Watson, "A Revolution to Touch Men's Souls," p. 292.

18. Pye, *The Spirit of Chinese Politics;* and Solomon, *Mao's Revolution.* The "exceptionalist" character of cultural explanations is criticized in Jowitt, "An Organizational Approach," p. 1172. Although cultural explanations do not require a focus on the *unique* elements in a culture, they do have an exceptionalist tendency and have generated disappointingly little cross-cultural theory.

19. This explanation is rejected by Susan Lampland Woodward in her analysis of Yugoslav schools: "Any failure of schools to teach the habits necessary to socialist democracy, at least as it is defined in Yugoslavia, should not be attributed to the interference of other agents of socialization but rather to the nature of the learning situation in schools itself." Woodward, "Socialization for Self-management in Yugoslav Schools," pp. 307-308.

as problems—avoidance of activists, for example—have not diminished at all but have actually grown stronger over the years since 1949. When we look at educational and occupational selection policies we find that these changes in behavior over time correspond to changes in policy. Finally, a structural approach to behavior can help us refine cultural explanations by facilitating comparisons between societies with similar policies and different cultural traditions.

But, the reader may ask, what about motivations? Surely the motives underlying behavior are the product of cultural tradition. The question of motivation is indeed a subtle and difficult one. Life goals obviously are influenced by traditional norms passed down through early family experiences, and there is variation within as well as across cultural lines. But certain fundamental objectives are held in common by people in all societies. I assume that most people in China, adults and students alike, operate according to three such basic objectives:

1. *Economic advancement:* A job that enables one to provide financially for one's family. In contemporary China a good "future" (*qiantu*) is defined as university admission, a city job, and avoiding transfer to the countryside.

2. *Moral integrity:* The feeling that one is a good citizen and has done the right thing.

3. *Peer respect:* Good personal relations with one's colleagues.

Although these objectives constitute assumptions and not empirical findings, they accord with the life concerns expressed in interviews by people in various job and school situations in China and by the refugees in Hong Kong who were the main data base for this study. The former high school students I interviewed in Hong Kong, like all people in China and elsewhere, had mixed motives. They tried to reconcile ambition with patriotism and friendship. They wanted to serve the revolution, but preferred to do so in the city rather than in the countryside— not only because the city offered greater comfort, status, and income but also because it provided opportunities for more significant public service. Although the demands of friendship and ambition often clashed, students tried to serve both by playing the "popularity game" and the "career game" simultaneously.

When faced with a difficult choice, then, how did people determine their priorities? Although cultural orientations and personality differences certainly influence the way people rank their goals, such rankings are also influenced by the real-life situations people face. In the case of urban high school students, the opportunity structure pitted them in competition with one another, and in many circumstances forced them to put ambition ahead of idealism and sociability.

An opportunity structure like the one confronted by Chinese students was bound to produce intense competition and ambitiousness, whether educational and occupational selection was according to virtue or merit.[20] Four characteristics of the structure account for this. First, *limited opportunities.* Although elite positions are limited in all societies, in systems like the Chinese one which restrict the growth of the modern urban sector by controlling labor allocation and rural-urban migration, the desirable opportunities are particularly scarce. In China there were only a small number of university places or city jobs open every year (see Chapter Two).

Second, *high stakes.* When the level of economic development is low, as it is in China, there is a vast disparity in living standards between the countryside and the city. The social consensus therefore is that status divides along the rural-urban line: the winners work in the city while the losers have to struggle along in the countryside. The status gap is further widened by the prohibition on migration. No rural dweller can improve his or her lot by moving legally to the city, or even to a more prosperous village. The combination of migration controls and rural-urban living standard disparity produces a "stratification of places."[21]

Third, *monolithic distribution.* If, as in China, all school and job assignments are made by state organs and there is no education or job market, then people have only one mobility game open to them and can find no alternative routes to success. In state socialist societies there is a particularly tight fit not only between education and occupational role but also between occupation and access to goods and status. Occupation is the primary determinant not only of income but also of access to consumer goods, social respect, and political influence. The official and the scientist obtain a large share of consumption opportunities, status, and power, whereas the peasant, although officially the object of social

20. Feodocratic systems should be less competitive because people know that their career horizons are narrowed by birth. A caste system presents the most extreme case of mobility limited by ascription.

21. This is a notion proposed by John R. Logan in "Growth, Politics, and Stratification of Places," pp. 404-416, and applied to the Soviet Union by Victor Zaslavsky, in "Socioeconomic Inequality and Changes in Soviet Ideology," p. 391.

honor, is in fact socially disparaged, poor, and powerless. Occupational identification is made even more conspicuous when, as in China, there is little job mobility. Because careers in such systems offer few second chances or possibilities for freelancing, school graduation is the decisive point of career embarcation, and the contest of ambitions is focused on the school arena.

Fourth, *apportionment by localities.* Competition is direct and face-to-face if opportunities are apportioned to local units, as they are in China. Each province is given a quota of freshman places at the top national universities, and it then apportions these places to cities and localities. Provincial and municipal universities admit only local students. Except at the level of national university graduates, people are assigned to jobs within their home province, and labor allocation is carried out by cities and counties.

The following chapters describe what happens in Chinese urban high schools when students pursue the goals of career, integrity, and popularity in the context of a highly competitive opportunity structure. Certain aspects of studenthood—for instance, the secret life of friendships or the hostility shown toward apple-polishers who play up to teachers—may sound familiar to readers, especially those who attended highly competitive schools or parochial schools which attempted to improve students morally as well as intellectually. But even in the strictest parochial school, there is no powerful vanguard youth organization like the Young Communist League, and being caught in a sin cannot ruin your future as it can in China. The overall pattern of student behavior described here is distinctive to virtuocracies, systems in which moral evaluations play a major role in occupational selection.

THE NATURE OF VIRTUOCRACY

A regime's choice of a principle of occupational selection has profound social ramifications. The choice of a rule for distributing life chances is made very explicit in an authoritarian system like China's where government bodies make all decisions about education and job selection and promotion. The political leadership must decide on what basis to assign opportunities: Randomly? By election? By birth? By professional or intellectual merit? By moral virtue? In practice there are three major principles of occupational selection: virtuocracy, meritocracy, and feodocracy.[22] These three principles parallel Max Weber's three types of authority: charismatic (virtuocratic), bureaucratic (meritocratic), and traditional (feodocratic).[23] Each principle implies different rules of the game in which people pursue their interests, as well as a different mode of managing the frustrations of those who fail to win the more desirable opportunities.

The decision of China's revolutionary leadership to introduce virtuocratic criteria into educational and occupational selection and promotion served its political interests in several ways. First, it was a means of promoting *social transformation*. By rewarding political commitment, activism, egalitarian attitudes, and cooperative behavior, the leaders of the Chinese revolution created incentives for all citizens to realize these moral values.

Second, virtuocracy facilitated the leadership's efforts at *mass mobilization for economic development*. Mao hoped, as Benjamin Schwartz notes, that "the energy of organized virtue" would spur economic development like a kind of collectivist Protestant ethic.[24] If a country is poor, economically backward, and lacking in capital and technical resources, one way to increase productivity is by mobilizing underutilized labor power. Mass mobilization strategies of economic growth lend themselves to virtuocratic appeals. Calls for volunteers to work longer, harder, or under more arduous conditions offer chances for people to prove their virtue. When rewarding virtue rather than merit, organizations can more easily substitute cheap moral rewards for expensive material ones; the virtuous are satisfied—or have to pretend to be satisfied—with praise.

Third, virtuocracy contributed to the processes of *political consolida-*

22. A complete list of distribution rules would have to include lottery, election, need, age, physical strength, first-come first-served, as well as rotation or the market. It is also important to distinguish between merit tests based on educational achievement or aptitude, and tests based on actual work accomplishments (such as piecework). For a proposal on the use of educational lotteries (in combination with merit tests) see Dore, *The Diploma Disease,* p. 161.

23. Weber, "The Types of Authority and Imperative Co-ordination," in *The Theory of Social and Economic Organization*, pp. 324–423. I have coined the term "virtuocracy" because there is no existing word for a society in which individuals are selected for occupational roles according to a definition of moral excellence. The term "aristocracy" originally meant rule by the "best," but it implies intellectual (or even artistic) abilities more than moral rectitude, and by now it has come to mean rule by individuals of high birth. The term "feodocracy" has been adopted for lack of a more satisfactory word to describe societies in which roles are assigned according to ascriptive status.

24. Schwartz, "The Reign of Virtue," p. 165.

tion and legitimation in a post-revolutionary regime. Virtuocracy is more amenable to political control than distribution according to merit or ascriptive status. Because the definition of political virtue is broad and flexible, elites can use the virtue standard to promote their loyal supporters and demote those who are potential threats.[25] By creating a political ladder of success they can isolate and weaken commercial, intellectual, or aristocratic groups whose power derives in part from meritocratic or feodocratic status values. For example, the requirement that all college applicants be evaluated politically as well as academically made it more difficult for Chinese intellectuals to build power bases in schools and universities, and more difficult for bourgeois families to maintain their traditional advantage over worker and peasant families. Virtuocracy was also an important source of legitimation for the new regime. Like Weber's charisma, virtue is a personal quality that people value. The revolutionary leaders had already won popular respect by risking their lives to overthrow the wicked oppressors of the old regime. The egalitarianism of virtuocracy further legitimated the new system; the groups—in the Chinese case, the peasants and workers—who did poorly under the old meritocratic or feodocratic rules saw that virtuocracy improved their chances to get ahead.[26]

Thus distribution of rewards according to virtue became a central element in the Chinese revolutionary leaders' strategy of social transformation, development mobilization, and political legitimation, which together formed a coherent alternative to Western capitalist strategy and came to be called by Western observers "the Maoist model."[27] The consequences of virtuocracy, however, were not what Mao and his

25. The political advantages of virtuocratic distribution rules at the early stages of social transformation are vividly illustrated in *Fanshen*, the study of land-reform in Long Bow village by William Hinton. When cadres began to distribute property according to degree of political participation (a form of virtue), rather than according to economic status or need, as formerly, they motivated people to speak out against the landlords and commit themselves to the revolutionary cause. The unfortunate consequence of such a tactic, however, was that people later came to assume that most people who speak out in meetings are opportunists seeking personal profit from activism.

26. Despite the appeal of virtuocracy in the early stages of revolutionary change, the influence of meritocratic principles remained strong even among those who knew they would benefit from virtuocratic distribution. An autobiographical novel about land reform has a poor peasant saying, "You say I can get the land without paying for it and I don't believe it. . . . I always tell my children not to take anything they haven't worked for. I don't want them to be led astray." Chen Yuan-tsung, *The Dragon's Village*, pp. 88-89.

27. For a clear statement of the Maoist model, see Weisskopf, "The Relevance of the Chinese Experience," pp. 283-318. Also see Oksenberg (ed.), *China's Developmental Experience*.

colleagues had intended. The widespread social distrust and political cynicism found today in China are the unintended consequences of virtuocracy.

What is it about virtuocracy that alienates citizens from one another and from the political system? Most important are the *vague and subjective standards* of virtuocratic selection. It is intrinsically difficult to devise a clear and objective test of moral excellence. It may be easy to distinguish the very bad from the very good, but degrees of virtue are much more difficult to measure.[28] All the standards of virtue must be behavioral; for example, how enthusiastically people respond to political directives, what they say in meetings and mutual criticism sessions, and whether they volunteer for unpleasant tasks. The only way to judge thought is to evaluate behavior. But one can assess behavior in different ways: by taking the act at face value, by examining the effect of the act, or by inferring the motive. For example, if one wanted to criticize someone with good outward behavior, one could claim that the action had a bad effect and thereby "demonstrate" that the person had bad intentions.[29] Because the link between thought and behavior is problematical, people in a virtuocracy run the constant risk of having their actions misconstrued.

The vagueness and subjectivity of virtuocratic standards also make it easy to cheat. Compare a contest of political purity to one of intellectual or athletic skill: in a mathematics examination or a foot race the standards are clear and unambiguous, and the outcome can be seen by

28. The complexity of political evaluations is illustrated by the "Guiding Principles for Inner-Party Political Life" adopted at the Fifth Plenary Session of the 11th Communist Party Central Committee in early 1980. The document explains that there are not just two types of political mistakes (those representing non-antagonistic and antagonistic contradictions), but *four* types that must be clearly distinguished. "One must not describe *an ordinary mistake in work or a mistake in understanding* as a political mistake; nor must one describe *an ordinary political mistake* as a mistake in political line; or mix up *a mistake in political line which is still in the nature of inner-Party struggle* with *a question of a counter-revolutionary nature involving attempts to subvert the Party and the socialist state." Beijing Review* (BR), No. 14 (April 7, 1980), p. 17. The document offers no clues to help Party members classify the mistakes of their comrades.

29. "Lin Piao and the Gang of Four first accused the person whom they wanted to destroy and then tried to find the proof from that person's works, which means they found out the author's motive and then tried to create some effect to prove it. Thus they could sentence anyone to political death or academic death at will. . . . Sometimes the objective effect doesn't reflect the motive at all. Social life is so complicated that a good motive can sometimes bring the opposite result." "Eliminate the Obstacles to Academic Democracy," *Guangming ribao* (GMRB), March 10, 1979, in *Xinhua yuebao*, Number 4 (1979), p. 15.

everyone; contestants cannot win by fakery.[30] In political competition not only do the rewards for the virtuous inevitably attract opportunists, but it is impossible to devise a method for screening all of them out. This difficulty of distinguishing sincere activists from false ones creates considerable leeway for arbitrary judgments on the part of the authorities.[31] Even sincere believers become disillusioned as they watch undeserving opportunists being promoted through favoritism.

The subjectivity of evaluations of virtue means that political competition comes to be pervaded by attempts to play up to authority. Virtuocracy breeds sycophancy. People try to demonstrate their moral zeal by flattering teachers or bosses, or by giving them critical reports of the behavior of their fellow students or fellow workers. Strategies that are conspicuously oriented toward pleasing superiors alienate activists from their peers.

A second divisive feature of the virtue contest is that it is judged by *judges within the group* as well as by outside authorities. In the Chinese virtuocracy, a person's moral character is evaluated by fellow-students and fellow-workers as well as by teachers or bosses. The politically excellent are recruited into vanguard organizations, the Young Communist League (YCL) and Chinese Communist Party (CCP); membership in these elite groups signifies moral achievement and is weighed heavily in university admissions and promotion to leadership posts. League and Party members are supposed to be well-integrated in the peer group, to be the friends and helpmates of their classmates or colleagues. But they are also supposed to make moral judgments of their peers: they are consulted when the authorities write the annual or biannual conduct evaluations that are placed in each individual's permanent dossier; and they decide who is pure enough to enter the League

30. According to interviews with coaches at two prominent athletic schools in China, during the Cultural Revolution when the use of the back door (favoritism for the children of officials and other people with personal influence) became rampant at regular schools and universities, it was much less common at sports schools. The coaches said that because athletes had to prove their skill in public contests, it was impossible for an official to pass off an untalented son or daughter as deserving of admission.

31. As one articulate expression of post-Cultural Revolution dissent, the "Li Yizhe Poster," put it: "It is not always easy to distinguish between fragrant flowers and poisonous weeds, between the correct and the erroneous, and between the revolutionary and the counterrevolutionary." And under a democratic dictatorship, if you demand democracy, they will label you a reactionary; and if you are a reactionary you must be deprived of democracy. Therefore it was said that the fixing of political labels cannot be left to leaders: "There must be a process; and the distinction must be tested by time." Li Yizhe, "Concerning Socialist Democracy and Legal System," quoted in Shirk, "Going Against the Tide," pp. 91–97.

or the Party. Because they have the power of political judges, League and Party activists are avoided by many of their peers; for the security-conscious, the safest strategy is to keep activists at arm's length.

The subjectivity of evaluations of virtue permits virtuocratic elites within institutions to monopolize the advantages of the chosen few. Party and League members are supposed to take the lead in revolution-izing all citizens, but in fact they are reluctant to throw open the doors and relinquish the distinction of vanguard status. In Max Weber's terms the Leninist strategy of social transformation produces a "sect" (an organization only for the truly righteous who must pass a moral trial to enter) superimposed upon a "church" (an organization open to all, which is aimed at trying to save all souls, to make everyone a better person).[32] The members of the sect (the Party and the Youth League) are responsible for leading the church (the entire society, or at least "the people" who are capable of salvation). The members of the elite sect, who are understandably ambivalent about diluting their special advan-tages by expanding group membership, find it easier to exclude people under virtuocratic rules than if they were operating under objective meritocratic or feodocratic standards. When aspirants find their actions continually unappreciated and misinterpreted by the activist peers who judge them, they grow frustrated and alienatated from the system.

The third feature of virtuocratic competition that generates social conflict is *mutual harm*. In China and other revolutionary regimes virtuous behavior necessarily involves actions that are costly to one's colleagues. The virtuous are required to watch over others and criticize them in public discussions and to authorities. Mutual criticism and mutual surveillance (what the Puritans called "holy watching") are central to the political life of virtuocratic institutions.[33] Everyone is expected to participate. As one respondent said in an interview: "The main difference in the political atmosphere on the Mainland and Tai-wan is that on Taiwan everybody was supposed to say nothing while on the Mainland everybody was supposed to say something." People de-velop peer-group norms to minimize the divisiveness of public criticism meetings: it is considered proper to criticize only the minor shortcom-ings of fellow group members. But those trying to prove their virtue

32. Weber, "The Protestant Sects and the Spirit of Capitalism," in *From Max Weber*, pp. 302-322.
33. Walzer, "The Revolutionary Uses of Repression," p. 127.

have to violate these norms; in order to make themselves look good, they have to make others look bad.

THE INSTABILITY OF VIRTUOCRACY

Because it is so difficult to devise standards for evaluating virtue that are not vague or subjective, meritocratic and ascriptive (feodocratic) selection criteria appear increasingly attractive after a revolution, and groups who stand to gain under these other criteria become increasingly able to advocate their use. Examination scores and family class origin are much clearer and simpler bases for recruitment and promotion than revolutionary virtue. This explains why, as Max Weber predicted, "In its pure form charismatic authority may be said to exist only in the process of originating. It cannot remain stable, but becomes either traditionalized or rationalized, or a combination of both."[34]

Virtuocracy has almost always been tempered by meritocracy in post-Liberation China. Few communist leaders in China have ever advocated the total abandonment of intellectual and professional standards in educational selection or job promotion. Managing the economy requires competent specialists, and it is hard to justify providing an expensive university education to someone with no intellectual aptitude or giving responsibility to someone with no professional ability. Even Mao, who went further than anyone else in stressing the primacy of virtue over skill, urged followers to "unite politics and technology," and derided people "who have no practical knowledge" as "pseudo-red, empty-headed politicos."[35] Because virtue was so difficult to measure, in practice school admissions officers were sometimes able to put more weight on academic achievement, and factory managers intent on fulfilling production targets could emphasize skill and productivity in work assignments. They justified themselves by arguing that students and professionals expressed their "redness" through their expertness.[36]

The vagueness of virtuocratic standards also fostered the application

34. Weber, "The Routinization of Charisma," in *The Theory of Social and Economic Organization,* p. 364.
35. Ch'en (ed.), *Mao Papers,* p. 57.
36. The traditional Confucian examinations for aspiring officials were an example of testing for virtue by examining intellectual merit. Although Weber describes the Confucian examination as a "cultural examination for the literati," he points out that it had a "magical-charismatic meaning" in the eyes of the masses. Max Weber, "The Chinese Literati," in *From Max Weber,* p. 433.

of ascriptive tests: it is harder to fake and easier to check a family pedigree than a moral character.[37] Mao and other communist leaders in China have never been able to decide which was the better measure of political purity, individual political performance or class background. The good class-background category includes the children of cadres, as well as the children of workers, poor and lower-middle peasants, soldiers, and revolutionary martyrs. The regime's ambiguous "class policy," which has been summarized in the slogans "pay attention to origin (*chengfen*) but don't pay exclusive attention to it," and "put the major stress on political behavior (*biaoxian*)," has been interpreted differently over the years (see Chapter Two).

Given the subjective standards of virtue and the populist egalitarianism of Marxism, it is possible for certain groups in a communist system to claim that although "redness" is achieved and not innate, some people are more predisposed to it than others.[38] Compensatory favoritism for groups that were discriminated against in the past seems fair and just. Virtuocratic elites who claim to represent the "have-nots" can include themselves on the list of those who deserve special treatment. In China, cadres and soldiers by identifying themselves with peasants and workers have been able to take advantage of "affirmative action" policies. Communist officials are always tempted to establish policies that judge people solely on the basis of birth status. But if they succumb to this temptation, those not blessed with "natural redness" will give up in defeat, and one of the most powerful weapons of social transformation will have to be abandoned.[39] Therefore a virtuocratic elite attempts to maintain an ambiguous combination of behavioral and ascriptive criteria for distributing opportunities.

Although authorities are supposed to consider both family background and personal virtue when making selection decisions, because of the problem of vague and subjective standards of virtue, in practice they

37. Although the assignment of family background labels could be complicated, the Party was able to establish rules that made it relatively simple and unambiguous. See Chapter Two.

38. Weber views charisma as a "personal gift" which cannot be taught or trained: "Either it exists *in nuce,* or it is infiltrated through magical rebirth—otherwise it cannot be attained." "The Chinese Literati," p. 426. The Chinese position on the possibility of attaining redness is more ambiguous. It asserts that people are malleable and that revolutionary values can be instilled in schools, but that differences in family environment make some people more inclined than others to accept these values.

39. Weber would call "natural redness" "hereditary charisma." See "The Routinization of Charisma," in *The Theory of Social and Economic Organization,* p. 368.

often pay more attention to background.[40] As one of the Chinese victims of the use of the class background criterion complained during the Cultural Revolution:

> "Look at origin and look at behavior also" in reality cannot avoid slipping into the mire of "only look at origin, don't look at behavior." *It's very easy to check on origin.* One flip of the file, the problem's solved and all's well. . . . *Checking a person's [political] behavior is rather bothersome,* particularly for that impossible group of doubters who don't believe either your everyday behavior or your behavior in times of turmoil; who doubt both your past and your present behavior and even prepare to doubt your future behavior; who doubt until you die and only then, when the coffin lid is closed, give a final verdict. Some people, moreover, have *no fixed criteria for evaluating behavior.*[41]

Throughout the years between 1949 and 1966 an ambiguous combination of selection criteria governed people's behavior. Career success depended on three factors: political record, academic (or professional) achievement, and family class label. The shifts in emphasis among these criteria (detailed in Chapter Two), which reflected elite conflicts over national priorities, produced widespread uncertainty. Because local authorities had trouble keeping up with the current formula, there was often a lag between policy and practice which further confounded people's difficulties in applying policies to their own situations. Students and employees also had to consider the biases of their teachers and supervisors, some of whom tended to favor the academic or work achievers while others favored political activists.

In the 1966-1969 Cultural Revolution, Mao Zedong completely rewrote the rules of the game. The Cultural Revolution was Mao's crash treatment for what he diagnosed as the serious ills of Chinese society seventeen years after Liberation: the growth of bureaucratic elitism and class privilege, the persistence of bourgeois intellectual and social values, and the degeneration of revolutionary élan into privatism and opportunistic competition. He diagnosed these maladies not as lingering vestiges of tradition but as products of the current system. His

40. This is in large part a matter of self-protection. If anyone rewards too many people of bad class background, he or she runs the risk of being criticized for showing a wavering attitude toward class struggle.

41. (Emphasis not in the original.) "Chushen lun" (Origin Theory), *Zhongxue wenge bao* (Middle School Cultural Revolution News), February 1967, in White, *The Politics of Class and Class Origin,* p. 79.

prescription, however, was to intensify rather than dismantle virtuocracy. He advocated more political education, more mutual criticism and struggle, more mass mobilization, and more promotion of activists as the remedies for China's problems. By strengthening virtuocracy he hoped to counter the threats of meritocracy and feodocracy. He saw meritocratic practices, such as academic examinations and industrial skill hierarchies, as the basis for the continuing dominance of bourgeois groups in academic and economic institutions. He viewed the feodocratic practice of class favoritism as largely responsible for the growth of a lazy, complacent elite of officials who were more concerned with opening doors for their children than with serving the people.[42] The problems of selfish ambition, opportunism, and privatism he analyzed as the consequences of too little rather than too much virtuocracy.

Mao's decision to lead a second revolution to purify Chinese society had disastrous consequences. The revival movement not only damaged the nation's economy and international position but also destroyed people's trust in one another and their leaders. When the Cultural Revolution began, many people—youth in particular—eagerly enlisted in the crusade to defend revolutionary ideals against the evils of selfishness and competition.[43] As this book will show, life under virtuocracy before 1966 alienated people from the political system without destroying their attachment to its moral principles. They blamed the opportunism, sycophancy, and backbiting they saw around them on the faulty implementation of policy or on the weak character of the participants, not on the basic premises of virtuocracy. The students described in this book still revered the revolutionary virtues of selflessness and service to the people, and saw the Cultural Revolution as a chance to realize them. But ten years later there appeared to be few people who continued to believe that it was possible to realize these ideals through political action.

The virtuocratic crusade backfired because it was carried out not by the leader of a reform movement who could offer followers only spir-

42. Nevertheless, Mao did not advocate the complete abolition of class background labels for recruitment and promotion. He never decided which was the most serious threat to Chinese socialism, the old middle class (sustained by the persistence of meritocracy) or the new official elite (aided by both virtuocracy and feodocracy), and he failed to resolve the ambiguous combination of inherited and behavioral definitions of class. See Kraus, *Class Conflict in Chinese Socialism* (forthcoming).

43. There was, of course, an element of career motivation involved as well. Students worried that under the new virtuocratic rules, failure to participate in the Cultural Revolution would be interpreted as a sign of political apathy or timidity.

itual redemption, but by the leader of a state who could use the weapons of power and opportunity to induce moral transformation. What was at stake for participants was not just their moral reputations but their life chances as well. All behavior was construed as an expression of revolutionary commitment or opposition, and the gap between rewards and penalties was increased in order to arouse more enthusiastic commitment. As a result, political competition did not disappear but instead became more virulent. Although extreme virtuocracy improved outward political conformity, it exacerbated the problems of individualistic calculation and social conflict.

The triumph of virtuocracy over meritocracy also produced less rather than more equality of opportunity. The consequence of abolishing all meritocratic protections was clearest in university admissions. The system which had combined the entrance examination with political screening was replaced by a recommendation process in which the applicant's fellow workers or peasants determined who was the most worthy of recieving a college education. The recommendation method was designed to "place the 'moral' aspect in the forefront" and to operate to the advantage of peasants and workers.[44] In fact, the subjectivity of the process and the absence of objective screening favored officials who could wield personal influence. Local elites in rural villages, where traditional patterns of power and deference persist, were the major beneficiaries. Many production brigades recommended the son (rarely the daughter) of the brigade leader. At the same time, higher-level cadres were able to exploit their connections to get their offspring into college through the "back door." University professors now say there were more children of workers and peasants enrolled in their departments before the Cultural Revolution than afterward.

Within work organizations, leaders, totally unconstrained by objective requirements of merit or birth, promoted their favorite followers into higher positions by defining virtue in terms of personal loyalty.[45]

---

44. *Jilin ribao*, March 7, 1972, *Union Research Service* (URS), Vol. 67, No. 15, p. 211.

45. In addition to posts in political and administrative offices, places in the work unit's Mao Zedong Thought Propaganda Team, an employees' song and dance troupe, were used by leaders to reward their favorite followers. Members of the team rehearsed and performed on a full-time basis and were relieved of other more tedious job responsibilities; they also had many opportunities to travel. According to informants, youth, physical attractiveness, and loyalty to the leader were the only criteria for selection; talent was not required. In many factories the propaganda team became the backbone of the leading faction. Some factory leaders took advantage of the vagueness and subjectivity of promotion criteria to extort gifts from employees (for an egregious example, see GRRB, January 24, 1980).

Virtuous actions came to be seen by people as no more than a cover for self-interest. Factional conflicts at the upper leadership levels further deepened people's cynicism about virtue. Character assassination is the standard technique of virtuocratic politics, in which it is necessary to impugn a rival's motives and character as well as his or her views.[46] During the decade beginning in 1966 the gap between the moralistic rhetoric of political competition and the reality of power struggles in Peking seemed to widen.[47] The Cultural Revolution accelerated the erosion of virtuocracy. Mistrust became so widespread that the moral basis of the regime's legitimacy was threatened.

THREE QUESTIONS

At this point, three important questions must be addressed. First, can data from the 1960-1966 period really help us understand the China of the post-Cultural Revolution era? The following chapters are written in the past tense because the interview data on which they are based come from the earlier period; nevertheless, the issue they identify as the core of Chinese political life—the unintended social consequences of political criteria for advancement—is the subject of great contemporary interest. Since Mao's death and the overthrow in 1976 of his radical allies (the "Gang of Four"—Jiang Qing, Zhang Chunqiao, Yao Wenyuan, and Wang Hongwen), there has been much discussion in China about the need for standards of distribution which are fairer and less socially divisive than the subjective political standards that prevailed in the past. Research on organizational behavior in the 1980s will tell us whether this effort to replace virtuocracy with meritocracy has succeeded. Meanwhile my research from the 1960s reveals general principles that can be used to evaluate the impact of such policy changes on behavior. If educational and occupational selection standards shift from political performance to skill examinations, there should be fewer political activists, less separation between activists and their peers, more group cohesion, and perhaps less intense friendships. But there are indications that political performance, although officially diminished in importance, may still continue to be a factor in selection, with socially

46. On the important function of character assassination in the politics of the Roman Catholic Church, see Greeley, *The Making of the Popes, 1978.*
47. See Dittmer, "Thought Reform and Cultural Revolution," pp. 67-85.

divisive consequences similar to those of the earlier period described in this book. Some people in China claim that the virtuocratic rules of the game are fundamentally unchanged. As one construction worker told a foreign journalist in 1980:

> Our team leader was appointed during the Gang of Four time because he was a radical and knew all the slogans. . . . He is still there, still in the position of power. When these bonuses come to our unit, he will be the main one who decides who gets them. And he is exactly the same kind of radical he was before—he has just digested the new slogans. People like that never want to judge you on your actual contribution, but on your "political attitude." When they start throwing in things like political attitude . . . well, anything goes. That is always the end of reality in China. It is just his way of giving the bonuses, the opportunities, to people he likes. That is why I had to get out of China. I want to be judged on my work, not my politics.[48]

A second important question is the extent to which my analysis of urban high schools applies to other institutions in China. I suspect that future research will show that the social ramifications of virtuocratic competition, at least until 1966, characterized not only schools but also adult work organizations. However, because the intensity of competition in an organization depends on its structure of mobility, the competitive pressures were probably weaker in adult organizations. For example, in factories there probably was less political competition than in schools. Although factories were more often the target of political campaigns, workers faced no risk of dismissal; promotions and raises were infrequent and based almost entirely on seniority rather than individual performance; and factory authorities employed political criteria mainly when making leadership appointments. I also suspect that there was less political competition in rural high schools, in which only a tiny percentage of the graduates could escape to the city through the army or college, than in urban high schools, in which anywhere from 20 to 80 percent of the seniors had the chance to enter a university or an urban work unit. The students in urban high schools were very ambitious because the career stakes were high and immediate. And like all adolescents they were more sensitive to the opinion of their peers and more idealistic than their elders. In the vivid drama of urban high

48. *The Christian Science Monitor,* August 1, 1980.

school life we can discover the themes of virtuocratic competition which appear in paler forms in other Chinese institutions.

The third question is crucial: "Is it possible to obtain a true picture of Chinese life through interviews with refugees?" This book is based on interviews I conducted with thirty-one student refugees and three teacher refugees in Hong Kong; most were conducted during 1971, but a few more were added in December 1977 and January 1978. I held a minimum of two sessions of three-hours each with each student; most were questioned in four to seven three-hour sessions. With a very few exceptions, I conducted the interviews myself in Mandarin. Despite the problems of small numbers and unrepresentativeness, refugee interviewing remains the best method for studying actual patterns of citizen behavior in societies such as the Soviet Union and China which limit the access of foreign researchers. The Harvard project on attitudes and behavior in the Soviet Union, which was based on émigré sources, produced findings that have been largely confirmed by subsequent research conducted inside the U.S.S.R.[49] Interviews conducted during my visits to the People's Republic in 1971, the spring of 1978, the fall of 1978, and especially in the winter of 1980, when people were more willing to speak frankly, as well as articles and short stories from the Chinese press, corroborate the refugee interview accounts. There is every reason to expect that when foreign scholars are permitted to do field research in Chinese organizations, their research will validate the findings of this book and other excellent books based on refugee data.[50] A detailed description of my interview procedure and a discussion of the problem of bias may be found in the Methodological Appendix.

By analyzing the behavioral choices of Chinese high school students, the following chapters will explore the social ramifications of recruitment policies which distribute opportunities according to judgments of political virtue. Chapter Two describes the educational policies that set the context, and Chapter Three analyzes the way in which students adopted a "schoolcraft" strategy—how they decided whether to invest their time and energies in academic study or in political activism. Chapter Four discusses the negative impact of the competition for scarce

49. Inkeles and Bauer, *The Soviet Citizen.*
50. Including Parish and Whyte, *Village and Family in Contemporary China;* Whyte, *Small Groups and Political Rituals in China;* Frolic, *Mao's People;* Barnett, *Cadres, Bureaucracy and Political Power in China;* Bernstein, *Up to the Mountains;* Solomon, *Mao's Revolution;* Vogel, *Canton Under Communism.*

opportunities on relations between student activists and their class-mates. Chapter Five, on friendship, shows that political competition could have unifying as well as divisive effects, because the need for close friendship was intensified by the political pressures in the school environment. The balance of cooperation and competition is described in Chapter Six. The structure of career incentives helps us understand why students cooperated in some activities and competed in others, and why political competition generated more social conflict than did academic competition. Chapter Seven discusses how changes in recruitment policies in 1966 and 1976 were likely to be reflected in new patterns of schoolcraft, and offers some speculations about the future of virtuocracy in China.

2

THE POLICY CONTEXT

The world of Chinese high school students was shaped by national educational policies which determined the structure of educational opportunity, the types of schools available to students, the school life they found there, and the selection criteria by which further educational opportunities were allocated. This chapter will provide a brief survey of these policies in order to help the reader understand the school system as it was between 1960 and 1966, when the students portrayed in subsequent chapters were engaged with it.

THE STRUCTURE OF EDUCATIONAL OPPORTUNITY

The structure of the educational system has not changed since 1949. Some children attend nurseries and kindergartens operated by work units and neighborhoods, but most children enter school at the primary level when they are seven years old.[1] Before the Cultural Revolution, primary and secondary schools were each six years in length.[2] Secondary education was divided into junior high school (*chuzhong*) and senior high school (*gaozhong*), three years each, which were sometimes administratively combined and sometimes separated. University education was four to six years in length. Education was neither compulsory nor free. Before 1966, annual tuition was approximately 14 yuan ($5.60) for junior high school and 20 yuan ($8) for senior high school.[3]

---

1. In 1978 a decision was made to enroll children in school at age six rather than seven, but the scarcity of teachers and school facilities has impeded its implementation.
2. After the Cultural Revolution the twelve-year curriculum was shortened to nine or ten years, but in 1979 the Ministry of Education declared its intention to return to twelve years, first in the cities and later, if the resources are available, in the countryside.
3. At 1965 exchange rates.

TABLE 1. Growth of Education, 1949–79

	1949	1958	1965	1979
Primary				
Schools ('000)	347	777	682	924
Enrollment (millions)	24.4	86.4	116.2	146.6
Enrollment ratio (%)	25	67	70	93
Secondary				
Schools ('000)	5.2	28.9	n.a.	147.3
Enrollment (millions)	1.3	8.5	14.4	60.3
Enrollment ratio (%)	2	17	16	46
Higher				
Universities/colleges	205	791	434	633
Enrollment (millions)	0.12	0.66	0.67	1.02
Enrollment ratio (%)	0.3	1.6	1.4	1.6

SOURCE: World Bank, *China: Socialist Economic Development*, Annex G: Education Sector, 1981, p. 6.

Parents also had to bear the expense of books and supplies. Scholarships were offered to many students on the basis of financial need.

Although school facilities and educational opportunities were expanded dramatically after 1949, even today most people go no further than primary school.[4] (Table 1 summarizes the expansion of primary, secondary, and tertiary enrollments from 1949 to the present.) High school students of the decade before the Cultural Revolution like those portrayed in this book were a privileged minority. In 1965, seven out of ten children were enrolled in primary schools, but less than two out of ten were enrolled in secondary schools. Most secondary school students were studying at junior high schools or at specialized technical or vocational senior high schools.[5] In 1965, although total secondary enroll-

4. A considerable number of children drop-out before completing primary school. According to 1979 Chinese statistics obtained by the World Bank, 72 percent of children entering primary school complete the fourth grade, and 64 percent of them graduate from primary school. The completion rate is, however, about 20 percentage points higher than in other less developed countries. World Bank, *China: Socialist Economic Development*, p. 91.

5. In 1965, 65 percent of secondary school students were studying in regular junior and senior high schools and 35 percent were studying in specialized technical or vocational schools. *Hong qi* (HQ), No. 8 (1980), *Chinese Education*, Vol. XIII, No. 3–4 (Fall–Winter 1980–81), p. 58.

ments were 14.4 million, there were only 360,000 graduates of general college-preparatory senior high schools such as those described in this book. Once a Chinese teenager reached a general senior high school, his or her chances to become a college trained specialist were excellent. In 1965, 45.56 percent of the senior high school graduates were admitted to universities and colleges (this lucky group constituted a mere 1.4 percent of the total age cohort).[6]

Secondary and higher educational opportunities were concentrated in the cities. According to a 1955 Chinese study, although only 13 percent of the population lived in cities and towns, 50 percent of junior and senior high school students and 75 percent of college students were from urban households.[7] Although this disparity must have shrunk during the 1960s, city students still had a better chance for educational mobility than their rural counterparts. The probability of winning college admission was as high as 60 to 80 percent at some of the very best city schools.[8]

The slope of the educational pyramid has changed over time in tandem with economic conditions and economic development goals. During the 1950s school enrollments and urban job opportunities were expanded by the First Five-Year Plan (1953-1957). New city factories were constructed or old ones rebuilt; both needed skilled workers and technicians. Government bureaus had to be created and staffed. The number of schools and enrollments increased at every level, and this expansion, in practice, guaranteed university admission or city jobs for most senior high school graduates. Table 2 shows the number of high school graduates, the number of university entrants, and the proportion of university entrants to high school graduates for 1953-1957.

As the statistics in Table 2 indicate, by 1957 opportunities were constricting; staffing demands for new bureaucracies and industries

6. *Zhongguo baike nianjian 1980* (Beijing, Shanghai: 1980), p. 538, cited in Rosen, "The Influence of Structure on Behavior," p. 31.

7. Feng Jixi, "The Growth of China's Economy as Viewed from the State Budget," *Tongji gongzuo* (Statistical Work), June 1957, p. 30, quoted in Emerson, "Manpower Training and Utilization of Specialized Cadres, 1949-1968," p. 193. The disparity has been narrowed by the expansion of rural education during the 1960s and 1970s. A visitor was told that in 1972 only one-third of the 36 million young people then in high schools were urbanites. John W. Lewis, "China Trip Notes," (unpublished manuscript, 1973), cited in Bernstein, *Up to the Mountains,* p. 61.

8. See Rosen, "Students, Administrators, and Mobility," p. 17. Nothing has been said about the chances for upward mobility through the military because few urban youth are recruited into the branches of the People's Liberation Army. The Air Force has relatively high technical requirements of its recruits and does therefore admit some urban high school graduates, but otherwise military recruitment is concentrated in the rural areas.

TABLE 2. Opportunities for Higher Education, 1953–1957

	Senior High Graduates	University Entrants	Entrants to Graduates Ratio
Summer-Fall 1953	58,400	71,400	122.3%
Summer-Fall 1954	72,100	94,000	130.8%
Summer-Fall 1955	106,000	96,200	90.8%
Summer-Fall 1956	156,000	165,600	106.2%
Summer-Fall 1957	202,600	107,000	52.8%

SOURCE: Bernstein, *Up to the Mountains*, p. 48, based on statistics from Leo Orleans, *Professional Manpower and Education in Communist China* (Washington: U.S. Government Printing Office, 1961), pp. 32, 38, 61. The ratios are larger than 100 because in addition to high school graduates, older workers, cadres, and army veterens were recruited to attend university.

leveled off, inadequate resources constrained educational expansion, and excessive 1956 enrollments had to be compensated for. It was in this context of limited opportunities for high school graduates that the idea of assigning urban youth to agricultural work units was first broached in 1957.[9] Young people began to realize that their ambitions might not be fulfilled. During the summer of 1957 in a county seat of Hubei Province, 1000 frustrated junior high school graduates rioted for two and a half days to protest their inability to continue their education.[10]

In 1958-1960, the Great Leap Forward created new educational opportunities and postponed students' worries about their futures. The Great Leap Forward was an ambitious, dramatic, and in retrospect misguided attempt to make China a modern, industrialized communist society through the mass mobilization of its then approximately 650 million people. Everyone—student, housewife, and bureaucrat included—was called out to build factories and other projects, including a multitude of new schools. School enrollments rapidly increased; in 1960, the Chinese press reported over 800,000 students in institutions of higher learning.[11] High school graduates were assured of university

9. Bernstein, *Up to the Mountains,* p. 35.
10. New China News Agency (NCNA), August 5, 1957, *Survey of the China Mainland Press* (SCMP), August 12, 1957, p. 32.
11. RMRB, June 4, 1960, SCMP, 2285, p. 16.

places, as the percentage of graduates who could enter university leapt to 135.3 percent in 1958 and 112 percent in 1959.[12]

The overly rapid and haphazard expansion of the economy and educational system made retrenchment and consolidation necessary after 1960. Many new Great Leap Forward schools closed for lack of government resources to support them, and newly admitted students found their hopes for educational opportunities dashed by the post-Great Leap economic depression. The high school students described in this book were the lucky few who had the chance to attend junior and senior high schools in the 1960s; but they faced post-graduation futures that were more uncertain than those of their predecessors of the 1950s.

The policy during the 1960-1966 period was to concentrate limited budgetary resources on high-quality, full-time secondary schools and universities. The policy-makers—led by Liu Shaoqi and Deng Xiaoping—who made the key educational decisions during this period rejected the mobilization approach to development, which Mao Zedong had imposed on them in the Great Leap Forward, but they did not return to the economic policy stressing urban industry on the Soviet model, which had been followed during the 1950-1958 period. They assimilated the lessons of these two unsuccessful approaches and decided to try a third way—to modernize agriculture while limiting the growth of the urban, industrial sector. The companion educational policy was to concentrate on producing well-trained experts, but only a limited number of them, no more than could be absorbed by the economy. The stress was on quality rather than quantity. Post-primary enrollments grew very slowly, and rural primary schooling was popularized mainly through work-study schools funded by local citizens.[13]

The policy of constraining growth of post-primary education was joined by a policy of limiting development of the urban economy and encouraging modernization of agriculture. A crucial element in the

12. Bernstein, *Up to the Mountains,* p. 52, based on the figure cited by Emerson, "Manpower Training and Utilization of Specialized Cadres, 1949-1968," p. 201 and Orleans, *Professional Manpower* (cited in Table 2 above), pp. 38, 61.

13. Articles in the press explained that since the government already spent over 40 percent of its annual education budget on primary education, the work-study school—which required less state funding because of the money earned by student labor and supplied by local communes—was the only economically feasible way to extend primary school opportunities to the countryside (NCNA, May 26, 1964, SCMP, 3229, p. 11). One article compared the per-pupil annual cost to the state of regular primary schools and the part-work, part-study schools: 234 *yuan* ($93.60) in full-time schools and 15 *yuan* ($6.00) in work-study schools (RMRB, September 3, 1964, SCMP, 3301, p. 7).

strategy was the transfer of urban youth to the countryside. Although at the time the Chinese press claimed that a major objective of the transfer program was the ideological tempering of the country's youth, the program had obvious economic goals.[14] By assigning a significant proportion of city junior and senior high school graduates to rural work units the national leadership could limit urban population growth, prevent urban unemployment by absorbing manpower into the rural economy, and send educated people into the drive to modernize the countryside. By hiring previously unemployed housewives, retirees, and temporary peasant laborers—rather than recent graduates—urban enterprises were able to keep down labor and social overhead costs. Although the data on the number of junior and senior high school graduates sent to the countryside during the pre-Cultural Revolution era are incomplete, one Chinese source claimed that between 1962 and 1966 "well over one million" urban youth were sent.[15] Before 1963, rural transfer was presented to students (at least those in Guangdong Province) as a three-year temporary assignment after which they could return to the city, and some graduates who failed to be admitted to senior high school or college or selected for urban jobs could avoid being transferred to the countryside because government control over labor allocation was imperfect.[16] However, in 1964 the government commit-

14. Bernstein's *Up to the Mountains* argues persuasively that the major reason for the transfer program was to solve the problem of surplus urban manpower.

15. NCNA, September 27, 1966, cited in Bernstein, *Up to the Mountains,* p. 24. In 1961, the Chinese press stated that the majority of primary and high school graduates must go to work in agricultural areas. *Zhongguo qingnian bao* (ZGQNB), August 16, 1961, *Joint Publications Research Service* (JPRS) 11590, p. 60. The following three statistics are cited by Chen Pi-chao, "The Political Economics of Population Growth," p. 266, and Bernstein, *Up to the Mountains,* p. 25. From Spring 1962 to early 1964, 292,000 junior and senior high school graduates were transferred (GRRB, March 22, 1964); in 1964 over 400,000 primary and high school educated youth were transferred (RMRB, February 19, 1965); and from January to August 1965, 250,000 urban-educated youth were transferred (RMRB, September 25, 1965). It was stated that between Liberation and December 1963, forty million students from all educational levels had been sent to rural villages (*Wen Hui Bao,* Hong Kong, December 10, 1963, SCMP, 3120, pp. 14-15); this figure probably includes peasants returning to their villages as well as urban youth. Rosen, "Students, Administrators and Mobility," p. 26, presents the following local Canton statistics on the numbers of youth sent to the countryside: in 1964, over 11,000, of whom 10,000 were "street youth" (unemployed graduates from previous years) (Canton radio, February 20, 1964); in 1965, over 12,000, of whom 5,100 were sent directly after graduation (Canton radio, December 4, 1965); in April 1966, a total over the past few years of 30,000 youth (Canton radio, April 3, 1966). Canton radio on December 4, 1965, said that there were a total of 34,000 Canton youth in the countryside.

16. Rosen, "Students, Administrators, and Mobility," p. 26; White, *Careers in Shanghai,* p. 76.

ted itself to a permanent transfer program.[17] After that time, students faced the likelihood of rural resettlement. It was widely recognized that the best graduates were given the places in senior high schools, colleges, and city enterprises, while those who failed to meet the academic and political requirements were relegated to the countryside. The contempt of rural villagers, who looked upon the urban migrants as "refuse" from the cities, was a bitter indignity for urban graduates, adding insult to the injury of downward mobility.[18]

During the Cultural Revolution decade (1966-1976) the educational system which had been in existence for seventeen years since 1949 was attacked by Mao Zedong and his allies as bourgeois and elitist. The primary goal of the Maoist leadership was economic and educational equality, and the strategy devised to achieve it was the rapid expansion of primary and secondary education, especially in the rural areas, and the de-emphasis of higher level training and research.[19] All schools were closed from 1966 to 1969 so that students could participate in the campaign, and many schools, especially at the college level, did not resume instruction until after 1971 or 1972. With very few exceptions (for youth with exceptional talents or parental connections) all senior high school graduates were sent down to live and work in the countryside. From 1968, when the rustication program began again in earnest, until the end of 1978, the official estimate is that 17 million urban youth were sent to the countryside.[20] After working for two years, secondary school graduates were eligible to apply to university, but because higher educational enrollments were cut back (there were only approximately 400,000 students in college in 1974), the probability of admission was very small.[21]

17. Peking wall poster, as reported by *Mainichi,* January 20, 1967, in *Daily Summary of the Japanese Press,* January 25, 1967, cited in Bernstein, *Up to the Mountains,* p. 78.

18. "A Letter from Chaling," *Geming qingnian* (Revolutionary Youth), No. 2, Changsha, November 10, 1967, URS, Vol. XLIX, No. 20 (December 1967), p. 271, quoted in Gardner, "Educated Youth and Urban-Rural Inequalities, 1958-1966," p. 269.

19. Even during the Cultural Revolution there was, however, no massive infusion of government funds into rural education, and the money for new village schools came out of the peasants' own pockets. The expansion of rural education in China has been accomplished more by political campaigns initiated by Party leaders than by government investment. Statistics on government spending for education are provided in World Bank, *China: Socialist Economic Development,* pp. 52–57.

20. Xinhua, December 14, 1978, FBIS, December 15, 1978, E5; Xinhua, January 24, 1978, FBIS, January 26, 1978, E2; RMRB, February 10, 1979, cited in Pepper, "Chinese Education After Mao," p. 48.

21. The 1974 enrollment figure comes from "Report of the Delegation of University and College Presidents to the People's Republic of China" (unpublished), cited in Bernstein, *Up to the Mountains,* p. 46.

After 1978, when Mao Zedong died and the Party moderates once again took charge of the economy and education, there has been a return to the policies of the early 1960s. Educational investment has been concentrated on high-quality secondary and university education because policy-makers believe that this makes the most efficient contribution to economic modernization. But even in 1979 the shape of the educational pyramid still showed the effects of the Cultural Revolution policies. The rapid expansion of primary and secondary education has made the competition for further schooling stiffer than ever. In 1965, 45 percent of high school graduates could attend college; the equivalent statistic in 1979 was 4 percent.[22] The demand for career opportunities and the opposition to the rural resettlement program have been so strong, especially among the politically vocal urban population, that the government has been forced to expand university enrollments, cut back the rustication program, and create more city jobs.

The problem of urban youth unemployment has presented a serious political challenge to the leadership. The government has had to find jobs not only for the millions of new junior and senior high school students who graduate every year, but also for the over twelve million past graduates who have fled illegally back to the city from their rural assignments.[23] It has responded by creating new positions in the urban service and collective sectors and by promising the employees of state factories and work units that if they retire, one of their children will be guaranteed a job in the same unit.[24] The rural resettlement program is so unpopular that political leaders have promised its abolition as soon as economically and demographically feasible, and for the present they are not nearly so strict in enforcing it as they were before 1978.[25] Of approximately seven to eight million senior high school graduates in

22. Minister of Education Jiang Nanxiang, "Speech at a National Discussion Meeting of Ideological and Political Work in Middle and Primary Schools," May 1979, Beijing Domestic Service, July 17, 1979, FBIS, July 20, 1979, L7.

23. Of the 17 million sent down from 1968 to 1978, 10 million remained at the end of 1978, and only 5 million were still there by the end of August 1979. Xinhua, August 29, 1979, *Bulletin,* Hong Kong, August 30, 1979, cited in Pepper, "Chinese Education After Mao," p. 54.

24. This policy of replacement, *dingti,* by which children can inherit their parent's occupational position, runs counter to the current meritocratic trend and is testimony to the political influence of the urban population.

25. Today the economic necessity of the program is emphasized and its political goals are played down. One article accused the Gang of Four of making too great a "fanfare" over the program and "preaching that only when urban youths go to the countryside and rural peasants go to the cities will it be possible to narrow the differences between workers and peasants, between town and country and between mental and manual labor." The actual

1979, according to the national plan only 800,000 were supposed to be sent to the countryside, and it is probable that even fewer actually reached their assigned destinations.[26] Compared with the students of 1960-1966 described in this book, the graduates of today stand a smaller chance of winning the top prize of college admission, but they also face a smaller risk of having to take the booby prize of rural resettlement.

TYPES OF SCHOOLS

A student's future depended on what type of high school he or she attended. Because budgetary resources were scarce and only a small number of students needed preparation for higher education, the pre-1966 secondary school system was differentiated. Although this differentiation was later attacked as an elitist practice of ability tracking which discriminated against workers and peasants, and for that reason was abolished during the Cultural Revolution, it was revived in 1978. The same types of schools that existed during 1960-1966 are again in existence today.

Ordinary Full-Time Schools

Most students in Chinese cities attended schools of this type, which were financed by government funds and had an instructional schedule and curriculum regulated by the Ministry of Education. Only students who passed municipal academic entrance examinations were admitted to these junior and senior high schools. Their curriculum was academic and they prepared students to continue their education at the next level. They were coeducational neighborhood day schools. Rural youth who managed to pass the entrance exam could attend full-time junior high schools located in commune towns and senior highs located even further away in county seats; both provided boarding facilities for the students whose homes were too distant for daily commuting. Most of the students I interviewed had attended ordinary full-time schools in urban areas.

rationale for the program was, it says, simply the inability of the urban economy to absorb all school graduates (ZGQNB, n.d., FBIS, November 28, 1978, E27-29).

26. Xinhua, August 17, 1979, *Bulletin,* Hong Kong, August 18, 1979, cited in Pepper, "Chinese Education After Mao," p. 57.

*Key (*Zhongdian*) Schools*

The highest quality urban full-time schools were designated key schools and were given the most experienced teachers and supplementary budgets for special equipment and programs. Key schools were selected by each level of government—the national Ministry of Education, provinces, counties and cities, and municipal districts—so that a large city had an elaborate hierarchy of key schools above its ordinary schools. Key schools were supposedly designated as such because of their strong leadership, good teachers, and superior facilities, but in fact they were chosen according to the proportion of their students who won admission to universities.[27] Key schools enrolled the best students, selecting them on the basis of municipal junior and senior high entrance examinations, school grades, and political evaluations (the examination scores were weighed most heavily). Many key schools were boarding schools because their students' homes were often far away in other parts of the city or suburbs. A few key schools were all-girl schools, but most were coed. Key schools usually included both junior and senior high school levels and favored their own junior high graduates in admission to the senior level. During the Cultural Revolution key schools were condemned as "little treasure pagodas" which cultivated "spiritual aristocrats" rather than "revolutionary successors." Today they are praised for fostering talent and helping achieve the modernization of the Chinese economy. Almost half of the students interviewed in this study had attended key schools.

*Rural "People-Run" (*Minban*) Schools*

Most students in Chinese rural villages attended schools of this type, which were financed by local funds and student tuition. The rural people-run schools offered a skimpier curriculum than urban full-time schools and prepared their students for agricultural work rather than advanced study.[28] They operated on an irregular schedule which com-

27. This tendency to "regard the proportion of students entering schools at higher grades as the sole yardstick for judging whether a school is run well or poorly" is, according to the press, still strong today. The Minister of Education criticized government officials who gave cash rewards to schools purely on the basis of percentage of graduates admitted to higher-level schools (Xinhua, May 28, 1979, FBIS, June 1, 1979, L19; also Beijing Domestic Service, July 17, 1979, FBIS, July 20, 1979, L7).

28. Before 1966 most of these local rural schools were primary schools, but since 1978 the policy of consolidating the rural government schools established during the Cultural Revolu-

bined agricultural work with study so that students could help out in the fields when their families needed them. The school facilities were primitive and the teachers poorly trained. Because these schools were obviously inferior to full-time schools, it was almost impossible for their students to compete successfully with graduates of full-time schools for admission to the next level.

Urban "People-Run" (Minban) Schools

Because the government was unable to accommodate all city youth in public secondary schools, it permitted a small number of "people-run" private schools to continue to operate in the cities.[29] Some were founded before 1949 or during the 1950s; others had their origin in 1960-1961, when the economic failure of the Great Leap Forward provoked a cutback in government spending for public education.[30] Urban people-run schools administered separate entrance examinations which were held at a later date than the public school examinations; their applicants generally were those who had failed to gain admission to the public schools. These privately supported schools charged much higher tuition than public schools—in some cases as much as 25 yuan a term, as compared to 10 yuan or less in public high schools, or $10 compared to $4—and many of their students came from affluent bourgeois families. Attendance at such a school was viewed as a way to avoid being sent to the countryside and to keep alive the dim hope of further education. In reality it was almost impossible for private school graduates to compete successfully for college admission or good city jobs.

---

tion has resulted in more people-run junior high schools. In effect, the leadership has told rural production brigades: We will give you the money to run a primary school, but if you want a junior middle school, you will have to bear the burden yourselves. In brigades which do not run junior high schools, only those children who demonstrate outstanding talent on the entrance examination will be able to continue their education at the government-funded full-time school, probably located in the commune town.

29. In 1960 private school enrollment at the primary level was as much as 17 percent of Shanghai's total (NCNA, Shanghai, April 9, 1960, cited in White, *Careers in Shangai*, p. 30).

30. It is not clear whether or not the consolidation of urban education after 1978, especially at the senior high school level, has resulted in the revival of these people-run schools. There has been talk, however, about "continuation classes" run on a tuition basis "to solve the problem of many young people being unable to enter a higher school." (Xinhua, April 9; 1980, FBIS, April 10, 1980, L6).

*Specialized (*Zhongzhuan*) High Schools*

These schools (some at the junior high level, but most at the senior high level) provided terminal degrees in technical fields, as well as in such fields as financial administration, teacher training, and athletics. They offered courses of three to five years in length. Many students chose to take the special entrance examinations for these schools, which were held at approximately the same time as the entrance examinations for the ordinary and key schools, because although graduates of specialized schools rarely could enter college, they were virtually guaranteed good city jobs in their hometowns after graduation.[31] (Because most specialized schools recruited students from an entire city, county, or province, they usually provided boarding facilities.) Even though the curriculum of these schools remains highly specialized and vocational, they are being promoted in 1980 as an effective way to dampen the excessive demand for higher education and to channel talent into technical and managerial fields that are of immediate importance to the economy.[32]

In addition to these five types of schools which constituted the formal system of secondary education, there were other opportunities for nonformal adult education, especially in the cities. Factories offered technical classes at both secondary and college levels for their employees, and many people studied English and other subjects by television and radio instruction. But there was a clear social demarcation between formal and informal education because informal credentials had almost no career benefits. The only way to advance was through formal schooling.

SCHOOL LIFE

Schooling during the three years of junior high school and three years of senior high school was very intensive and time-consuming, much more

31. Two respondents reported, however, that they had applied to specialized high schools (a teacher training school and a naval navigation school), but were redirected to key academic high schools because their school grades and examination scores were *too high*.

32. Many recent articles and speeches argue that during the past decade the development of general senior high schools has been too rapid while specialized secondary schools, which meet the immediate needs of the economy, have been underdeveloped. The ratio of general schools to specialized schools in 1979 was twelve to one in Beijing and five to one in Tianjin,

so than for American students. Classes were held five and a half days a week, from eight in the morning until three in the afternoon. Most students remained at school until dinner time for sports, cultural activities, labor chores, and political meetings, many of which were mandatory. Most of the students who lived at home also went home for lunch and later for dinner, but they were expected to return to the campus in the evening for supervised study halls. Boarding students were free to return home only from Saturday noon until Sunday evening. For both boarding and day students, then, urban life was high school life.

Students entering the first year of junior high (junior-1) or the first year of senior high (senior-1) were divided into classes of approximately fifty students each. In order to foster collective loyalties, the members of each class studied all subjects together and remained together for all three years. The pupils stayed in the classroom while the Chinese language, mathematics, foreign language (usually English), physics, chemistry, history, geography, hygiene, art, music, and politics teachers came in turn to instruct them. Ability tracking was rare and the students in each class were academically and politically diverse. The only differentiation of classes occurred in some schools during the last year or two of senior high, when students were divided into science and arts classes to prepare for the science or arts university entrance examination.[33]

Instruction was by traditional rote recitation, and classroom discipline was strict. Students rose to greet the teacher at the beginning of each class period, and at the end of the class period they could not leave the room before the teacher without permission.

Each class had assigned to it one teacher who was responsible for its students' overall development—their academic, social, political, and moral progress. This teacher, called the class director (*banzhuren*), supervised all class activities including political discussions and labor stints. The class director was supposed to guide the political development of individual students and was responsible for evaluating their political character and behavior every term. These conduct evaluations,

but the policy is to make it one to one, as it was in these two cities in 1965. Xinhua, August 17, 1979, FBIS, August 21, 1979, L9; Xinhua, February 5, 1980, FBIS, February 8, 1980, P7; Heilongjiang Provincial Service, March 23, 1980; FBIS, March 27, 1980, S1.

33. A few schools tracked the best students into a key class in which new teaching methods were tested.

called *jianding*, were recorded in students' permanent dossiers and formed an important basis for university selection and job assignment upon graduation.

Political education was not confined to the formal lessons in Maoist and Marxist theory given in politics class, but pervaded every aspect of school life. Chinese political leaders and pedagogues recognized the limitation of formal instructional approaches to political socialization: students are unlikely to internalize what is taught in the classroom if it is contradicted by what they find in real life.[34] They also understood the strong influence of peer group norms, particularly on youth who are highly motivated by the desire for peer esteem. Students listen more to their classmates than to their teachers or parents.[35] Because Chinese educators believed that the informal moral-political lessons learned in school—what some Western educational theorists would call the "hidden curriculum"—had a more powerful effect on students than lectures or textbooks, their approach to socialization was to penetrate and control the informal side of schooling. They attempted to create an informal student culture that approved the same behavior that was being encouraged by official policy.[36] If the formal and informal definitions of good behavior were identical, then an individual would not be able to find support for deviant behavior.[37]

The Chinese contrasted this approach to political socialization, which they called "collective education" (*jiti jiaoyu*), with what they

34. If the lessons of personal experience contradict those of formal instruction, students are apt to become cynical and reject the formal lessons. For example, in the American Army during the Second World War, "orientation was an isolated hour a week in an environment in which almost every other influence ran counter to its ultimate goals. While, for example, the orientation program had for its purpose, among other things, the reaffirming of the values of democracy and the integrity of the individual, the ordinary enlisted man returned from his discussion hour to the depersonalized world of the Army in which he found little democracy and not much regard for him as an individual. Little wonder, then if enlisted men accepted the larger part of their Army lives as the reality and took orientation with a large grain of salt." Quoted from Stouffer and others, *The American Soldier,* p. 472.

35. The landmark study of the impact of the peer group on individual political orientations is Theodore M. Newcomb, *Personality and Social Change: Attitude Formation in a Student Community.* Also see Langton, "Peer Group and School and the Political Socialization Process."

36. "Insofar as the leaders of the political system can directly penetrate and control the interaction process within the face-to-face group, the norms set by that process will tend to support the larger system." Verba, *Small Groups and Political Behavior,* p. 55.

37. In schools and work units, "if the individual can be successfully isolated from social support for unorthodox views and confronted with unanimous social pressure from peers in support of orthodox views, the pressure for change in his attitudes and values should be great." Whyte, *Small Groups and Political Rituals in China,* p. 55.

called the "individual reckoning" (*gebie suanzhang*) method, which was based on a one-to-one relationship between student and teacher.[38] They believed that learning by individual reckoning with the teacher, the adult representative of the political system, was shallower and less lasting than that acquired through collective education: individual reckoning taught students only to obey authorities, whereas collective education taught them to act on the basis of internalized belief.

Under collective education, student leaders rather than teachers were supposed to be the primary agents of socialization. These leaders were not allowed to emerge spontaneously; they were recruited into official vanguard organizations that were delegated significant powers over their peers. At the junior high school level, there was no official elite organization, and almost all students were members of the Young Pioneers (Shaonian Xianfengdui). Beginning in the last year of junior high school, when students reached the age of fifteen, they could apply for admission to the Chinese Communist Youth League (YCL, Zhongguo Gongchanzhuyi Qingniantuan). Only the most outstanding political activists (*jijifenzi*), one half of the students at most, were admitted to this leadership group. Except for the weekly YCL classes held for those who aspired to membership, the activities of the class League branch were secret and separate from other activities for the class as a whole. YCL members were, however, supposed to integrate themselves in the class and keep abreast of informal developments among their classmates. They were expected to initiate "heart-to-heart" political talks (*tan xin*) with fellow-students and report the contents of these talks to League officers and the class director.

The class was organized as a collective in order to maximize its impact on students. Each class elected officers—a president, vice-president, and officers responsible for study, sports, labor, cultural activities, and student welfare. At least once a week a class meeting was held to discuss new Party policies, problems within the group, and upcoming

38. Chen Yi, "Speech to This Year's Graduates from Peking's Higher Institutions," August 10, 1961, ZGQNB, September 2, 1961, SCMP, 2581, pp. 1-7. Collective education was a pedagogical approach acquired from the Soviet Union. On the teaching of collectivism in the Soviet Union, see Bronfenbrenner, *Two Worlds of Childhood*. Although collective education was adopted during the period of Soviet influence in the 1950s, even when the Chinese struck out on their own with the 1958 Great Leap Forward and Mao attacked all Soviet policies as revisionist in the 1960s, it was not renounced. The basic elements of collectivist education—the peer group rather than the teacher as the main agent of socialization, the emphasis on the role of student activist leaders, and the inculcation of cooperation instead of competition—persisted through the 1960s and remain even today after the Cultural Revolution and Mao's death.

activities. Although the class director usually chaired the meeting, all students were encouraged to speak up. Sometimes the meetings discussed problems shared by many students; the entire class might engage in self-criticism—for example, for reading too many romantic novels and not enough political theory, or for reluctance to volunteer for rural jobs. At other times the class singled out one student for criticism. If students committed very serious wrong-doings, a schoolwide struggle meeting was held to reprimand them and hold them up as negative models. In these ways, the public opinion of the collective was brought to bear on signs of deviance within it.

Public opinion was also expressed in small groups (*xiaozu*). Each class was divided into four to six such groups. Group membership was based on classroom seating assignments; each group was composed of the eight or ten people in one row of desks. Small groups met once every one or two weeks, usually following class meetings, for discussion and criticism. Everyone was expected to criticize his or her own flaws and those of other group members. Mutual criticism, carried out primarily in the small group context, was supposed to prevent students from backsliding and ensure that interpersonal tensions did not fester and corrode collective unity.

Another important element in collective education was manual labor. Even before the communist victory in 1949, Mao Zedong believed strongly in the transformative powers of manual labor. He felt that if students, intellectuals, and other people who worked with their minds were required to spend time working with their hands in factories and farms alongside ordinary workers and peasants, they would shed their attitudes of superiority and individualism. Through labor Mao believed that students would learn that cooperation was more satisfying than competition, and that serving the people was more rewarding than pursuing selfish ambitions. Although the amount of time allotted to manual labor has varied over the years, labor has remained a part of the school curriculum from 1958 until the present. During the 1960-1966 period, which is the focus of this book, high school students were required to spend at least one month a year doing manual work, usually during weekly periods in school vegetable gardens and in annual expeditions to nearby factories and rural communes.[39]

39. Shirk, "The 1963 Temporary Work Regulations," pp. 530; and Shirk, "Work Experience in Chinese Education," pp. 5-18. As of 1978, the amount of time allotted to labor in secondary schools has been increased to a maximum of eight weeks and a minimum of four weeks a year. See Shirk, "Educational Reform and Political Backlash," p. 195.

The goal of educational socialization was to replace competition with cooperation and selfishness with concern for the group and the nation. But although students absorbed these cooperative ethical messages through classroom lessons, group meetings, and manual labor stints, they also recognized that their life chances depended upon competing successfully in school. In state socialist countries like China, students know that their futures depend on educational achievement. In the absence of inherited wealth and private capital, the educational system allocates almost all occupational positions, and social status comes to be more closely tied to occupational position.[40] Therefore issues of educational and job selection (as well as job retirement) become extremely important. Because of the high stakes involved, students were naturally disappointed if they failed to win admission to senior high school or university and were therefore faced with the likelihood of rural transfer.

Schools had to motivate the achievers and console the failures at the same time, a problem that Western educational sociologists have called the "cooling-out problem."[41] The Chinese approach to this problem between 1960 and 1966 was the "One Red Heart and Two Preparations" campaign, an annual springtime event in which students were

---

40. Lane, *The Socialist Industrial State,* p. 185. Although there have been no studies of occupational prestige in China, my impression is that it follows a pattern similar to that in the Soviet Union and Eastern Europe (which in turn resembles the pattern in Western capitalist countries). (For a summary of survey results from the Soviet Union and Eastern Europe, see Lane, p. 182.) At the top of the Chinese status rankings are non-manual professionals such as research scientists, professors, engineers, doctors, Party and government officials, and factory technicians. They are followed by skilled urban factory workers who are ranked higher than their counterparts in Western capitalist countries. Among manual workers, the skilled have more prestige than the unskilled, and those who work in heavy industry have more than those in light industry, who in turn have more than those in service work. At the bottom of the status ladder are rural peasants. Perceptions of status hierarchy are diagnosed by the Chinese press as vestiges of "feudal ideology." (See BR, No. 6 [February 11, 1980], p. 19.) They are accordingly treated with massive doses of ideological education and "role-switching" into manual labor. (See Munro, *The Concept of Man in Contemporary China.*) However, campaigns to change status values seem to have strengthened rather than weakened them. For example, the resettlement of urban youth in the countryside reinforced the urbanites' disdain for peasants; the only change in status attitudes that resulted was an elevation of the status of urban industrial labor. (See Bernstein, *Up to the Mountains,* p. 103.) Moreover, the restrictions on mobility instituted by the state have also had a strong effect on occupational prestige. When people are asked why they would prefer a job in a state-owned factory to one in a collective factory, they answer, "You can transfer from a state factory to a collective one, but you can't move up from a collective factory to a state one," and they explain the higher status of urban over rural work by saying, "You can move from the city to the countryside but not from the countryside to the city."

41. Clark, "The 'Cooling-out' Function in Higher Education," p. 513.

urged to study diligently for the entrance examinations but also to be ready to accept rural assignments with revolutionary joy.[42] According to the students I interviewed, this campaign had little effect on student reactions to graduation assignments: those who won admission to senior high school or college were ecstatic; those who were assigned by local labor bureaus to jobs in city factories, shops, and offices were satisfied; and those who were sent by the school to rural work were depressed.

COLLEGE SELECTION CRITERIA

College admission was based on a combination of three criteria: (1) academic achievement (evaluated by school grades and scores on the national entrance examination); (2) individual political performance (*geren biaoxian*, assessed by the high school on the basis of biannual conduct comments); and (3) class background (*jieji chushen*, determined by the father's occupation and source of income three years before Liberation). To assist college officials in screening applications, school administrators quantified the political factors in the equation (academic grades and test scores were already in numerical form). Political reliability (based on individual behavior, family background, social relationships, and relationships with relatives living abroad) was graded on a three-point scale: (1) can be trusted in a secretive or restrictive course of study; (2) can be trusted to be put into an ordinary, less sensitive field of study; and (3) cannot be permitted to enter university under any circumstances. Class background was similarly classified: (1) Good, meaning cadre, military, revolutionary martyr, worker, poor or lower-middle peasant; (2) Ordinary, meaning hawker (ped-

42. Everyone was urged to take the examination and not to be afraid that it would be construed as a lack of determination to do agricultural labor (ZGQNB, May 11, 1965, SCMP, 3480, p. 5). The press emphasized that ideological work with the graduating class was a serious matter, because "as the students are about to graduate and are involved in the question of whether they will continue their studies or go to work they are most susceptible to the corrupt influences of bourgeois ideology and the habits of the old society" (*Zhejiang jiaoyu* [Chekiang Education], April 1965, JPRS, 33142, p. 1). The expansion of secondary education during the Cultural Revolution decade has made the cooling-out problem even more acute today. Policymakers have attempted to lower the expectations of students (and their parents) for college admission by channeling more of them to terminal degree programs in specialized technical high schools, and by giving provincial screening examinations in advance of the national college entrance examination to reduce the number who sit for the national examination.

dler), teacher, intellectual, clerk, middle peasant; or (3) Bad, meaning rich peasant, landlord, capitalist, Kuomintang, rightist.[43]

Chinese policymakers and educational leaders, trying to adjust the educational system to fit several different national goals, frequently shifted the emphasis among these recruitment criteria, even during the brief period of time between 1960 and 1966. They argued about the primacy of academic or political criteria; and they disagreed on the question of how to judge political excellence, whether by individual performance or by family background.

The question of which students should be rewarded with educational opportunities—those who are the most "red" or those who are the most "expert"—has long been a source of leadership conflict. What Cultural Revolution rhetoricians called "the struggle between the two lines on the educational front" was largely a conflict between leaders about academic or political priority. Liu Shaoqi and others (including Deng Xiaoping), who dominated educational policy-making between 1960 and 1966, believed that although political reliability was important, schools had to concentrate on academic learning and colleges had to select the most intellectually promising students in order to accelerate economic modernization. Mao Zedong and his allies, who tried to change the policy direction after 1962, and then again during the Cultural Revolution decade (1966-1976), believed that schools had to concentrate on the ideological remolding of youth if China was to retain its revolutionary character. Liu was not the apolitical technocrat caricatured by his Cultural Revolution attackers, and Mao was not the impractical Luddite fanatic depicted by his foreign and domestic critics. Liu never claimed that political education was unnecessary; and Mao never suggested that book learning was irrelevant to building socialism. But clearly, the two leaders disagreed about which should have the first priority, academic achievement or political commitment.

The clearest policy signal, carefully watched by school authorities, students, and their anxious parents, was the university enrollment regulations issued every spring from Peking. These annual regulations from 1960 to 1965—the Cultural Revolution began in 1966, and in that year no regulations were issued and entrance examinations were canceled—are summarized in Table 3, which shows how the delicate balance of academic and political requirements shifted every year.

43. Rosen, "Background to Rebellion," p. 6.

TABLE 3. Enrollment Regulations for Institutions of Higher Education

Year	Unified Examination	Priority for Certain Groups	Age Limit	Exemption from Foreign Language Exam	Re-test	Talk About Class Line
1960	no	yes	none	none	no	yes
1961	yes	no	30 (except for workers, peasants, PLA, cadres)	except for foreign language specialties	yes	no
1962	yes	no	30 (no exceptions)	except for foreign language specialties and major institutions	no	no
1963	yes	no	30 (no exceptions)	except for foreign language specialties and major institutions	yes	no
1964	yes	no	25 (except 27 for workers, peasants, PLA, cadres)	except for foreign language specialties	yes	yes
1965	yes	no	25 (except 27 for workers, peasants, PLA, cadres, and educated youths with over two years work experience)	except for foreign language specialties	yes	no

In 1961, following the Great Leap Forward, there was a clear shift toward academic selectivity. Whereas the 1960 rules called for "affirmative action" for certain classes (children of workers, peasants, cadres, military personnel, revolutionary martyrs, and in this case, national minorities and Overseas Chinese as well), after 1961 the regulations made no such provision. The main focus of educational policy in the early 1960s was improving the academic quality of schools.[44] National leaders such as Chen Yi were making speeches urging students to show their "redness" in their "expertness," to demonstrate their revolutionary zeal through diligent study.[45]

The 1962 enrollments were the most meritocratic of the decade. The regulations no longer stipulated that all applicants who passed the entrance examination had to undergo retesting of their political record and medical history before they could be accepted. There was no provision for giving priority to applicants of good class background, and whereas in 1961 the thirty-year-old age limit had exempted workers, peasants, soldiers and cadres, it was applied to all candidates in 1962. The state policy of investing in higher education only for the brightest students was also reflected in the foreign language examination requirement. In 1961 an exemption from the foreign language test was given to everyone except those who planned to specialize in languages at university. But in 1962, all applicants to the top national universities were required to pass the foreign language exam—a requirement that in effect excluded aspirants from most rural schools, which did not offer instruction in foreign languages.

In 1963 students and teachers perceived a renewed official concern for political performance and class background. Although the enrollment regulations were otherwise identical to those of 1962, the check of politics and health was reinstituted. Chairman Mao initiated the campaign to Cultivate Revolutionary Successors.[46] The clear message of this campaign was that schools should worry more about students' political behavior, and authorities should select the staunchest revolutionary youths to enter university and take up leadership positions.

---

44. See Shirk, "The 1963 Temporary Work Regulations."

45. Chen Yi, "Speech to This Year's Graduates from Peking's Higher Institutions," August 10, 1961, ZGQNB, September 2, 1961, SCMP, 2581, pp. 1-7.

46. See "Cultivate and Train Millions of Successors who will Carry on the Cause of Proletarian Revolution," RMRB editorial, August 3, 1964, SCMP, 3274, pp. 4-5.

Newspaper articles of that year reminded students that the majority of college students belonged to the Youth League or Communist Party.[47]

In 1964 the enrollment regulations gave out mixed signals. They expressed a concern for emphasizing political credentials at the expense of academic achievement, which was apparent from admonitions to implement the class line in granting admissions; this meant favoring proletarian applicants and no longer requiring applicants to the top national universities to take the foreign language exam. But they also required that the pool of applicants be further restricted by lowering the age limit from 30 to 25, and by requiring that even workers, peasants, soldiers, and cadres could be no older than 27. The 1965 regulations were almost identical to those of 1964, except that they did not make even symbolic obeisance to the class line.[48]

It is clear, then, that between 1960 and 1965 there was a shift in emphasis from academic to political criteria, although the specific rules varied from year to year. Despite the shifts, the graduating class of every year (except perhaps 1962) knew they had to be acceptable both politically and academically.

After the Cultural Revolution the old rules were abolished. Under the new rules, political considerations totally eclipsed academic ones.[49] College applicants were no longer required to take entrance examinations, and school grades were ignored. Instead, applicants were chosen according to the recommendations of their fellow workers or of fellow peasants in the work unit to which they had been assigned after high school graduation. These recommendations were based on work attitude and political activism rather than intellectual potential. Because educational leaders were worried by the decline in quality in higher education caused by the recommendation method and the hiatus be-

47. Over 62 percent (NCNA, August 11, 1963, SCMP, 3040, p. 6).
48. Despite the stress on redness, 1965 newspaper articles reminded students that "in the achievement of success at the matriculation examination, what plays the primary role is still intellectual education. There are a few people who fail to gain admission because of inadequacies in their moral culture or physical culture, but the majority of failures are due to their poor intellectual attainments. The average student can generally meet the requirements in moral culture and physical culture, but he may definitely not be sure of satisfying the intellectual requirements" (*Shandong jiaoyu* [Shandong Education], February 20, 1965, JPRS, 30, 222, p. 54).
49. "The great teacher Chairman Mao pointed out 'In all its works, the school should aim at transforming the student's ideology.' Whether we should give first place to transforming the student's ideology or give first place to transforming him intellectually . . . is a basic distinction between proletarian and bourgeois education." Heilongjiang Radio, November 27, 1971, FBIS, December 2, 1971, Gl. Cited in Unger, *Education Under Mao.*

tween high school graduation and college entry, they attempted to modify the new rules so that students in certain subjects such as mathematics, the natural and physical sciences, and art and music could go directly from high school to college.[50] For the same reason, they administered "cultural tests" to applicants in 1973. But the radicals who dominated education and the press obstructed this attempt to reinstitute intellectual selection methods by publicizing a college applicant named Zhang Tiesheng, who had refused to take the cultural test and had instead lambasted it for turning youth into "bookworms" in the pre-Cultural Revolution fashion.[51]

After Mao's death the pre-Cultural Revolution admissions practices were restored. Entrance examinations were held on a provincial and municipal basis in 1977, and on a national unified basis in 1978 and every year thereafter. The 1980 college enrollment regulations resembled those of the 1961-1965 period. The only "affirmative action" was for national minorities. Although examination scores were considered the most important criterion for selection, candidates also were required to pass a political and physical screening. It was explicitly stated that when several applicants had attained the minimum examination score set for a certain department in a university, the university admissions officials should choose the student who has "worked enthusiastically for the student body"—in other words, the one who has been an activist.[52] Because the pool of applicants who pass the entrance examination is much larger than the number actually admitted to universities, at each stage in the admissions process authorities may apply their own subjective standards of acceptability.[53] A poor political record

50. RMRB, February 21, 1976, SCMP, 6086, p. 15.

51. In July 1973, cultural tests were defended (RMRB, July 28, 1973, SCMP, 5433, p. 187), but by August they were attacked (RMRB, August 10, 1973, SCMP, 5442, pp. 112-114). Ironically, some people attacked Zhang Tiesheng from the left, accusing him of being a "college fanatic" because of his concern about the unfairness of admissions tests (RMRB, September 22, 1973, SCMP, 5473, p. 148).

52. Xinhua, May 9, 1980, FBIS, May 13, 1980, L3.

53. On September 10, 1979, four hundred students and parents demonstrated in Beijing against university admissions procedures. They complained that although the students had passed the entrance examination, they were not admitted to universities, and applicants with lower scores were admitted instead because of their family connections (*Los Angeles Times*, September 11, 1979). In April 1978, I was told at a Hangzhou key high school that in the 1977 examinations 71 students passed, but only 49 were admitted after the political and health screening. In a Hunan rural production brigade three persons passed but not one was admitted; in 1977 in the entire province of Hunan, only 10 persons out of every 28 who passed the exam were actually admitted. The 1980 regulations addressed directly for the first time the tendency for subjective political evaluations to lead to "going through the back door."

is still likely to count against applicants, and Youth League membership gives them an edge.[54]

Policies on Class Label

Superimposed on changing policies about the relative importance of academic or political standards were shifts in the definition of what was meant by "politically good." Because it was so difficult to judge a person's redness, family class background was often used as the best predictor of political stance.

During the Civil War and after the 1949 victory, the communists used a system of class labels to classify groups within Chinese society.[55] These designations were based primarily, but not entirely, on economic position. In the rural areas, class labels based on economic status three years before the land reform were used as the basis for the redistribution of property during the land reform. Villagers were categorized as landlords, rich peasants, middle peasants, poor peasants, or hired agricultural laborers. Even though there was no land reform or comparable economic redistribution in the cities, city-dwellers were divided into capitalists, workers, hawkers, teachers, and clerks. Added to these economic labels were the political role designations assigned to selected people in the city and the countryside: revolutionary armyman, revolutionary martyr, revolutionary cadre. These economic and political labels, by identifying a person's place in the social structure, were seen as necessary for carrying out campaigns of social transformation after Liberation. Class designations answered Mao's questions, "Who are our enemies? Who are our friends?"[56]

They stated that "those who are engaged in enrollment work (including admissions staff members in colleges and universities) and the cadres and physicians who participate in conducting political screenings and physical examinations must uphold principle and must never practice favoritism or other irregularities in any form." Xinhua, May 9, 1980, FBIS, May 13, 1980, L3.

54. In 1977, 74 percent of the new freshman class were Youth League or Communist Party members; the statistic was over 87 percent in some provinces. "Education Ministry Official on College Enrollment Reform," NCNA, May 11, 1978, FBIS, May 17, 1978, p. E6; "Anhwei Education Cadres Criticize Erroneous Views on Enrollment," Anhwei Provincial Service, June 5, 1978, FBIS, June 12, 1978, p. G1.

55. Richard Kraus has provided an excellent analysis of the class label system and the political interests underlying different policies toward class in China. The following discussion draws heavily on his article "Class Conflict and the Vocabulary of Social Analysis in China," pp. 54-74, and his book *Class Conflict in Chinese Socialism*.

56. Mao Zedong, "Analysis of the Classes in Chinese Society."

With the elimination of private property, the collectivization of agriculture, and the nationalization of industry in the mid-1950s, the pre-Liberation labels seemed increasingly anachronistic to Party leaders and fell into disuse. During the 1960-1962 liberalization period after the Great Leap Forward, the emphasis in educational selection was on academic excellence, and insofar as political criteria were considered at all, the emphasis was on political achievement, not on class background. In his famous speech advocating an improvement of educational quality, Chen Yi argued that the class labels of parents were irrelevant to evaluations of children:

> Now it is already twelve years after Liberation. . . . If a youth from an exploiting class family origin is twenty-two years old today, he was ten in the year of Liberation, a very young age. It must be said that the influence of his exploiting class family on him will be relatively small. Today's students are all children of our party, our people, and our nation. If they make an effort themselves and if we educate them properly as well, then they can all become good cadres.[57]

Whenever individual schools and colleges pursued an admissions policy of compensatory favoritism to recruit students from disadvantaged groups, they used the current economic status of the parents rather than their pre-Liberation class status as the measure of deprivation. A student's class label, marked in a dossier, was based on the father's current job, not on his pre-1949 label.

Mao's "Never Forget Class Struggle" speech given at the Tenth Plenum of the Communist Party Central Committee in September 1962, revived the system of class labels and shifted the emphasis in educational selection to the political criterion of family class background. Young people were assigned class labels according to their class background (*jieji chushen*), which was defined as their *father's* (or grandfather's) economic status three years before Liberation. By 1962 the list of class labels had expanded to include negative political labels (also called "caps" or *maozi*), which were affixed during political campaigns to individuals who had made political mistakes. These political brands, like the pre-1949 ones, could be inherited by children and grandchildren. People included in the "five types of black elements," those labeled as landlords, rich peasants, counterrevolutionaries, right-

57. Chen Yi, "Speech to This Year's Graduates," p. 4.

ists, and "bad elements" (and their offspring), were treated as political pariahs who had no rights and were subject to imprisonment or community supervision.[58] Although Mao said that excluding rightists, the other four categories comprised about 5 percent of the population (roughly 35 million people in 1967), the numbers must have been much higher when the children and grandchildren who were also stigmatized with these black class labels were included.[59] Those of ordinary class background, middle peasants, teachers, intellectuals, clerks, and hawkers (and their descendents) were not treated as harshly as the black elements, but the intensification of class-struggle policy put them under suspicion. Because their political loyalties were labeled as uncertain they were at a disadvantage in educational selection and admission to the Youth League and Communist Party. It was impossible for them to join the army, which recruited exclusively from those of "good" class background. Poor and lower-middle peasants, workers, cadres, armymen, and martyrs (and their children and grandchildren) constituted the "five types of red elements"—the good class categories who were the beneficiaries of class favoritism in educational selection and admission to vanguard organizations.

The revival of the class struggle line in 1962 turned the pre-Liberation class structure on its head, and then made it the basis of stratification of the new society. There were several reasons why Mao felt it was necessary to discriminate in favor of the red classes and against everyone else. First, the old bourgeoisie continued to be a threat to the socialist system, socially if not politically. With the elimination of private economic capital, differences in human capital based in genetic endowment and family socialization came to play a more important role. When the contest for opportunities was free of preferential treatment according to class background and was based solely on academic and political achievement, the children of capitalists and intellectuals took a disproportionate share of the winning places because of the abilities and achievement motivations acquired from their parents. Compensatory favoritism policies were required if the children of peas-

58. Capitalists and their offspring were also considered a bad class category, but they were not included in the black elements.
59. Mao Zedong, "Conversations with Comrades Hysni Kapo and Beqir Baluku (February 3, 1967)," *Long Live Mao Zedong Thought* (Taipei: Institute of International Relations, July 1974), pp. 663-667, cited in Chang Ching-li, "CCP's Treatment of the 'Five Categories of Elements,'" p. 13.

ants and workers—the groups who were supposed to be the beneficiaries of the revolution—were to get their fair share of education and
jobs.

The proportion of worker-peasant-cadre-soldier youth in college did
increase as a result of favorable affirmative action policies and the
improvement in rural education: their enrollment figures rose from
approximately 20 percent in 1953 to 48 percent in 1958 and to 66
percent in 1965. But compared with the almost 90 percent of the
population who were labeled proletarian, this category was still under-
represented in higher education. Despite class favoritism policies, an
opportunity gap remained in 1965; based on the above figures, it has
been estimated that approximately 3 percent of "exploiting class" youth
and only .5 percent of "proletarian" youth had access to higher education.[60] In fact, the disparity was even greater than it appears in these
national estimates, because students from worker-peasant families
were likely to attend inferior local colleges whereas the children of
urban intellectuals and officials attended the major national universities.[61] Although worker-peasant youth continued to be at a disadvantage in the contest for university admissions, in the intensely competitive
urban high schools attended by the respondents I interviewed, it often
appeared that good class origin gave one a special advantage during the
1962-1964 period, when background was emphasized in recruitment
policies.

A second reason for class favoritism was that it was supposed to help
guarantee that new generations of leaders would be staunchly committed to serving communism and the people. The presumption was that
family environment had a dominant influence on individual attitudes,
and therefore that family background was the best predictor of individual political orientations. The campaign to Cultivate Revolutionary
Successors in 1963-1964 made these assumptions explicit:

> Some persons who do not come from families of laboring people,
> through education by the party can forsake their original class and can
> be tempered through revolutionary struggles into proletarian revolu-
> tionaries. But attention must be paid to insuring that people of good
> class and family origin who have been tempered for a long period

60. Townsend, *The Revolutionization of Chinese Youth*, pp. 67-68.
61. Gardner, "Educated Youth," pp. 266-267, and Emerson, "Manpower Traning,"
p. 193.

through class struggles account for the greatest majority of the nucleus of the leadership of the revolutionary ranks of the proletariat. This is the class basis for guaranteeing that the revolutionary ranks and the nucleus of leadership will never change color.[62]

The movement to learn from Lei Feng, a model of revolutionary sacrifice, which also was prominent in the media and in classrooms during 1963-1964, stressed that "Comrade Lei Feng's deep class consciousness and his ordinary but great communist spirit were inseparable from the fact that he came from a family of hired peasants and suffered great hardships at the hands of the landlord class, and from the exploitation and oppression by the ruling class in the old society".[63] The equating of worker-peasant-cadre-soldier origin with revolutionary consciousness made it difficult for students of other backgrounds to pass political muster and gain admission to the Youth League after 1962.[64] Youth of non-proletarian origin approaching graduation after 1962 perceived that their chances for university admission had worsened. But because the policy was ambiguous, exploiting class youth were never prohibited from entering college—as they had been during the early 1930s in the Soviet Union—and they nurtured the hope that outstanding academic or political achievements might compensate for their bad class label.

In 1965 the political pendulum swung away from class labels back to individual political performance, as Mao shifted his attention from the old bourgeoisie to the new one that had emerged under socialism. He worried that the Party and government cadres whose children benefited from class-line policies based on pre-Liberation class categories were themselves becoming a new privileged class. In the old society, capitalists based their dominance on economic power, but under socialism officials who took the "capitalist road" based their dominance on political power. Mao used the old class language against this new class enemy, but he developed a new behavioral definition of class. The designations of "proletarian" and "bourgeois" were affixed according

62. "Cultivate and Train Millions of Successors Who Will Carry on the Cause of Proletarian Revolution," RMRB editorial, August 3, 1964, SCMP, 3274, pp. 4-5.
63. "Does a Good Family Background Obviate the Need of Ideological Remolding," ZGQNB, March 28, 1963, SCMP, 2968. Quoted in Rosen, "Students, Administrators, and Mobility," p. 21.
64. During 1963 and 1964 there were many articles on following the class line in YCL recruitment. For example, ZGQNB, November 7, 1963, SCMP, 3115, p. 4. Cited in White, *The Politics of Class and Class Origins,* p. 13.

to one's own political beliefs and actions, not according to the class label of one's parents.

Signaling this shift from class background to individual political performance was the 1965 movement to learn from the model of Wang Jie, who in clear contrast with Lei Feng was a youth of ordinary class background (middle peasant) who had conquered his class handicap.[65] After its national congress in 1964, the Youth League took a more tolerant attitude toward class background and broadened its base even to the point of "including the majority of the youth from families of the exploiting class."[66] YCL branches were reminded that "children of the members of the exploiting class are not members of the exploiting class, and they have long been educated in the Thought of Mao Zedong."[67] According to the respondents, most League branches implemented this policy and considered more exploiting class youth for membership during 1965 and 1966. Although not all such applicants were admitted, students without class credentials felt that they had a better chance to prove themselves politically than they had during 1963 and 1964.

The class policy of the regime—pay attention to origin, but don't pay exclusive attention to origin and instead put the major stress on individual political behavior—remained stable but confusing between 1960 and 1966. Because Mao saw both the old and the new bourgeoisie as threats to his vision of the good society, he continued to use the old ascriptive definition of class alongside the new behavioral definition.

Because the system of selection combined "contest mobility" (in which advancement is earned by individual achievement) with "sponsored mobility" (in which certain groups are granted advancement because of ascriptive status such as class origin), everyone felt victimized by discrimination.[68] Many students from ordinary or bad class backgrounds believed that despite their academic and political accomplishments, class sponsorship rigged the mobility game against them. Students from worker-peasant families, whose academic and political

65. *The Diary of Wang Jieh* (Beijing, Foreign Languages Press, 1967), p. 6. Also expressing this tolerant attitude toward those of non-proletarian origin was a speech by Peng Zhen stating that "the Party deals with youths of different class origins and different life experiences by chiefly considering their behavior." GMRB, April 5, 1965, SCMP, 3441, p. 19; and articles with such titles as "The Class Policy which Attaches Importance to Behavior must be Implemented," *Zhongguo qingnian* (ZGQN), September 1, 1965, *Selections from China Mainland Magazines* (SCMM), 495, pp. 35-38.

66. ZGQN, May 16, 1965, SCMM, 479, p. 13.

67. ZGQN, May 16, 1965, SCMM, 479, p. 15.

68. Turner, "Modes of Social Ascent Through Education;" Bock, "Countervailing Outcomes of Malaysian Education," p. 72.

progress was handicapped by poverty, lack of parental help, and inferior educational preparation, viewed the contest for advancement as inherently unfair. The ambiguity of selection criteria fueled the fights between rival Red Guard factions during the Cultural Revolution. The first Red Guard units to establish themselves in the spring of 1966 included many children of important cadres and permitted only children of the "five types of red" to participate. Forming later in opposition to these groups and their doctrine of "natural redness" were the rebel Red Guard groups, which consisted mainly of students from ordinary and bad class backgrounds.[69] Up to the time of his death in 1976, Mao never resolved his ambiguous position on the relative importance of old ascriptive class background categories and new behavioral ones, even though this issue was the crux of the Red Guard factional conflicts of the Cultural Revolution.

After Mao's death, Deng Xiaoping and the Party moderates moved to rehabilitate most of those who had been given bad class labels in previous campaigns and declared their intention to treat people equally regardless of class origin and evaluate people on the basis of individual political performance rather than class origin.[70] After years of living under an ambiguous class policy, the officials who must make decisions about admissions and hiring are, however, still reluctant to give good opportunities to people with bad class labels.[71] They worry that if the line on political evaluation is revised again in the future, they will be accused of being soft on class struggle. Nevertheless, students today are judged less on their family origins and more on their academic and political achievements than were those who preceded them in 1960-1966, and this change is bound to have an effect on student behavior in the future.

The Teachers

The ambiguity of educational selection criteria during 1960-1966 made it difficult for students to determine which was most important—

69. Hong Yung Lee, *Politics of the Chinese Cultural Revolution;* Montaperto, "From Revolutionary Successors to Revolutionaries"; Rosen, "Background to Rebellion"; White, *The Politics of Class and Class Origin.*

70. "Decision of the Central Committee of the Chinese Communist Party on Removing the Labels of Landlords and Rich Peasants and Changing the Class Label of the Children of Landlords and Rich Peasants," *Xinhua yuebao,* No. 1 (1979), pp 48–49; Chang Ching-li, "CCP's Treatment of the "Five Categories of Elements,' " pp. 13–27.

71. An example is described in ZGQN, No. 10 (1979), pp. 20–21.

academic achievement, political behavior, or class background—and what their own chances were. Students' uncertainty about selection priorities was heightened by the contradictory signals they received from their teachers and school administrators. There was a lag between policy and practice because school authorities could not keep up with the current formula; and the authorities injected their own biases into the process as well. Since the school's evaluation of each student's character—based on the conduct comments written by the class director—was a crucial part of college admissions (and probably of job assignment and Party recruitment as well), the personal standards of acceptability held by teachers and principals were carefully analyzed by every student. The bad luck of being assigned (often for two or three years) a class director who favored studious students when you were an activist with mediocre grades (or vice versa) could ruin your career.

According to the respondents, teachers' preferences were not difficult to discern. Every teacher had favorites whom he or she frequently called on in class, chatted with outside of class, and invited to visit at home. Favoritism influenced teachers' grading practices in some courses, mainly in politics and Chinese language, because in these subjects, one respondent said, "there was no absolute standard." Teachers also liked to delegate responsibilities to their favorite students, appointing them course representatives in the course they taught, or if they served as class director, nominating them for class office. By these kinds of actions, teachers signaled to students their personal priorities.[72]

According to the respondents and press reports, most high school teachers leaned toward students who were studious and obedient.[73] It is not surprising that since academic study remained the central purpose of the school, the institutional authorities favored those who did the

72. For example, Jiang, the son of a former member of the Kuomintang, served as class president at the class director's request for two years in junior high school. When a new class director was assigned to the class in its junior-3 year, he expelled Jiang and replaced him with a working-class student. And when in senior-1 yet another class director (at the same school) took over the class, he returned Jiang to office. By these moves each teacher announced to the students his or her position on the relative importance of background or behavior.

73. Even before the Cultural Revolution, a teacher's preference for bourgeois students who had "good grades," were "polite," and "clean," was criticized as being devoid of class or political content. See *Zhongguo funu* (Chinese Women), February 1, 1965; *Wen hui bao* (Shanghai), February 20, 1965; *Yangsheng wanbao* (Canton), March 19, 1965. A post-Cultural Revolution article describes a teacher who realized that judging student behavior according to quietness and obedience rather than according to political stance was wrong: "This way of doing things cannot bring up little pace-setters in the proletarian revolution and can only bring up bourgeois 'lambs'!" RMRB, June 9, 1974, SCMP, 5656, p. 172.

institutional task best. It is only natural that mathematics teachers, for example, chose as teachers' pets the students who excelled in mathematics.

Academic achievers (many of whom were from bourgeois families) also benefited from the personal biases of most high school teachers. Because of the shortage of trained teachers, the government has had to retain teachers educated before 1949 and to recruit new teachers who were themselves more expert than red. The older teachers in particular were somewhat prejudiced against working class students and preferred students who were studious, polite, and well-dressed. In one respondent's school, older teachers often criticized students with torn, dirty clothes—who were usually the children of workers or peasants. Some older teachers, especially those educated abroad or those interested in foreign ideas (usually the foreign language teachers), nurtured cosmopolitanism. They showed a preference for students who had a yen to learn about foreign cultures and who would eagerly listen to the teacher's reminiscences. Other older teachers, especially those who taught Chinese language and literature, favored students who were interested in traditional Chinese culture and morality. Many students, particularly those of bourgeois background themselves, held these senior bourgeois teachers in high esteem and formed something of a counter-culture around them. Because these teachers seldom were politically reliable enough to be appointed class director, students felt relatively free with them and used them, as they used their friends (see Chapter Five), to escape from the political pressures of the class.

A smaller number of teachers leaned toward students who were politically active and from proletarian families. These teachers usually were younger, of good or ordinary background, and members of the Youth League or Communist Party. According to one teacher who was interviewed, the young, politically aware teachers usually taught politics or arts subjects, were of a lower cultural level than the older teachers, and did not get along with the older teachers. In some schools, such teachers allied themselves with the school CCP secretary against the principal, who was supported by the senior teachers. Because class directors were required to be "politically progressive," the younger teachers were often given this authority role.[74] Therefore most but not

74. "Jiangsu Province Temporary Regulations on the Class Director's Duties," *Zhongxue jiaoshih* (High School Teacher), No. 8 (1957), pp. 22-23.

all the teachers who were responsible for evaluating student conduct emphasized activism and background rather than diligence in study.

Favoritism was motivated by career considerations as well as personal preferences. Teachers and principals were promoted according to their students' rate of success in the contest for university admissions. Although admissions depended on a combination of political and academic criteria, the teachers and administrators felt they could do more to improve their students' course grades and entrance examination scores than they could do to improve their political credentials.[75] Like a coach with a team of athletes, they were dependent upon those they taught and were solicitous of their academic "stars." However, teachers bent on political careers—politics teachers, class directors, and those trying to move up in the Party—had to worry more about their students' political progress. They favored the activists and those who showed themselves willing to be saved.[76] They could not afford to be conspicuously sympathetic to students—particularly those from bad backgrounds—who had reputations for political unreliability.

Although most teachers stressed expertness over redness, the majority of class directors took the opposite view. The variation in teacher preferences—a class director who liked your type of student might be replaced next year by a teacher who did not like your type—added to the uncertainty generated by ambiguous recruitment practices.

THE IMPACT OF POLICIES ON SCHOOL BEHAVIOR

Policy decisions concerning the supply and distribution of mobility opportunities determine what career incentives are available to the leaders of socializing organizations for use in molding their members.

75. "The revolutionary teachers and students realize that in the past the students studied for grades and the teachers taught for grades. The reason was that the high grades ensured the teachers of promotion." Xinhua, October 29, 1967.

76. For example, Huang told me that he found himself the target of schoolwide struggle meetings because his class director happened to be a candidate member of the Party: "She decided that she had a new and better way to carry out criticism and she needed a case to demonstrate it to the other teachers. So she picked out me and my friend and criticized us for writing an article for the class blackboard newspaper about how to study well, without mentioning politics in it. Ordinarily such a small thing would not have led to struggle meetings, except that the class director was ambitious. The struggle meetings went on for a month. After the struggle we really put ourselves out to prove that we were reformed, by attending League class, working very actively, and acting very red. The class director, of course, wanted us to appear to be revolutionized as a result of the struggle meetings, to show that her method worked. So she wrote us a good final conduct comment and we both were

The decisions to limit higher education and urban job opportunities, to send high school graduates to the countryside, to control college and job assignments through the state, and to apportion college and job opportunities to localities put students at Chinese urban high schools in competition with one another. Because educational selection was based on political criteria as well as academic ones, students had to engage in political as well as intellectual competition. One consequence of combining academic and political factors in selection—a positive one from the communist leadership's point of view—was that it motivated students to strive for excellence in both realms. Because no one could be sure which selection formula would prevail at graduation, few students gave up in defeat. Most kept their hopes alive and worked hard to earn the best academic and political records they could. Students chose a strategy that maximized their comparative advantage, but the ones who concentrated on academics and the ones who stressed politics had to compete with one another. As the following chapters will show, the social ramifications of this kind of competition were negative from the perspective of the leadership's goals of moral transformation.

The social conflicts described in this book took a particularly acute form after 1963. Changes in recruitment policies explain why political competition became more intense after that year: a larger number of graduates were sent to the countryside; the government strengthened its control over job allocation; there was a shift in admissions standards from academics to politics; class background favoritism became more pronounced, although students from non-proletarian backgrounds were still not supposed to be excluded from vanguard organizations or from college. The intense competition of 1963-1966 was especially destructive of social cohesion at the elite key schools, which offered students higher probabilities of success, and especially during the senior high school years, when the climax of graduation approached.

The drastic transformation in student behavior wrought by the Cultural Revolution provides vivid evidence in support of the argument that behavior is shaped by policies concerning the distribution of career opportunities. When the rules of the game changed, student behavior changed too. After 1969 college selection was completely separated

admitted to university." Some teachers who were concerned about their careers also thought it prudent to give special tutoring to the children of important officials, and, in rural schools, to be especially nice to children from the powerful clans and lineages.

from high school performance.[77] Therefore students were no longer pitted against each other in academic or political competition, and school authorities were robbed of the "carrots and sticks" they had previously used to motivate student achievement. Because almost all students confronted uniformly dismal futures in the countryside, a situation similar to that in the pre-1966 urban private schools developed in the public schools: there sprang up a delinquent peer culture in which young people were more concerned with social acceptance than with success in school.[78] Teachers had trouble enforcing classroom order: many students were truant, and if they came to class at all, they slept, chatted, or played cards.[79] When the Cultural Revolution destroyed the school's incentive structure, the respect for learning and desire for scholastic achievement that have often been described as constants of Chinese culture disappeared almost overnight, and were replaced by mischievousness and apathy.

This book concentrates on student behavior between 1960 and 1966 at the majority of urban high schools which were regular schools (that is, either ordinary or key schools). The impact of recruitment policies on behavior, however, can be even more vividly illustrated by a brief comparison with other types of schools. Unlike the students described in this book, who confronted school situations of risk and uncertainty, students at specialized and private schools faced uniform futures— either certain success or certain failure.

77. But old assumptions are hard to change. Sometimes the local Communist Party committee responsible for selection "visited schools and units where persons under recommendation formerly studied and worked to find out their past records." Anhwei People's Radio Station, March 29, 1972, URS, Vol. 67, No. 15, p. 205.

78. In fact, students did not face uniform futures: some were sent to farms in other provinces, while others were assigned to nearby suburban communes, and a few others were recruited into the Army or given urban jobs. But the basis for differentiation was not so much school record as it was exigencies of family situation or parental influence (only children or children from families with special hardships were permitted to remain in the city, and the children of well-connected officials managed to obtain city jobs). See Bernstein, *Up to the Mountains*, pp. 105-116. Another reason for the decline of student ambition and competition was that students were no longer tracked by ability into key and ordinary schools, but were assigned to neighborhood schools. Under the previous tracking system, those students studying at key schools had had higher expectations because they knew that their chances for success were better than for those at ordinary schools. In schools with more heterogeneous student bodies, expectations were lower.

79. Unger, *Education Under Mao*, Chapters 7 and 9.

Specialized Schools—Guaranteed Success

Although graduates of specialized schools rarely had the chance to enter college, they were virtually guaranteed good city jobs in their hometowns after graduation. The picture of student behavior in such schools—based on the accounts of one respondent whom I interviewed and one who was interviewed by other scholars—contrasts with that in regular schools.[80] Because their futures were assured, students in specialized schools—especially those for training administrative cadres—eagerly exchanged their commitment to political values for the certainty of positions of relatively high status.[81] All students strove to be politically active. Youth League activists generally were liked and admired by their peers. Students wanted to associate with activists rather than avoid them. There was a taut political atmosphere in which students strictly criticized one another's failings, but criticism lacked the rancor created by political competition among insecure youth. Students were not forced to choose between friendship loyalties and staunch mutual criticism because peer group norms supported the criticism process and other regime values, and because in this type of student political culture, friendship had been transformed into less intense comradeship. Although this picture should not be exaggerated—life at specialized schools was not free of all conflicts, and some schools, such as those for training athletes or musicians, were quite apolitical—still the behavior of specialized school students more closely approximated regime standards than the behavior of less secure students at schools where failure was a realistic possibility.

Because they were confident of success, these students might have been expected to relax their political and academic efforts and let the school give them a "free ride," but this apparently was not the case. It was difficult to gain entry to many specialized high schools, especially

80. See Montaperto, "From Revolutionary Successors to Revolutionaries"; Whyte, *Small Groups and Political Rituals,* pp. 96-134; Bennett and Montaperto, *Red Guard: The Biography of Dai Hsiao-ai.*

81. John Bock has written: "The social power of a school which is seen as virtually assuring elite recruitment of its clients is quite substantial and [is] a powerful resource in its task of resocialization. . . . Educational institutions which can assure their students subsequent entry into elite status possess higher exchange values and, therefore, greater power over their students, than those schools which are not able to implement the success of their product" (Bock, "Education and Nation-Building in Malaysia," Chapter 2). Also Meyer, "The Charter: Conditions of Diffuse Socialization in Schools," p. 575.

those for training cadres; students were accepted only after demonstrating academic and political excellence in junior high school. Having overcome such obstacles, the future cadres sensed a "covenant between themselves and the leaders of the country" and were eager to repay the Party for its trust in them.[82]

Private Schools—Certain Failure

At the opposite end of the secondary school spectrum were the private, or *minban* (people-run) schools. The "charter" of the private school was very low: attendance at such a school was defined as failure. As Wu, a private school student, explained: "A private school is where people who couldn't get into a good school and who didn't want to go to the countryside stayed to kill time."[83] Private school students knew their situation was hopeless: it was almost impossible for a graduate of such a school to be admitted to university or be assigned a good city job.

In these circumstances, school authorities had no incentives with which to shape student behavior, and students had no reason to strive for good grades or political activism. Such schools were pervaded by an apolitical atmosphere, with students concerned mainly about their social lives (especially dating and romances) and material possessions. There was more cooperation—especially more cheating on examinations—than in public schools; it was cooperation that grew out of a camaraderie of losers. Students' desire to win the approval of their peers eclipsed their concern for political values or for their own futures, thereby creating a delinquent student counter-culture.[84]

This counter-culture was not completely devoid of competition, however. Individual competition can be generated by school peer

82. Montaperto, "From Revolutionary Successors to Revolutionaries," p. 590. As Albert Hirschman has explained, a high price of entry leads to loyalist behavior in organizations. On the relationship between selectivity and commitment in organizations, see Etzioni, *Modern Organizations*, p. 69. In vocational and teacher training schools which were less selective and which prepared students for less prestigious occupations, I expect that there would be less enthusiastic commitment to regime values.

83. One of David Raddock's respondents said that being forced to attend a private school was like "falling from heaven to earth." Raddock, *Political Behavior of Adolescents in China*, p. 85.

84. In other school systems, students in lower tracks whose mobility prospects are bleak often develop an anti-system delinquent peer culture. For example, see Stinchombe, *Rebellion in a High School*, and Hargreaves, *Social Relations in a Secondary School*.

groups as well as by the external demands of adult authorities.[85] In private schools students competed for popularity (girls strove for popularity with boys as well as with members of their own sex), rather than for political or academic points with the teacher. Because the future appeared hopeless, these students invested all their energies in the "popularity game."

One respondent, Wu, the daughter of a former Kuomintang official, had attended such a private senior high school from 1963 to 1966.[86] All the students in her class were from bad family backgrounds. She described the atmosphere in the class as politically "backward," an idiom commonly used to depict an attitude of apathy or resistance to official political standards. As Wu said, "Nobody was concerned about school life. They went to school only because they had nothing else to do." There was only one political activist in the class—a girl whose father lived in Taiwan—and she was seen as a deviant in the private school political culture: "Other students didn't like her constant criticism of the class. They said she was just wasting her time since everyone in the class did those bad things [cheating and talking in class] except her."

The lack of political or academic competition did not, however, create harmony among the students in the class. As Wu described it, there were many cliques and conflicts among them, mainly over relations with the opposite sex and possessions such as clothes, family cars, and bicycles. Girls spent most of their time talking about clothes and boys, and friendship relations between girls were afflicted with the constant jealous rivalries that can be found in many American high schools. Wu and her best girl friend "split-up" because of jealousy over a boy. Wu's clique of girls was resented by two other female cliques "because we all hung around a lot with the richest boys who had bicycles and could take us on picnics on the weekends."

It might be argued that the different behavior patterns characteristic of specialized, private, and regular high schools resulted from the types

85. In her analysis of American city schools, *Scene of the Battle,* Joan Roberts makes the mistake of assuming that student society is naturally cooperative. For good analyses of social competition in American high schools, see Coleman, *The Adolescent Society,* and Gordon, *The Social System of the High School.*

86. Three other informants had attended Overseas Chinese private high schools, but these schools had a different charter because their graduates could win admission to universities. One of these respondents, Guo, went on to study chemical engineering at a university after graduating from his high school. The situation at these schools was not hopeless.

of students they admitted, rather than from the futures open to these students. High school selection procedures certainly account for some of the differences among schools. Primary school graduates were admitted to junior high school, and junior high graduates to senior high school, mainly on the basis of school grades and scores on entrance examinations, although political record and class background were also examined. The best applicants were channeled to key schools, the average ones to ordinary schools in their neighborhoods, and the worst ones left to private schools (if they could afford the tuition, and rural transfer or urban unemployment, if they could not). The high level of political commitment found at specialized schools was, in part, due to the fact that these schools, especially those for training cadres, selected students who had established a good political track record in junior high school. The delinquent counter-culture found in private schools stemmed in part from the fact that these schools were forced to admit students who had in their previous schools failed in academic and political endeavors. Interpersonal competition was more intense in key schools than in ordinary neighborhood schools, and more intense in senior high than in junior high, because these schools admitted only those individuals who had been achievers at the previous level of education.[87]

Variation in the selectivity of school admissions standards is not, however, a sufficient explanation for the different social patterns found in different types of schools. Students' expectations about their futures were the dominant influence on their behavior. They adapted their behavior to the structure of opportunities and the rules of the game. Students with as mediocre an academic record, as poor a political history, and as bad a family background as many students at private schools, when presented with the chance of success at a regular high school, tried hard to achieve intellectually and conform politically. And students at regular high schools, who were in every way the equal of students at specialized schools for training cadres, accommodated to the risk of failure by avoiding activists and by nurturing friendships more often than students at the specialized schools.

87. My analysis focuses on the competition for post-graduation opportunities in senior high schools and pays little attention to the competition among junior high school students for senior high school admission. Although the opportunities for further education available to junior high school graduates were roughly as scarce as those available to senior high graduates, and the win-lose differential was just as wide (many of those who failed to be admitted to senior high were shipped off to the countryside too), the respondents described junior high life as much less competitive than that in senior high. A possible explanation is that junior high students were too young to appreciate what was at stake.

3

CHOOSING A STRATEGY
To Be or Not to Be an Activist

The high school environment confronted students with intense pressures and important choices. They were buffeted by the conflicting pressures of ambition, friendship, and idealism. They had to decide how to pursue their goals in the context of the incentives offered by the school, incentives which were structured by national policies and by the preferences of teachers. Although these calculations were not always conscious, all students had to decide how to invest their time and energy.

The key choice was whether to concentrate on academic studies or on political activism. This crucial strategic decision depended largely on how the student perceived his or her comparative advantage in the competition for scarce post-graduation opportunities. Many students invested their time and energy in political activities—mainly the Young Communist League—and became political activists. Some political activists also tried to maintain good grades, while others hoped that a record of activism would compensate for poor grades. Other students concentrated on their studies and kept a low political profile. But even those who took the academic route had to make sure that they were politically acceptable and were not seen as "backward." And when they felt the political climate change after 1963, some of these academic types concluded that the political minimum would no longer suffice and that a greater degree of political zeal was required. Among studious ones, there also were "failed activists" whose efforts to prove their political enthusiasm were rejected, and who therefore put all their eggs in the academic basket. And, finally, there were a small number of students who focused their energies on athletics or the arts because outstanding athletes were often recruited by universities for their teams, and outstanding performers and artists were sometimes assigned to enter conservatories and professional troupes.

Table 4 summarizes the strategies pursued by 28 of the 29 re-

TABLE 4. Student Strategies

Class Background	Strategy		
	Political Activism	*Academic Achievement and Political Activism*	*Academic Achievement*
Good	1	1	0
Middle	2	3	10
Bad	1	2	8

NOTE: The academic achievers are those who reported themselves as having high grades or as striving for academic excellence. The political activists are those who reported themselves as playing a political leadership role in the class. Not all activists were Youth League members: five were YCL members; one had applied and was being considered for membership when the Cultural Revolution closed the schools in 1966; one was a Young Pioneer activist in junior high school but left China before senior high school; two had applied to the YCL and were rejected because of class background; and one never applied. Two of the academic achievers were "failed activists" who had tried to join the League but were rejected because of class background.

spondents who attended regular high schools. There was also one respondent whose academic standing was so low and class background so bad that he knew he was doomed to rural transfer; therefore, he psychically withdrew from school society, sought solace in his family, and planned his escape to Hong Kong.[1] The inventory of student strategies would be incomplete without mentioning the female students who made only halfhearted efforts to achieve in academics or politics because they believed that success depended more on the man they married than on their own careers. In other words, they substituted the marriage market for the career market.[2] They worried about catching a husband who was a cadre, or at least a Party member, rather than striving to become one themselves. There were no such girls among our respondents, although several respondents remarked that girls were generally more relaxed politically than boys.

1. This type of student was under-represented in our "sample" of refugees. Most of the young people who left China for Hong Kong were driven by very strong career ambitions (and a profound antipathy toward rural life), and therefore were most unlikely to concede defeat.

2. Stinchcombe, *Rebellion in a High School*, p. 151. According to a memoir of student life in the early days of the People's Republic, whereas before Liberation young women clung to the hope of marrying a student returned from abroad, in the 1950s they told themselves, "I will only marry a Party comrade" or "I will only love a Youth League member." Yen, *The Umbrella Garden*, pp. 190-191.

The respondents' accounts of their own decision-making and their descriptions of that of fellow-students indicate that the choice of strategy was based on judgments of comparative advantage. Students searched for strategies that would build on their strong points and compensate for their weak points. The critical variables were intellectual ability, political skill, and family class background.

For example, if your background was a liability and you were intellectually clever, you were likely to concentrate on academic study. The distribution of natural abilities and patterns of family socialization made it likely that the children from non-proletarian families would take the academic route. Although no Chinese researchers have dared to undertake a study of the determinants of educational achievement, apparently family background is the dominant factor, as it is in other countries. Many respondents observed, as Wang did, that "The students with bad class background and most children of cadres tend to have the best grades, whereas the students with good working-class background usually don't have good grades."

Those who were poor in study, even if they had an illustrious revolutionary pedigree, had to demonstrate political activism because family origin in itself was not sufficient to assure success. Many respondents referred to political activists who "had bad grades and so needed to become active to accumulate political capital." But even if their grades were good, youth from good family background tended to develop their natural advantage and become political activists.

The change in political atmosphere after 1963 was keenly felt by high school students. Before that time, academic achievers who were politically passable (but not necessarily active) were likely to be admitted to university. As Huang, a 1964 graduate who went on to college, described the situation at his key school in the early 1960s: "There were only a few students with good grades in my class who didn't get admitted to any university. It took good grades and *not bad* political background plus activism to get into university. It was not necessary to be very active if your grades were excellent."

The academic strategy appeared less viable after 1963, however, when the political performance and class background criteria for university admission and job assignment became more important. Students of non-proletarian origin found their background becoming more of a liability at the same time as the pressure for active political participation increased. The Youth League responded to the increased demands for membership by implementing a relatively open recruitment policy.

This policy of welcoming youth from middle and bad family background no doubt further stimulated the efforts of such individuals to prove that they were more than politically passable. It is in this context that we find a significant number of students from non-proletarian families venturing down the political road after 1963.

CHOOSING TO BE AN ACTIVIST

In any organization, "natural leaders"—people who enjoy being out in front and who have a knack for mobilizing others—will emerge. In Chinese city schools, certain individuals—from the time of junior high school, or even as early as primary school—were chosen every year to be class officers or Young Pioneer officers. These individuals were acceptable to both students and teachers. Frequently they were recruited into the Young Communist League and became the political activists of senior high school.

Many students became political activists not only because they liked to lead, but also because they felt that activism was the legitimate responsibility of a good Chinese citizen. Even the most cynical respondents reported that many political activists were sincerely committed to the revolution. The accounts of several activist-respondents illustrate the way in which natural leadership aptitudes and genuine enthusiasm for political service were mixed with an element of self-interest. Peng had this to say:

> I was such an out-and-out activist, that when the news of my escaping to Hong Kong came, everybody in the school was surprised. I was active in those days because I saw it as my responsibility to do those things, and I wanted to be a League member. Also deep inside I knew that being an activist would be better for my future, especially for going to university. I was such an activist that now when I meet old friends from the Mainland they tease me for being an opportunist. But before senior-2 I really believed in what I was doing and hadn't thought a bit about myself. I liked the job, I liked to work for people. But in senior-3 I vaguely thought that what I was doing might be helpful for my future, for university.

Even an activist strategy consciously aimed at maximizing one's chances for university admission was not necessarily cynical. Many students were willing to exchange active political participation for the chance to enter university because they believed it proper that the state ask for higher levels of commitment from people in elite roles. As Yang, an academic achiever who became an activist, described his motives:

> I applied to join [the Youth League] because I wanted to go to university and I realized that the minimum level of political activism for a university student was being a Youth League member. To be a university student one should be studious and also active at least to the extent of being a League member. Of course, everyone on the Mainland cares about politics, and so it's simply a matter of the level of activism appropriate to your position—for example, if you don't want to be a cadre then you don't have to be very, very active.

Another motivation for joining the Youth League was the elite status of the organization itself. Even though students didn't admire all League members, they respected the organization as the revolutionary vanguard of Chinese youth. While they might resent certain League members for putting defense of official morality ahead of friendship loyalties, they were themselves believers in this morality and felt it proper that there be such an organization of people totally committed to it. Yang, a Youth League applicant, put it this way: "Students felt that the Youth League was basically a good organization. In my view, it helps people morally. What I mean is that being a member of the League would make you behave better. Generally people would think that the League is prestigious, that a League member is a good person who is fairly good in every respect."

The exclusivity of the organization also stimulated demands for entry. The Youth League admitted only those deemed particularly worthy of the honor—in most city high schools this amounted to no more than one-third of the class by the time of senior high graduation. The League had its own special rites and symbols, its meetings were secret, and its members were given political information to which ordinary students were not privy. Kang, the one respondent who had attended a rural school, described his motives for entering the League:

> I joined the League because it felt good to wear the League pin and have that status. Since it's not that easy to be admitted, when you see other people joining, you feel that if they can get in, "why can't I?" Also the League members were very powerful in the class because they could struggle against people they wanted to "get" for other reasons. Also there are three practical advantages of YCL membership. First, it's easier to get a job; second, only if you are a League member are you

trustworthy enough to join the PLA, which is the main road out of the
countryside for a peasant; and third, only League members can later
get into the Communist Party.

Although Kang was the only respondent who admitted that he was
attracted by the power as well as the status of the League, no doubt
other aspirants also appreciated the power that automatically accrued
to YCL members, stemming from their access to teachers, their role in
class elections, and their political security.

Students were sometimes discouraged as well as attracted by the elite
character of the Youth League. They worried that they were not worthy
enough to join—that they were too selfish or too undisciplined. When
they got to know YCL members, however, they were less in awe of
them. One unintended consequence of "heart-to-heart talks" (*tanxin*),
in which League members probed the political thoughts of potential
recruits, was that familiarity bred—if not contempt—then at least a
more realistic view of League members. After spending a considerable
amount of time with YCL members, the ordinary student realized that
they were no purer than anyone else. Yang described how his view of
the Youth League secretary changed after heart-to-heart talks: "I was
pretty close to him in senior-3 because I wanted to join the League and
had to talk with him about my progress, my thought, etc. When I got
close to him, I saw that he was not really all that active; he had some
ulterior goals like joining the Party, going to university, and eventually
becoming a high-level cadre." A more realistic evaluation of League
members had two different implications for the decision to seek membership: it might diminish one's desire to join the organization, or it
might provide reassurance that one merited League status just as much
as those who were already members.

Even when students were strongly attracted to Youth League membership and political activism because they welcomed the opportunity
to use leadership abilities, were committed to political service, and
respected the status of the League organization, they also recognized the
practical advantages of activism. The primary advantage of being an
activist—especially of being a YCL member and class officer—was that
it was noted on your permanent record, and thus became an asset for
university admission, job assignment, and acceptance into the Party. As
one League respondent succinctly stated her reason for joining: "I

wanted to get into university so I joined the League in the first term of senior-3. It was the easier road to take." The peasant Kang emphasized that League membership was required for recruitment into the Army, which for rural youth was a more promising route out of the village than university admission. Moreover, parents often urged their children to pursue a political strategy to enhance their careers. Even parents who were former capitalists, such as Luo's parents, offered this type of advice. Luo said:

> I applied to join the Youth League in junior-2 because it would be easier to go to senior high. My family advised me to do so. A League membership would help you anywhere you go, factory or countryside, not only in senior high. Being a League member means that you are politically all right. . . . Getting rejected by the YCL wasn't a terrible blow to me because although I did want to join to get security for my future, I hadn't been all that enthusiastic about it. It was mainly my family that urged me to apply. Many people in my family were progressive and active and they advised me to be practical. My League application form was filled out by my aunt.

The secondary advantages of League membership and class officership were also substantial. Frequent contact with the class director gave you control over the information reaching the teacher. Thus you could make sure you received good conduct comments; and if you were cunning, you could give the teacher a bad impression of your rivals for class or League office. Even sincerely committed activists such as Peng acknowledged that good conduct comments were a dividend of League membership: "In fact, everybody was thinking about the same thing, which was to get good comments on conduct. . . . Being an activist of course would help you get better comments, which in turn would help enhance your future after graduation, especially when you want to go to university."

Holding class office helped you obtain League membership. "It was easier to get into the Youth League if you were a class officer. Most officers were League members, and those who weren't would later join," said Yang. In addition, the League members' role in selecting the nominees for class offices could lead to their own election (or reelection), thereby further enhancing their political record. Participation in evaluating candidates for YCL recruitment enabled you to exclude individuals—such as someone whose grades were better than yours—who, if they were granted YCL status, might outshine you in the competition for scarce opportunities.

Indeed, the rewards of political activism—in terms of both expressing citizenship loyalties and maximizing future opportunities—were so great that it may be difficult to comprehend why anyone but a private school student would choose not to be an activist. Nevertheless, many made that choice.

CHOOSING NOT TO BE AN ACTIVIST

Most of the respondents, and many students in city high schools, decided not to pursue a political strategy, but rather to invest all their efforts in academic study (or in sports or cultural activities) in the hope that an outstanding academic record, unsullied by any serious political mistake, would suffice for university admission. Political activism might produce great rewards, but it also entailed grave risks, especially for students who lacked political self-confidence. Becoming an activist took a great deal of time and effort. It required making oneself conspicuous, which was potentially dangerous if one were vulnerable to political criticism. And in a system like the Chinese one, in which the definitions of good and bad behavior were broad, imprecise, and frequently changed, the safest approach for the politically unsure was to avoid attracting notice. Moreover, activism sometimes created painful moral dilemmas. It was difficult to harmonize political obligation with friendship loyalty and personal integrity. Becoming an activist could alienate you from your friends and make it difficult for you to be true to yourself. These costs seemed especially high to students without good background credentials, who figured that their chances of winning acceptance as an activist were slim. Therefore, given the risks of activism, many students preferred to follow a safety-first strategy of remaining politically inconspicuous.

The time issue was a real one. Serving as a class or Youth League officer could take all your afternoons and even your weekends, leaving little time for study. One YCL branch secretary "would rarely get home before 7 or 8 at night." This was a serious burden, especially for those students who calculated that their best chance for university admission was academic excellence. Even after 1963, when recruitment policies emphasized class background and political performance, many intellectually gifted youth attending key high schools decided that their best bet was investing time on study rather than politics. As one such student, Xi, said: "Everyone tried to get high grades and were proud of high grades. . . . If your background and political performance weren't too bad, then you had a chance to get into university."

Some key high schools channeled their students to universities with which they had special relationships, much as some American prep schools once placed many of their graduates at Ivy League universities.[3] Students who were the potential beneficiaries of such arrangements knew that the universities liked to recruit a particular type of student, such as the scholar-athlete, from these "feeder" schools. If students fit the image, they could afford to opt out of politics. As one such student, Chen, described his strategy:

> It is easier to get into university if you belong to the Youth League, but I didn't think much about joining, but instead took the approach of trying to impress the teacher with my active role in the class (I was sports and culture officer), my studies, and so on. . . . I decided to spend most of my senior year on studying for exams. I wanted to attend Zhongshan Medical College or Qinghua University, and I knew that both universities especially liked students from my school who had both good grades and good athletic ability. Both universities came to my school sometimes to get students to represent them in sports competitions even before the results of the entrance examination were in. So I figured I had a pretty good chance.

Many students' decisions to allocate scarce time to academics rather than to politics were influenced by the values they acquired at home. Chinese parents—middle class parents in particular—continue to believe that academic study is the central purpose of schooling; they tend to encourage their children to strive for intellectual excellence, and pay less attention to political accomplishments. Scholar-athelete Chen said that his mother influenced him: "When I went home on weekends, she would ask about my studies, why I got a certain grade on an examina-

---

3. Students with parents who were outstanding intellectuals could sometimes rely on parental influence to get into college, and so were free to concentrate on study and abstain from politics. According to one respondent, Zhongshan Medical College in Canton had a rule that the children of professors at the college had first priority to be accepted. Therefore, he explained, "These students knew that their level of political activism would not affect their chances for further study, and they could concentrate on their studies while others had to show a certain degree of activism."

tion, etc. She was less concerned about my nonacademic activities in school so long as they didn't affect my grades."

Political activism was not just time-consuming; it also entailed making oneself conspicuous. Attracting attention was potentially dangerous, especially if you were not confident of your ability to sustain a level of activist behavior or if you were in any way vulnerable to criticism. If you kept a low political profile, then your slips of the tongue or moments of laziness might go unnoticed. But if you stepped out in front, then any mistake might make you a target of criticism—a dilemma that presents itself in all competitive organizations.[4] The politically insecure student could not tolerate the risks of being conspicuous.

The risks were multiplied because you could not wait until just before graduation to stick your neck out. It took time to prove your political commitment; overnight transformations were suspect, especially when your family background was not good. As Luo, a girl who applied to join the YCL but was rejected because of poor class background, explained it: "To be an activist, you had to be active for a long time, not just over the short term. I never had that kind of patience. It was possible that people who were not activists in junior-1 might become so in junior-2 or junior-3, but these people had to be at least politically concerned in junior-1, too. You can't be a star overnight."

The dangers of conspicuous activism were exacerbated by the vague and subjective standards of political behavior in China. People faced the constant risk of having their actions misconstrued. A student who befriended a politically backward classmate in order to reform him or her could be accused of failing to "draw a clear class line." Aspiring activists often found their motives misinterpreted. Someone who spoke out strongly for the first time in self-criticism or against others might be accused of being a political opportunist.[5]

Whereas in some organizations a conspicuous person risks attracting criticism only from the authorities, in a Chinese school aspiring activists

4. For example, in the United States Army, "The man who wants to get ahead necessarily makes himself conspicuous—to get ahead one must stand out from the crowd. In doing this, the ambitious recruit gets his name or face well known to the noncom, who therefore must easily remember him when there is an extra detail to be done. Too, the mistakes—all recruits make scores of mistakes in learning their new culture—of the conspicuous recruit are more easily associated and remembered than those of the inconspicuous recruit, and so the former gets more punishment and more rebuke." Stouffer and others, *The American Soldier,* p. 414.

5. In the Soviet Union, self-criticism is often not accepted as "frank and honest" because it is seen rather "as an attempt to save position for oneself." Novak, *No Third Path,* p. 50.

had to worry about criticism from peers as well as from authorities. The practice of mutual criticism—in small group discussions and class meetings—provided opportunities for fellow students, as well as for teachers, to point out the flaws of those who had made themselves noticeable. Becoming an activist required exposing yourself to criticism and taking the lead in criticism. One of the most serious risks of activism was that you might create enemies who sought revenge by publicly criticizing you in return.[6]

Although mutual criticism had divisive effects in the competitive environment of Chinese city high schools, peer group norms softened the impact of mutual criticism. Although it was in any individual's interest to impress the authorities by criticizing a classmate, it was also in everyone's interest not to be the target of criticism. Therefore peer group norms evolved that accepted the need to strive for success but condemned as "over-eager" all efforts that hurt others and seemed insincere. In specialized schools where success was a "sure thing," peer group norms supported mutual criticism, but in regular schools where failure was a real possibility, the norms required individuals to show that they were more loyal to their peers than to the authorities. Thus small group members were expected to criticize others, but only infrequently and only for minor shortcomings. These norms, by raising the price (in the currency of popularity) of breaking rank, gave everyone some protection from the political exertions of peers. Students who chose to remain politically inconspicuous conformed to these norms; according to respondents, only those trying to prove their activism "were forceful in speaking and spoke a lot during mutual criticism meetings; other students barely responded."

Natural leaders were particularly sensitive to the socially alienating consequences of becoming an activist. By joining the Youth League or serving as a class officer you might well damage your relationships with friends and erode your popularity. Serving as class president, for example, improved your career prospects, but the responsibilities of the office—which included mobilizing classmates for political activities, taking the lead in public criticism, and reporting to the class director on your classmates' political thought and behavior—could turn your class-

6. Michel Oksenberg notes that in all Chinese organizations most people say the minimum in criticism sessions in order to avoid making enemies who could harm them in return; those with political ambitions have to risk creating enemies by initiating criticism to prove their activism. "Getting Ahead and Along in Communist China," pp. 331-332.

mates against you. Activists frequently found themselves caught between institutional demands and peer group expectations: In Xu's
words, "Most students prefer not to be chosen as a class officer because
if you do poorly in the job, the League and the class director are after
you all the time, and if you're too harsh, then your fellow-students don't
like you."[7] One result, reported by Tang and echoed by others, was that
"a new class president was usually elected every term, because by the
end of the term almost every officer would be criticized by and resented
by the students—it was a difficult job and hard to please everyone."
Because of the cross-pressures it was difficult to persuade people to hold
even the relatively minor political post of small group head: "You get in
the middle. You end up with bad relations with your classmates because
you have to keep discipline and stop group members from chatting." A
few activists, like An, declined to join the Youth League for these reasons: "one, there is too much restraint on League members; two, as a
League member you have to take the lead; three, you have to inform on
your classmates; and four, it makes the other students avoid you and
distrust you."

This tension between official responsibilities and peer group loyalties characterized most regular high school classes, especially at the
senior high level. The only exception was girls' schools, where, as two
activist respondents explained, the female students were "simpler and
more obedient" and expected their leaders to follow the teacher in
everything. One way that students at coeducational schools managed
the risks of activism was to accept election to the comparatively low-risk
posts of class study officer (responsible for overseeing the blackboard
"newspaper" and improving students' study habits), or class sports
officer or culture officer (both responsible for organizing non-political
extracurricular activities); they could thus show some activism while
avoiding positions of greater political responsibility, such as class president or Youth League officer. Many of the respondents who pursued an
academic strategy served as study officer, because this job could enhance
their chances for university admission without requiring them to criticize people or make enemies.

Many students preferred to abstain from politics altogether because

7. Press articles urged students to be more tolerant of the shortcomings of their class
officers; many students were unwilling to serve because of the fault-finding attitude of their
fellow-students and because it would detract from their time for academic study. *Zhongxuesheng* (ZXS), September 1957, pp. 6-7, and October 1957, p. 14.

they saw that it presented moral as well as social pitfalls. They feared that demands from official authorities and the pressures of their own ambitions would force them to say or do things which they believed to be false or wrong. As one respondent, Xi, said, "Being in the League was too demanding for me; and you had to say things you didn't mean."

In competitive school settings, students confronted the possibility of failure and had to hedge their bets.[8] Many would necessarily be "losers" in the competition for career opportunities, and so they needed to protect themselves against this eventuality. Making a wholehearted academic effort was emotionally less risky than activism, because academic competition was less mutually destructive and good grades were respected by all. Conversely, a total commitment to political life could leave one socially isolated. In specialized high schools, which guaranteed their graduates success, students threw themselves wholeheartedly into political life; but in regular schools, many students were reluctant to make an all-out political effort. The risks of taking time away from study, provoking retaliation and attracting criticism, endangering personal values, and alienating friends were just too great for many students—especially for those who were politically vulnerable and had to protect themselves against the strong possibility of failure.

CLASS BACKGROUND AND CHOICE OF STRATEGY

It is now appropriate to describe in more detail the function of the notion of class background. Mao Zedong asserted that class struggle does not disappear after revolution, but persists during the historical stage of socialism. He believed that children of the former elite (landlords, capitalists, and professionals) were politically unreliable but maintained an advantage in educational competition because of the aptitudes and attitudes they acquired from their parents. The policy remedies for class stratification—in particular, compensatory favor-

---

8. "Each student must hedge his commitment—if it gets too high, failure would be too costly, and failure is a possibility. So, in protecting himself, each student tends to adopt as behaviors and orientations a set of characteristics which represent a realistic combination of the probable futures which at that moment attach to him. This is also made necessary by his relationships with peers and others, who also understand his high probability of failure, and who would regard over-eager attempts on his part to adopt the charter of the school as illegitimate grasping and aping of his betters. In this way the peer culture tends to resist the pressure in institutions." Meyer, "The Charter: Conditions of Diffuse Socialization in Schools," p. 575.

itism for people of worker, peasant, army, or cadre origin, and evaluation of political virtue in class terms—created the conditions for actual
class-based social conflict among Chinese youth. Class divisions were
sustained by policies that distributed power and opportunity in part
according to class origin, and class conflict became bitter because of the
moral connotations attached to class labels. The children of former
capitalists, landlords, and even intellectuals, were not only discriminated against in educational and occupational selection; they were also
assumed to be politically backward—bad people. Especially during
periods such as 1963-1966, when policy and rhetoric emphasized family class origin, the behavioral choices of individual students and the
patterns of social conflict among students were shaped by class considerations. Everyone had to come to grips with his or her class label—if it
was a liability, to compensate for it, if it was an asset, to take advantage
of it.

Students of good class background maximized their advantage by
becoming activists. It was relatively easy for them to win acceptance as
activists and gain admission to the Youth League. The students from
cadre families were the most fortunate. They were the beneficiaries
both of the policy giving preference to people of good class origin and of
the "pull" exerted by their parents' influential friends. Their home
environments were often as conducive to academic achievement as those
of their bourgeois classmates, and many of them excelled academically
as well as politically. Their ability to function in the political arena was
enhanced by the ideological fluency and political skills learned from
their parents, by the information on political trends they also acquired
at home, and by class background invulnerability. Tang, a non-activist
with excellent grades, portrayed cadres' children as "to the manner
born":

> The children of cadres are not hypocritical activists but genuine
> activists. Generally they are brighter than the worker-peasant kids,
> and they usually have either very good or very bad study grades. They
> do tend to stick together a lot and act somewhat superior when to-
> gether, but they really do care about study and they respect kids with
> good grades. In fact, the only non-cadre classmates they do respect are
> the ones with good grades like me. After 1965, they tended to wear
> military uniforms more; when you saw a student in a uniform, you
> knew that he was a child of a cadre or at least one of the Five Good Red
> backgrounds. Many ordinary students resented the children of cadres,

but I didn't. Generally the daughters of cadres are very pretty because cadres marry beautiful women, and the sons are taller because they are not Cantonese. Children of cadres usually are Youth League members. They have a special air about them. They have leadership ability, think well, and speak Mandarin. *They are the individuals who fit best into the Mainland environment* (emphasis added).

Despite all these advantages, the children of cadres were not *guaranteed* a good future; the element of uncertainty was increased by the possibility that shifts in policy or conflicts between political leaders might suddenly rob their parents of their influence. Therefore, although they were relatively confident, it was still in their interest to earn a school record of academic and political achievement. Respondents reported a few scandalous exceptions of generational rebellion and free-rider laziness, particularly among high-ranking cadres' children who could take more for granted; as Tang said, "Generally, children of lower rank cadres are more Red than children of higher rank cadres." Most children of cadres, however, joined the Youth League and became outstanding political activists, and many earned excellent grades as well.

Although the children of cadres had the imperious manner of young nobles, they were less threatening to their classmates than students of worker-peasant background. Because they thought of themselves as "naturally red" (*zilai hong*)[9] and were confident of their future prospects, cadres' children evolved a relatively relaxed political style, and rarely raised the class background issue against their peers. (Chapter Four will discuss styles of activism.)

Students from worker, peasant, or low-level cadre families, however, who had neither parental connections nor intellectual talents to rely on, were much less secure and tended to become activists with a more rigid political style. Those with mediocre academic grades were particularly anxious, and therefore tended to harp on the "bourgeois" failings of their competitors. They could not afford to moderate their style of participation in public criticism or bend the rules to help out their classmates, as the children of cadres could do. Some respondents pointed out that activists from peasant backgrounds were particularly dogmatic because they were so unsophisticated. Whereas bourgeois youth sometimes found it hard to accept the twists and turns of the

9. This notion of "natural redness" was attacked during the Cultural Revolution, and was criticized even earlier, in 1956. See *Yangcheng wanbao* (Canton), August 20, 1965.

political line, unquestioning obedience came easier to peasants: "It was easier for peasant youth to become activists because they were simpler in mind."[10]

While it was the rare city student of good family background who did not take advantage of this status to join the Youth League and become an activist, the strategies pursued by those of "ordinary" (*yiban de*) family origin were more diverse. With no ascriptive assets or liabilities, the sons and daughters of professors, teachers, doctors, middle peasants, clerks, and petty merchants based their choice entirely on their predictions about the relative importance of political and academic selection criteria and on their own aptitudes. Some chose the academic route and kept a low political profile. Some tried to balance low academic achievement with a record of outstanding activism. Others hoped to be able to present at graduation a record of substantial accomplishment in both study and politics.

Class background was the dominant consideration in the strategic choices of students from landlord, capitalist, rich peasant, Kuomintang or rightist families. Persons who are discriminated against because of race, religion, or class tend to respond in one of two ways: they give up, or they try harder.[11] The Chinese students who were stigmatized with a bad class label adopted either a passive or an assertive stance in political competition; either they abstained from politics and invested all their energies in academic endeavors, or they attempted to demonstrate through enthusiastic activism that they had overcome the negative political influences of their families. The optimists calculated in the way Ding did: "I joined the Youth League because I had a bad family background. So if I entered the League, then I would have a better

10. The dichotomy between "simple" (*jiandan*) and "complicated" (*fuza*) frequently arises in Chinese communist descriptions of people. It is assumed that "simple" people—for example, peasants and children—will accept the ideology more easily than those, such as intellectuals, who are more "complicated." This premise probably explains why roles which require total obedience—such as soldiers and prison guards—are filled mainly by young peasants. Several bourgeois respondents poignantly described how they wanted to commit themselves wholeheartedly to the revolution but were bedeviled by their analytical, critical, or satirical temperaments.

11. Stouffer and others, in *The American Soldier,* make this point in regard to Negro soldiers during World War II: "Many Negroes were adherents of the doctrine which held that improved status for the group would follow upon demonstration of their loyalty and ability, and the war seemed to offer an ideal situation in which to demonstrate these qualities" (p. 513). On the other hand, a Negro G.I. could feel that he "had no status to lose in the white society for failure to conduct himself by the whites' standards and little likelihood of acquiring status by means of individual performance" (p. 52).

chance to study at a university." The pessimists abstained from politics because, as Lin expressed it, "Activists and teachers are always telling you that anyone can become revolutionized, but that really isn't true; if your background is bad, that's it."

Many students with background vulnerabilities believed that it was too dangerous—and probably futile—to venture into the political fray. They kept a low political profile and devoted themselves to their studies because, as Guo, the son of a rich peasant, said, "If your family background isn't good, then the only way to succeed is to study hard, which is what I did."

Others worried that just a clean political record would not be sufficient for someone whose political reliability was suspect because of bad class origin. They tried to show the authorities that unlike their politically passive peers from bourgeois families, they were *actively* committed to the revolution. Peng, for example, was genuinely enthusiastic about politics, but he was also aware of the need to dispel the cloud that his bad class origin cast over his future: "I thought that conduct comments were more important than grades because I had such a bad background and needed good conduct comments to compensate for this."

Some individuals with a class background burden tried to rid themselves of it by becoming activists, but failed to win acceptance.[12] Jiang, a natural leader who had been class president throughout primary and junior high school, found his path to political recognition blocked by the fact that his father had worked for the Kuomintang. His application to join the Youth League was rejected. There were some students with bad backgrounds who gained admission to the League, he said, but only those who had a relative who had fought in the People's Liberation Army or had other mitigating factors in their family histories. Deng, a landlord's daughter, described her experience of political rejection:

> I tried hard in junior high school, but later I found out that an active performance could not compensate for your class background. Even if they became nice to you superficially, it wouldn't make any difference just to have better treatment. There were people who broke off from their families by condemning their class background and criticizing their parents, but even these people couldn't get into university or get a good job. Although the government said "you cannot decide your ori-

12. See Raddock, *Political Behavior of Adolescents in China,* for an analysis of the psychological impact of school rejection on youth of bad class origin.

gin, but you can choose your own road," it wasn't true. My junior high teacher told me that I wouldn't have been able to get into senior high except for the fact that my excellent grades saved me. I realized then that I couldn't get anywhere by political performance. The only way for me to get to university was to get outstanding grades to outshine others.

Many students from bad family backgrounds resented the policy of class discrimination not only because it diminished their chances for a successful career but also because it frustrated their desire to express themselves politically. Respondents noted that many of the young people who later joined the rebel faction of the Red Guards during the Cultural Revolution had previously been stifled politically by class prejudice in schools, and jumped at the chance to serve the revolution.[13]

When youths with bad class labels tried to decide whether or not to venture into the political arena, they considered not only the ambiguities of official policies on class origin, but also the social attitudes on the issue. There is a pervasive assumption in China that people of good class background are "naturally red," and that people of bad background are inherently apolitical, anti-revolutionary, or selfish and opportunistic.

It is striking that almost all our respondents, even those who complained vehemently about being discriminated against because of bad class background, had accepted the notion that class origin to some extent determined political beliefs. For example, Deng raged against the unfairness of class favoritism: "They shouldn't punish me for my family. I couldn't help what my family had done years ago! . . . Many individual talents will be buried unknown because of this class discrimination." And yet she had accepted the premises of this favoritism, saying "it was unnatural for bad elements (people from bad family origin) to act so progressive." Even students from middle-range backgrounds, for whom the class background issue was not as salient, shared this assumption about natural political tendencies: "Students with good background are naturally progressive in politics. Students with bad background are often the most enthusiastic about politics because they

---

13. However, even during the Cultural Revolution, class background was still a factor. In Canton, the youths of ordinary background constituted the main force of the rebel Red Guard factions because many students of bad background were still afraid to risk political involvement. Rosen, "The Radical Students in Kwangtung During the Cultural Revolution," p. 395. And, according to respondents, even the rebel factions elected official leaders of good family origin "in order to protect the organization from outside criticism."

need good political credentials to compensate for having bad background. And students with so-so background like me don't care that much about politics."

Because of this widespread assumption that the sincerity of political commitment depends on family origin, bad-background students had a hard time winning acceptance as activists. As Deng explained, "Being a class officer naturally helped facilitate one's future, because it showed that you had progressive tendencies. However, it was still background that counted more, because sometimes a good performance would still be interpreted as phony."

Fang's account of one classmate's futile efforts to prove her activism suggests that people were suspicious of the motivation of activists from non-proletarian families because they projected their own attitudes onto them:

> Our class study officer had very good grades and was very competent, but she was from a capitalist family. She applied many times to join the Youth League, so people said that she must be seeking private gain (*tou ji*). People are prejudiced (*pian jian*). They assume that people with bad background must be dissatisfied, so their behavior must be phony. They assumed she was applying] to serve her own future, not totally to serve the people. I had known her since junior high school. I thought she had an individual goal, because after all, I did. We all wanted to go to university.

The anxiety of bad background activists who had to work harder at politics in order to live down their origin was communicated to their peers, and further contributed to their image as phony opportunists.

The opportunistic image of bad background activists was encouraged by good background aspirants to activist status, and also by many Youth League members who had already established their own political credentials.[14] Even after the liberalization of the Youth League's recruitment policy in 1964, many local branches rejected applicants of non-proletarian background. One respondent, Ding, who had succeeded in gaining admission to the League, said that even after she became a member she was distrusted by her comrades because of her bad background:

---

14. ZGQN, No. 2, January 16, 1956, SCMM, 29, pp. 24-25; ZGQNB, May 26, 1956, SCMP, No. 1308, pp. 5-6. Also see White, "Social Inequality and Distributive Politics in China, 1949-69," pp. 114-115.

In senior-3 my political thought changed because the League never trusted me. If you have a bad background the League people don't believe in you. They think you're an opportunist. They don't give you important jobs to do, and they don't tell you the important things in meetings. They seldom send you to district meetings. They criticized me for spending too much time in study, saying I was expert, not red.

In a system that ascribes the good and evil in people's current behavior to their parents' (or grandparents') pre-revolutionary role and also encourages mutual criticism, the reputations of those from non-proletarian backgrounds are fragile. The risks of having one's behavior criticized in class terms were so great that the system discouraged even some students of not particularly bad family background from becoming active. As An, the son of a technician, explained: "Good class background is an important condition for being an activist, because although you might become an activist without good background, if you make any mistake you will be put down easily because of your background. So if your background isn't good you won't last very long as an activist." Without proletarian credentials, a student was likely to be defeated in the social conflicts engendered by political competition. Gao, who came from an overseas Chinese family with an ordinary class label, said that this fear deterred him from becoming politically active:

I believed that even if I performed well in political activities, that wouldn't help me much because my class origin wasn't good. . . . It is possible that even when you got into a high position and then had trouble with a person who came from a good background, he would remember that your father or great-grandfather killed his grand-uncle. Then he would still use your family background to hurt you.

In school situations where the probability of winning university admission or a good city job after graduation was either zero (private schools) or one (specialized schools), students had no choices to make. At private schools that offered no chance of success, students competed for popularity and did not have to choose between politics and academics. At specialized schools that guaranteed career success, all students became activists. But in the majority of urban high schools, where students were placed in competition with one another for future success, there were several options available. They had to estimate the relative importance of university and job selection criteria—academic grades and test scores, political record, and class background—and had to devise a strategy that would exploit their comparative advantages while compensating for their disadvantages (and at the same time allowing them to maintain friendship relations and self-respect). The "givens" in this calculation were one's intellectual ability, political skill, and class background. No decision was irrevocable. Students were constantly re-estimating the odds and modifying their strategies as recruitment policies shifted and as they learned from experience. The following chapters will show how the patterns of social relations between students were shaped by the strategies they chose. Chapter Four analyzes the interaction between activists and non-activists in terms of the conflict of interests between them.

4

AT ARM'S LENGTH
Relations between Activists and
Their Classmates

There have been three waves of political dissent in China since 1949: the Hundred Flowers Campaign (1957), the Cultural Revolution (1966-1969), and the as-yet unnamed period of post-Cultural Revolution dissent in the 1970s.[1] The voices raised during these periods of dissent were mainly those of students or recent graduates, and a recurrent target of their criticism was the evils of political competition. Political activists were attacked as hypocritical opportunists who pursue politics for personal profit. The 1957 dissidents lambasted activists "who still seek every opportunity to get a position, who praise and please their superiors obsequiously, who know how to read their superiors' minds from their faces, and who attack others."[2] Ten years later the Red Guards echoed this refrain, denouncing activists who "bluff and curry favor . . . and struggle for their individual 'future' and 'prominence.' "[3] The most recent group of dissenters was also contemptuous of political activists, attacking them for their "hypocritical, evil, and ugly behavior," and for being speculators who invest in activism in order to obtain "10,000 times profit for one unit of capital."[4]

The estrangement of Chinese youth from political activists stems primarily from one feature of the Chinese system: the distribution of educational and occupational opportunities on the basis of individual political credentials. Because participation in the Young Communist League was perceived as a route to power and career success, it inevitably attracted a certain number of opportunists who lost the respect of

1. See Shirk, "'Going Against the Tide,' " pp. 82-114.
2. Doolin, *Communist China: The Politics of Student Opposition,* pp. 46-47.
3. "A Piece of Meat," *Tiaozhan* (Challenge) (Canton), No. 1 (March 1968), p. 4.
4. Li Yizhe, "Concerning Socialist Democracy," pp. 117-118.

their peers. But even when they were not motivated by careerism, political activists created real costs for other students who had chosen not to pursue an activist strategy but who still needed to present a clean political record upon graduation. All the respondents, the activists as well as the non-activists, reported tension and separation between student political activists and their classmates.

Ideally, student activists should have been well integrated with their classmates. The Chinese approach to teaching political values requires attempts to merge official values with the informal values of the social group. To achieve this, it was necessary to have a core group of activists who would exemplify official standards of behavior and who would motivate other students to emulate them.[5] As one activist, Peng, said: "An ideal activist should be a leader, a model, be able to influence his fellow students, and be able to unite them for collective action."

But Chinese educational policies regarding activists were contradictory. Although activists were supposed to merge themselves with the group in order to socialize its members politically, they were also singled out for positions of power and opportunity. The policy of recruiting political achievers into elite adult roles (through university and Party) entailed choosing a small number of activists from among their peers, organizing them into an official vanguard (the Young Communist League), and training them to wield power by granting them power over their peers. These recruitment policies made activists concerned about distinguishing themselves from other students, and made non-activists interested in keeping activists "at arm's length" (*jing er yuan zhi*).

BECOMING AN ACTIVIST

Beginning with the third year of junior high school, the Young Communist League became a significant factor in the life of the class. New YCL members, who had to be at least fifteen years old, were selected from among the applicants by students who were already YCL members, in consultation with and with the approval of the school YCL organization (which included teachers and administrators as well as students). The school Communist Party organization assigned one Party cadre to oversee YCL activities, and that cadre played a major

---

5. "It is impossible to form a collective without activists." Guo Sheng, "On Collectivism and Collective Education," p. 82.

role in making admissions decisions. Non-YCL students in the class did not participate in this selection process; YCL deliberations were kept secret from non-members. As students grew older and moved through high school, more and more of them joined the YCL. Although some classes had five or six members and could form a YCL branch as early as junior-high-3, by the end of the senior-1 or the beginning of the senior-2 level, all classes (with the exception of classes at private schools) had YCL branch organizations. Respondents reported that approximately one-third of the students in their senior-3 classes were YCL members.

As the respondents defined it, an activist is a person who always takes the lead in political, labor, and social activities and who is eager to carry out directives from teachers and school authorities. A person became an activist not upon joining the Youth League, but when he or she started to associate with YCL members and take on the behavior patterns associated with YCL membership in order to gain admission. Michel Oksenberg describes the analogous situation of "effective membership" in the Communist Party:

> In behavioral terms, a person was recruited into the Party not when he formally joined the Party, but when he started acting like a Party member, and that occurred even before his admission into the Party. An undeterminable number of Chinese, the so-called "activists," in fact had adopted the code governing the behavior of Party members and were behaving much as if they were Party members.[6]

The respondents confirmed this observation: students who were not yet YCL members often were more active than those who were already members. As Xi said: "An activist is someone who responds quickly to political movements. Most activists are Youth League members, but activists are not necessarily League members. In fact, people act more active when they are trying to gain admission to the League, and may become less active after they are admitted."

The new activist must convince the League members and school Party authorities that he or she puts commitment to the League and to official political values ahead of all other personal obligations. The process of anticipatory socialization, as YCL aspirants shifted their reference group from other students to League members, naturally

6. Oksenberg, "Getting Ahead and Along in Communist China," pp. 306-307.

evoked a hostile reaction from the non-active students who were "left behind." Almost all our respondents recalled with bitterness their rejection by a pal who had "turned active."[7]

When a student applied to join the League, he or she had to find one or two members, called "introducers," to sponsor him or her for membership. In the earlier years, when the class YCL organization was still small, older students from other classes were assigned to serve as introducers. They would visit before and after classes, and have heart-to-heart talks with potential recruits. According to several respondents who had been YCL members, the introducers sought out people with good class background and encouraged them to attend the weekly League class held for recruits, and later to apply for membership. Those from bad background had to find their own introducers, because as one respondent explained, "the League didn't take the initiative."

After the League received a student's application, it observed the applicant's behavior and investigated his or her background, a process that took one or two semesters to complete. Meanwhile, the applicant was required to discuss his or her political ideas in weekly heart-to-heart talks with the League introducer. During that time the applicants tried to find occasions for demonstrating their political enthusiasm. They offered to help class officers and League members in their work, thereby becoming what were called "backbone elements" (*gugan fenzi*). One respondent remarked that during every stint of manual labor outside the school, one or two new League members were "developed." People would apply to join before leaving for the countryside, so that their work performance could be closely scrutinized and judged as a manifestation of good political attitudes.

The standards of political "goodness" were unclear and subjective. It was difficult for League members to identify the "real" activists from the fakes simply by observing their behavior and talking with them.

7. Robert Merton has explained how the negative response from the old reference group encourages "climbers" to intensify efforts to be accepted by their new group: "What the individual experiences as estrangement from a group of which he is a member tends to be experienced by his associates as repudiation of the group, and this ordinarily evokes a hostile response. As social relations between the individual and the rest of the group deteriorate, the norms of the group become less binding for him. . . . And to the degree that he orients himself toward out-group values, perhaps affirming them verbally and expressing them in action, he only widens the gap and reinforces the hostility between himself and his in-group associates. Through the interplay of dissociation and progressive alienation from the group values, he may become doubly motivated to orient himself toward the values of another group and to affiliate himself with it." Merton, "Anticipatory Socialization," pp. 348-349.

One YCL member, Yu, explained the criteria she used: "If she isn't real, she uses all her free time for studying. Actually labor is a good test because it doesn't involve grades and most of the time the teacher isn't looking." There also was a widespread assumption that a phony activist would be unable to keep up the act for long, and therefore that someone who behaved like an activist for a long time must be genuinely committed.[8]

Because it was so difficult to infer applicants' internal values from their outward behavior (and because it was commonly assumed that redness depended in part on family origin), YCL members often relied on class background labels in making their recruitment decisions. In some League branches the issue of class background was controversial. For example, in Fang's branch, "there was a contradiction between members of different backgrounds who held different views. For example, the good background members would decide to do thought work with someone of good background who was a promising new recruit, but we of ordinary or bad background would argue that this person's behavior wasn't good enough." In other instances, the admission of someone of bad background was blocked by good background League members who argued that the person's behavior "was just a superficial attempt to win admission to the League." The members of proletarian origin tended to stress background credentials, while other members emphasized behavior, each group trying to maximize its own advantages in the competition for political recognition. A case of complicated family origin could generate conflict within the branch that was difficult to resolve.[9]

Two steps in the admissions process were particularly difficult for applicants with background problems. First, all applicants had to write a family history that would meet with League approval. Constructing a history that was sufficiently detailed and which demonstrated the correct revolutionary perspective—by drawing a "clear class line" between yourself and your family—could be a protracted and traumatic experience. As one respondent, Ding, the son of a former Kuomintang em-

8. See GRRB, February 18, 1980.
9. Fang gave the example of a girl whose father had been labeled a rightist and whose mother was a cadre: "Her political behavior was good, but it took her a long time to be admitted to the League because one branch member objected. They finally voted to admit her by majority vote, and the school League committee approved her admission." The more diverse and cosmopolitan a person's experience and the more mixed the family influences, the more politically unreliable that person is assumed to be.

ployee, described it: "It was painfully difficult (*kunnan*). I had to write my father's history over ten times because each time they didn't accept it. They said it wasn't incisive (*shenke*) enough." It is noteworthy that even in the early 1960s, when Ding joined the League, applicants were required to analyze their family histories rather than merely reporting their parents' current jobs. Even during that period, when class background was supposedly de-emphasized, students from bad backgrounds who aspired to YCL membership were required to undergo the psychological ordeal of renouncing their families.[10]

But the League did not rely only on personal accounts for screening out individuals of bad background; they also scrutinized the applicants' political records and those of their families. Yu, who had participated in several investigations as a League member, gave a detailed description of the process:

> First the branch looks at the applicant's dossier (*dangan*). In the dossier is your home address, native place, your grandfather's class label and age. Then for your father: his class label, his political appearance (*zhengzhi mianmu*)—especially whether Party member or Kuomintang member and whether a bad element—age, job, and work unit. The same for your mother. There also are the class label and political appearance for important relatives like uncles and aunts. Then the political appearance, age, and school or work unit for your brothers and sisters.
>
> For yourself, there is your history in each campaign, any awards or penalties you have received, and what has been said about you in criticism meetings. Also your class director's comments (*jianding*) on you for every year in primary school, especially the final comments when you graduate from primary school. These comments are signed by the class director. Only the final comments from junior high are included; they describe how your behavior changed from year to year. The ones done every semester are not included in your dossier; they are given to your parents and used as reference. The school keeps them for about six years after you graduate, and then throws them out. Your comments are much more detailed if you are a League member.
>
> After looking over the dossier, the League branch reports to the school League committee, which then carries out a more detailed investigation of the applicant's family background. They delegate people

---

10. For a psychological analysis of youth forced to publicly renounce their exploiting class parents, see Raddock, *Political Behavior of Adolescents in China*.

to carry out the investigation. Sometimes, if it's a very simple case and the committee is very busy, the branch may carry out the investigation. For anyone to go out to investigate, they need verification from the school's Party personnel committee, which has a special [stamp of authorization]. They go to the father's work unit, and to the neighborhood where the family lives; they only go to the mother's work unit if there is a problem. For example, in one case the father was an engineer and had no problems, but the mother was a bad element in the lane where they lived and was the daughter of a landlord. But anyway her dossier was kept by the neighborhood committee because she didn't work.

The investigation results are not written up but delivered orally. It's a very big responsiblilty for the investigators. They can't say anything about it to anyone else; to do so would violate Party rules. If the applicant's parents are Party members, then a Party member must be called in to do the investigation. And if the parent is a high level Party cadre, then he must be investigated by the city League committee, and they can only see part of his dossier; they can't see the detailed part of the history, which can only be seen by someone above the cadre.

According to another YCL respondent, in a straightforward case YCL branch approval took about one month, and school committee approval took two to three months. The review process itself was for some a deterrent to joining.

It may be, as it is in many other organizations, that the basic level was more susceptible to popular social pressures than the higher level, and was therefore less stringent in its political screening of new members. Ding recalled a 1962 case in which the school League committee overruled the branch: "[A boy in senior-2] was rejected for admission one time. But the second time he applied, the branch approved him. But when his background was investigated, he was not approved by the school YCL committee because his background was too complicated. The committee said that our branch had been too young and inexperienced and didn't take background sufficiently into account."

Because it was so difficult for students with family background problems to clear the hurdles of the League screening process, they had to try harder than the applicants with no background handicap. It is no wonder that many respondents described students from bad background who were working toward League membership as *more* active than other League aspirants.

Proving Activism through Criticism

One way in which students trying to gain acceptance as activists—particularly those who needed to overcome a bad background—proved their commitment to revolutionary values was by criticizing their classmates in public. High schools offered students frequent occasions for mutual criticism: weekly small group sessions and class meetings, special rectification meetings to deal with behavioral problems, year-end class discussions, and the extended class discussions before junior high and senior high graduation. Although in theory everyone was expected to participate in criticism, activists were expected to "take the lead." Criticism sessions provided clear tests of political commitment. People recognized that social loyalties were a particularly strong force in public, face-to-face encounters. To speak out against a fellow-student in a criticism session demonstrated that you put political principles ahead of loyalties to your friends.[11]

Being the target of criticism, of course, was psychologically and practically damaging. In fact, to be singled out for criticism by your peers was *intended* to be psychologically painful. The Chinese communists believe that public criticism within social groups is an effective technique for shaping people's political beliefs and behavior, because ostracism from the group is much more distressing than reprimands from authorities.[12] Being criticized by your classmates meant reduced chances for a successful future as well as hurt feelings. Serious criticisms were noted in your conduct comments and included in your school record; they could make the difference between university admission and a rural work assignment.

The subjectivity and variability of behavioral standards exacerbated the anxiety generated by criticism meetings. You never knew when an activist might turn the discussion to your actions or statements, no matter how innocently they were intended. A Soviet journalist described the feelings evoked by criticism meetings:

11. Reinhard Bendix points out that the Soviets view mutual criticism as the true test of an activist's loyalty to the Party. It is "the touchstone of socialist consciousness in our people, because it is an indication of their capacity to put the interests of society above their own peace of mind." M. A. Leonov, *Kritik und Selbstkritik* (Berlin: Verlag Kultur und Fortschritt, n.d.), p. 34, quoted in Bendix, *Work and Authority in Industry,* p. 417.

12. See Schurmann, "Organization and Response in Communist China," p. 57.

The problem is simple; it is called *fear.* . . . You go [to the meeting] and you don't know what awaits you. Perhaps nothing, perhaps this time as well, like many other times before, no one will point his finger at you, no one will call your name, no one will mention you in his report. . . . Somewhere, however, at the bottom of your Soviet soul, anxiety hovers: What if? What if *this time* it'll be different? *Somebody* will point his finger at you? *Somebody* will utter your name? It doesn't matter whether it'll be praise or reprimand, promotion or degradation. What matters is that you're facing two or three hours of waiting for something like this. . . . Of course your conscience is clean, you're—or so it seems to you—all right. But at the same time you know that the world changes and that the criteria of *being all right* may have changed."[13]

Being a good activist entailed hurting other students by criticizing them. Whereas leadership in other systems is usually defined by a set of behaviors that benefits group members—for example, staying up late to put up decorations for the dance, writing articles for the union newspaper, organizing a picnic for the congregation—the definition in China included behaviors damaging to group members, such as public criticism and reporting errors to the authorities.[14] Someone who wanted to prove political commitment had to criticize his or her peers. This destructive element of activism has been decried by Vice Premier Chen Yun, a political iconoclast and ally of Deng Xiaoping. What kind of people are those who take "an active attitude," he asked. "What are they being active about? Not active in production but active in picking others' faults."[15]

Though it was in any single student's interest to impress the teacher

13. Novak, *No Third Path,* p. 31.
14. One reason why activists often have difficulty establishing their legitimacy as peer group leaders is that they criticize fellow-students in public. This type of behavior violates one of George C. Homan's rules of leadership: "The leader will neither blame, nor, in general, praise a member of his group before other members. The leader has much to do with establishing the social rank of his followers. When he blames a man in public, he is lowering, or attempting to lower, the man's social rank, that is, the degree of esteem in which he is held by the members of the group. But the leader is not the only man who determines social rank; the opinions of the other members count for something too. They may not be ready to accept the leader's evaluation. When he blames a follower in public, he is not only humiliating the man; he may also be putting in doubt his own reputation for justice—his capacity for living up to the norms of the group." Homans, *The Human Group,* p. 433.
15. "Ch'en Yun's Speech at the CCP Central Committee Work Conference," p. 84. Although there are some doubts about the authenticity of this version of the speech, it appears to be genuine.

and League members by criticizing a classmate, it was in everyone's interest *not* to be the target of public criticism. Peer-group norms accepted striving for success as necessary, but then condemned people who harmed others by making major criticisms of them in public, especially people who used exaggerated rhetoric in their criticisms.

When these norms of mutual protection were followed, criticism sessions were casual or routinized. In Li's group, even though the Youth League branch secretary was a group member, "We would chat about inconsequential, even non-political things until the last few minutes of the session, when the League secretary would say, 'Look now, you have to say something because I have to make a report of what you said.' It was all very friendly and relaxed." If group members did criticize one another, they would talk only about minor behavioral problems. As Gao put it, "We would criticize one another about small things in our lives when we were supposed to be talking about political thought. It was a way to avoid the serious issues." When they discussed political questions, they used abstract, formulaic language. Respondents described these political discussions as tedious, but rarely traumatic.

Many respondents felt that mutual criticism was very effective, nevertheless. Jiang, an activist, said this:

> Criticism and self-criticism is a very good method. People usually criticize themselves more than others. They disclose their own mistakes and failings and then ask other people's opinions on it. It's true that most students don't take criticism sessions very seriously, and usually just bring up superficial things, but still some people do take it seriously; for example, a few people have confessed to stealing things. Of course, with close friends, we criticize one another in criticism discussions only superficially or even don't tell the truth.

The fact that groups often steered away from political subjects and focused on minor behavior problems did not mean that they were meaningless. Instead, the avoidance of larger political topics enhanced the naturalness of the sessions and increased group influence on the students. Deng, a young woman who had a negative view of other aspects of school life, praised the practice of small group criticism:

> Political thought problems were hard to solve because they were so abstract, and even though you make people give verbal consent, it doesn't mean that you have really convinced them. But on issues of substance like lack of discipline, laziness, bad grades, lateness in com-

ing to school, and so on—small groups could help to reveal the problems and offer actual help. This really worked. On these issues the
small group could pull people closer.

She gave an example of the positive consequences of small group criticism:

> One boy in my group, well, his study fluctuated a lot. When we
> raised this in group discussion, he confessed that he had to work late at
> night to help his mother do handicraft work to get money. . . . When
> members of the group understood his case, they advised him not to join
> too many activities—to cut all the non-essentials so that he could have
> more time to study and help the family. Also they offered to help him
> review the studies in which he lagged behind. Gradually he got better
> in his study.

When activists used criticism sessions to demonstrate their political
zeal, however, they violated group norms and shifted the discussion to a
more serious political plane. They could turn a minor question of
lifestyle into a major political issue. For example, Lin complained about
the bad background people who victimized him in group sessions:

> In order to impress the class director and League members with how
> active they were, they would criticize the backward students, especially
> me. They attacked me for my background and said that was why I was
> always reading novels and listening to classical music. They told tales
> to the teacher too. They were disgusting (*taoyan*).

Even in meetings where students discussed political topics in a formal,
mutually protective manner, activists could create tension by challenging the authenticity of other people's statements. Peng described one
particularly obnoxious activist:

> In senior-3 everybody was supposed to write a self-criticism and
> read it to the class for comments. Everybody knew that this was a
> chance to express loyalty to the Party and the country, and would take
> other people's expressions of loyalty for granted. But this one person
> would question people's loyalty on the grounds of their class back-
> ground, as if only people like himself, coming from a worker-peasant
> family, could be faithful to the Party.

Furthermore, even an activist's self-criticism could be a hostile act.
Deng told a story about an activist who used self-criticism to distance
herself from a friend of bad background:

One day the active girl met the other one and her father in the street, and she greeted the father as "uncle" (*boye*). But later she wrote a self-criticism to the teacher, saying that she shouldn't have greeted the old man so nicely—it showed she hadn't drawn a clear class line yet. She said that someone who was completely firm in the class line wouldn't have been so friendly to a bad element. When the daughter heard about this, she moved further away from the activist.

Students of bad background bore the brunt of activists' criticism. Because serious public criticism always involved making an enemy, it was safer for activists to pick on someone who because of background was politically weak and unable to make a credible counterattack. Those of bad background were also the frequent target of aspiring activists of similar background who had to demonstrate that they had "drawn a clear class line." Therefore, non-proletarian students, in order to protect their feelings and their political reputations, were particularly prone to avoiding activists who threatened to criticize them.

THE POLITICAL POWER OF ACTIVISTS

As explained earlier, the Party delegated power to student activists in order to enhance the socializing role of the peer group and to train these future members of the political elite. The power of activists was inherent in their responsibilities as class officers or League members. In selecting new League members, reporting to the class director on student attitudes and behavior, and choosing the nominees for class office, they had the power of "gatekeepers" who determined which individuals were admitted to the circle of activists. The gatekeeper power of activists—and the fact that political competition was judged by peers as well as by adult authorities—had profound ramifications for the relations between activists and non-active students.

Reporting to Teachers

The class director was responsible for monitoring the political progress of students and writing biannual evaluations of their conduct. Because teachers were removed in age and role from the student peer group, they were supposed to solicit activists' opinions. The three teachers who were interviewed said that they did indeed rely on information provided by activists when they evaluated students. The procedure was described by Yu, an activist who had often participated in such discussions:

> The class director meets with the class president and the League branch officers to discuss the conduct comments. [He or she] also gets the notes that the League members have taken at the annual rectification sessions held by the class. Most class directors rely on the officers when writing their comments. Sometimes they show these comments to [student officers] and ask their opinion, because students are clearly knowledgeable about the situation of other students. The teacher's position is too far away.

Pedagogical experts urged teachers to consult students but not to delegate to them the responsibility for writing conduct comments. The divisive effects of mutual evaluation were well-understood: "It may create grudges among students, and they may look only for the weaknesses of others; the students may attack one another, and this would affect good relations among students."[16] But these divisive effects were felt even when students played only an advisory role.

The willingness of activists to report their classmates' failings to the teacher meant to students that activists wanted the approval of teachers more than the approval of their peers. Any peer group member who strives for the blessing of authority rather than for informal prestige and popularity is bound to evoke hostility from peers.[17] It is no wonder that many respondents defined an activist as "someone who talks a lot about Mao Zedong Thought and who plays up to (*pai ma pi*) the class director." Literally translated, *pai ma pi* means "patting the horse's rump." It has all the negative connotations of American expressions such as "apple polishing" (and other less polite versions). Students were infuriated by activists who constantly told tales to the teacher. Zhang complained that "something we did tonight the teacher would know about by tomorrow." He defined activists as "the people who stood with the teacher."

16. *Renmin jiaoyu* (RMJY), Vol. 3, No. 2, p. 52.
17. For example, in the American Army during World War II: "To the enlisted men, 'bucking' and the frequently used term 'brown-nosing' were terms of opprobrium. They were used to describe the type of act which is too obviously aimed at making an impression on one's superiors. Currying favor of officers partook of class disloyalty and also represented a conflict with soldierly values of toughness and self-reliance; 87 percent of the enlisted men in the post-hostilities study last cited in the study concurred." Stouffer and others, *The American Soldier,* pp. 264-267.

Not all activists were equally resented for peer disloyalty. The more confident ones found ways of letting their classmates know that when they met with the teacher, they were discreet and considerate. They reported only serious violations of school rules and never exaggerated people's mistakes. Students reacted to such behavior with gratitude. On the other hand, less secure activists did more than required; they often ran to the teacher with reports of student misdeeds and inflated the political significance of them. These activists were both feared and despised.

Activists' access to and credibility with school authorities—and their *willingness* to denigrate their classmates to these authorities—gave them significant power, which was clearly recognized by their peers. As Deng said about activists: "If you are all right with them, they would not say bad things about you, or would even say good things. But if you had grudges with them, they would exaggerate your bad points." This power shielded activists from retaliation by other students. Deng said: "I saw that girl who had criticized my class background cheat once, but I didn't dare tell on her because she was the class director's favorite, and she could take revenge on me by saying bad things about me to the class director." Of course, friendship with an activist could provide a certain degree of protection, especially if the friend was an established activist who had high credibility with teachers. Luo was in that kind of situation: "No one dared to tell tales on me because I was good friends with the girl who was class president in junior-1 and vice-president in junior-2." But most students who pursued an academic strategy put safety first; they believed that the best way to maintain a clean political record was to not let the activists observe you say or do anything that could be reported to the teacher.

Electing Class Officers

At the beginning of every term (or every year) the class elected a class committee, consisting of five to eight officers (called class cadres). The committee was led by the class president (*banzhang*) and vice-president (*fu banzhang*), and included officers responsible for study (or propaganda), sports, culture, labor, and welfare. The Youth League branch provided political leadership and was perceived by respondents to be more powerful than the class committee. As Guo said: "The League branch secretary is more important and has more power than the class president. The League secretary is responsible for the class political life and concentrates on thought work, while the class president takes care of routine matters in the class." However, respondents who had served as class officers said that the class committee was responsible not only for organizing academic and extracurricular activities, but for doing "thought work" (*sixiang gongzuo*, ideological education) and reporting to the teacher on students' political progress as well.

Although students pursuing an academic strategy were not eager to serve as class officers—the risks outweighed the benefits—being chosen for class office was a way of achieving political prominence. Class office-holding was seen as a manifestation of political commitment, was noted in one's record, and was an asset in the competition for university and job selection. Because of their access to the class director, class officers also could obtain good conduct comments by filtering the information (on themselves and their classmates) that reached the teacher. Serving as a class officer was also a way to prove yourself politically and to win an invitation to join the Youth League.

In the regular elections of class officers students learned how democratic centralism worked.[18] The voting for the class committee was democratic, by hand or by secret ballot, with the candidates receiving the most votes being elected to office.[19] The usual practice was to elect the president first or to assign the presidency to the person receiving the most votes. The rest of the committee was then elected by choosing the students with the greatest number of votes; the actual determination of different posts was decided by the new group of electees. The committee was always elected except in the first semester (or first year) of junior and senior high school, when the students were not yet familiar with

18. I did not collect detailed information on the procedures for electing League branch officers, League school committee members, militia officers, or Student Association officers. Apparently, school League committee and Student Association officers were elected in the first case by all the League members, and in the second case by all the students. Nominations for League committee were made by each League branch, and nominations for Student Association offices made by each class. All the nominees had to be approved by the school Party authorities. According to one YCL respondent, the Party committee sometimes used its power of approval to intervene in the selection of school leaders. In one case, a girl who had been elected to the school YCL committee was reassigned to be Student Association cultural and sports officer by the Party committee because although her political performance was good, her father had been labeled a rightist. The Party committee didn't want to publicize her background problems, so they simply transferred her to the less politically sensitive Student Association post. For an excellent description of elections in rural production teams, see John Burns, "The Election of Production Team Cadres."

19 .If secret ballots were used at all, it was at the senior high level.

one another and the committee was appointed by the class director on the basis of students' previous school records.

Although the voting was democratic, the nominations were determined in a centralized fashion by the class director or the Youth League branch. According to the respondents, the most common pattern was for the class director to choose the nominees in junior high school, and the YCL branch, in consultation with the teacher, to choose them in senior high school. On election day the class director listed the nominees on the blackboard, or the League members offered the names from the floor. In some classes the teacher and the League presented the students with a mimeographed list of nominees at election time.

Almost 25 percent of the respondents said that the class director presented his or her nominations to the class in an indirect fashion, talking about the qualifications for each post or evaluating the incumbents in a way that broadly hinted at who was best suited for each post. Yang said that the class director preferred this approach to outright nomination because "if he suggested names, he would lose face if these people didn't win."

Sometimes the choices of the class director and the League were revealed to the students in a pre-election process of consultation and discussion called "fermentation" (*hunyang*). The teacher called a meeting of the League members, incumbent class officers, and several other students to discuss who should serve during the next term. According to Deng, students knew that those invited to these deliberations were future officers chosen by the teacher and League members. The nominees then had to be approved by the school Party committee. On election day, the class director hinted at his preferences, but the actual nominations were made by League members and backbone elements from the floor. The number of nominees varied. Sometimes students were presented with seven names, sometimes eight, and sometimes ten names, from which to choose a seven-person committee. According to a Chinese magazine article, whether the number of nominees should be the same as or greater than the number of positions was "not a question of principle. The number of nominees and number of those elected can be identical or may not be identical."[20] Students were always permitted to offer additional nominations from the floor, but they rarely did.

There were a few exceptions to this practice of centralized nomina-

20. "On the Issue of School Elections," ZXS, October 1957, pp. 6-7.

tion. Three respondents reported that in their classes, students either voted without nominations (each person would write three or five names on a ballot) or nominated freely. But according to Gao, even with free nominations, "we wouldn't be too risky in nominating. We would always nominate those who best fit the requirements. . . . Unlikely people could only get one or two votes, and even if they could win the election, they would be given unimportant positions in the class committee."

The practice of centralized nomination was based on the premise that the leadership must focus the will of the people; a satisfactory group of representatives could not be chosen by free election. A magazine reported a student's question: "If we had no nominations but each person just voted for whomever he wanted, wouldn't this be more democratic?" It answered by explaining that without nominations, there "would always be very scattered votes," and without a base of support, an elected student "won't receive the assistance of a large number of people."[21] A former class director who was interviewed described class elections as a mere formality: the teacher picked the committee, and the class automatically ratified his choice. He was taken aback when asked about nominations by the students themselves:

> Oh no! That would never work at all! Because if the students just put forth their own nominations, then it would be impossible to control, the votes would be scattered, and the naughty students would nominate and elect one another. Anyway, it was a school rule that the class director should first consult with the old class officers and League members and then do the nominating himself. It had to be that way. Otherwise it would all be chaos (*luan*).[22]

Because Youth League activists helped determine the nominations for class office, they had in effect more than the ordinary student's one vote and they were often able to get themselves elected. Respondents said that the Youth League's dominance in the class committee increased every year as the number of League members in the class grew larger; by senior-2 and senior-3, the elite organization had a virtual monopoly on class offices.

The respondents contrasted the junior and senior high patterns. As Yao put it: "In junior high the class presidents were always those with

21. *Ibid.*
22. The Chinese need for order and fear of chaos (*luan*) have been analyzed by Solomon, *Mao's Revolution.*

the best study grades, but in senior high the class president—the same person all three years—was the one most active in politics." Another respondent, An, bemoaned the shift in class power to the Youth League:

> It wasn't like in the junior high class, when the class director liked our group and all the students supported us so that we could decide who won elections. In the senior high class, the League members were in the majority, so that the core League members and the teacher decided who would be nominated, and ordinary students didn't dare to challenge their choices. Another difference was that in senior high League officers took up class posts—for example, the class president in senior-1 and senior-2 was the League secretary for the whole school.

Some respondents reported that once people were elected, they tended to hold office for a long time. Others said that incumbents were rarely re-elected, and that the class president, in particular, was frequently replaced. But even with frequent rotation, the same type of person tended to hold office every time. In Xi's class, the presidency changed hands almost every term, but nevertheless "those in the group of political leaders were always League officers and class officers, and they just traded jobs around so that although there was frequent turnover in office, the offices were always held by someone from this leadership clique."

The argument for allowing a small group to hold leadership positions over a long period is that it gives future members of the elite a chance to acquire leadership skills. But there are also good reasons for not allowing a small number of activists to become entrenched in office. When elite recruitment begins in early adolescence and the same few students always hold positions of power, then in adult society, political mobility is impeded and the gap between leaders and followers is widened. Individuals who have held power since high school become accustomed to the prerogatives of office and find it difficult to empathize with ordinary folk. Those who have always been followers see leaders as a separate breed and have no incentive to develop their own leadership abilities. In 1965, a series of letters to the editor of *Chinese Youth Journal* addressed the issue of people who have been "important cadres for a long time," beginning "from primary school all the way to university."[23] One letter pointed out that although these people had, because of their long tenure in office, been "well-trained . . . at the same time,

23. ZGQNB, November 18, 1965, p. 2.

there has been some degree of bad influence on them—it is easy to nurture a cadre's sense of superiority." The editor responded that it was preferable to give more people the opportunity to serve in order to "raise up more activists" and to "cultivate in them a good work style of being able to go up and down" (work in both superior and subordinate positions). He argued that offices should be circulated among a large number of people and that one person should hold no more than one office at a time.

This practice was in fact followed in many high school classes. Students could be either League cadres or class cadres but not both. In some classes, like Lin's, the League branch secretary was not permitted to hold class office, but other League branch cadres could serve as class officers. In Guo's class there was no prohibition against holding League and class office at the same time, but "sometimes the class director thought that this was too much work for one person and persuaded a League cadre to give up his class responsibilities to another non-League student."

Some respondents reported that teachers made a special effort to widen the leadership circle in senior-2 and senior-3, when the approach of graduation intensified time pressures on students. (In several cases, such efforts coincided with the more open Youth League recruitment policy of 1965). In the context of uncertainty about the relative importance of political and academic criteria for university admission, some teachers felt it was only fair to force activists to improve their grades and give the studious types a chance to improve their political credentials. Therefore, despite the resistance of League activists (to be discussed shortly), these teachers enforced the one-person, one-office rule and nominated students from the non-League "masses" for class officers and small group heads during senior-2 and senior-3.[24]

Most respondents accepted as natural and legitimate the role of the class director and Youth League activists in shaping election outcomes, and the dominance of League members in the class committee. This acquiescence stemmed not only from students' passivity but also from their lack of objections to the particular students proposed by the teacher and League activists. Most of the time, as Yao explained, "The class director knew how to choose his officers, and his choices always

24. According to An, "the kind of 'masses' chosen to serve were people influential among the ordinary students."

matched the students' taste, because they were persons who were both good in study and popular." Moreover, there was usually some scope for choice among the nominations handed down. As Xu said, "We just selected the ones we liked best out of the League nominees."

Students acknowledged the Youth League's dominance of the election process, and some respondents said they felt that class officers had little independent power and needed League support. As Lin expressed this view: "It would be impossible for someone to do a good job as class officer if the League didn't want him to hold the post; without League support he would have no power."

Students wanted officers who would be capable and influential not only with students but also with the Party and school authorities with whom they had to deal. For this reason, students preferred representatives with high political status: those with impeccable class background credentials and Youth League membership. In He's class, one person was re-elected as president every year "because his father was important in the People's Liberation Army, because he spoke well and was a Northerner, and because he was League branch secretary. Because of his powerful position in the League, students had to listen to him, and he had good relations with the school administration."

Students were cautious as well as politically realistic, and they recognized the personal risks involved in challenging the class director and League activists in the election arena.[25] Only on rare occasions was the choice of the teacher and League so abhorrent to them that they rebelled. When Shi's class rejected the centrally determined nominees and elected seven "people's choices" to the nine-person committee, it brought down the wrath of the school authorities:

> The class director was embarrassed by the election results and told the students to go home, think it over, and decide whether the winners

25. The power of activists and teachers to determine students' futures impeded the ability of these authorities to acquire accurate information through elections or other feedback mechanisms. Weaknesses in the functioning of the class committee or Youth League were likely to go undetected by teachers and administrators, because it was against the interests of ordinary students to reveal them. For example, a 1955 magazine article recounted the story of a junior-high-school class vice-president who was a terrible bully. The class director tried to help him improve by giving him more responsibility and praising him more. With the class director's support he became so powerful that nobody dared to complain about him and the teacher thought he was completely transformed. RMJY, September 1955, p. 64. Other organizations (factories, production brigades, even the national system for economic planning) have also been plagued by distortions in their information processes because people at the lower levels are reluctant to criticize higher-ups upon whom their careers depend.

could really represent them, do their jobs well. The next day the school Youth League secretary came to our class meeting to talk about vigilance in keeping class enemies out of our ranks; he implied that the election had turned out the way it had because class enemies had sneaked into our class. Then the election was repeated, and we just gave up and voted for all the nominees of the class director and League.

After this incident, Shi's class never again dared to challenge an election. None of the few election rebellions recounted by our respondents were successful, and none were ever repeated.[26]

Gatekeeping

There was a contradiction in the activists' role. On the one hand, they were supposed to encourage the "masses" to be more politically active—in other words, to nurture more activists. But on the other hand, because activism offered substantial career rewards, those who established themselves as activists were unwilling to dilute their advantage by recruiting new activists. The greater the number of activists, the lesser the chances of each in the contest for a limited number of opportunities.[27]

The tendency of some activists to exaggerate the shortcomings of their fellow-students in criticism sessions, in reporting to the teacher, and in League recruitment decisions, can be viewed as an attempt to prevent new political stars from eclipsing them. For example, a short story in a Red Guard newspaper describes how Youth League activists called a youth a "selfish hypocrite" merely because he inadvertently spooned out for himself the only piece of meat in the soup; this label destroyed his chances of entering the Youth League.[28]

Activists also used their power to cling to their leadership posts in the class and in the League. Because their futures depended on their political achievements, they did everything they could to avoid losing elections. One activist, who year after year had served as League branch

26. Official encouragement of local elections since 1979 may have strengthened democratic norms and stiffened popular resistance to centrally determined nominations. When Party officials forbade a college student who proclaimed himself to be a nonbeliever in Marxism to stand for election to a local governmental body, his fellow-students went on a hunger strike and protested outside local Communist Party headquarters. *New York Times,* October 16, 1980.

27. Whyte, *Small Groups and Political Rituals,* p. 121.

28. "A Piece of Meat," p. 4 (cited in note 3 above).

secretary, League school committee member, and Student Association chairman, was not re-elected branch secretary in his last year of senior high school. He anxiously inquired in a 1965 letter to the editor of *Chinese Youth Journal*: "Now I feel upset and depressed (*kuman*), especially when I see League members whom I personally developed taking leadership of the branch. I feel really bad. Comparing myself with them, does this mean I have fallen behind them?"[29] The editor replied that activists should enthusiastically encourage the development of new leaders: "It should be a joyful thing to let those behind catch up. . . . We should not feel insecure over the issue of being or not being cadres; this is the proper attitude that we should have." But it was hard for activists to "joyfully" relinquish the powers and career advantages of office-holding.

ACTIVISTS IN THE EYES OF THEIR CLASSMATES

Political activists were seldom the most popular students in the class. Activism did not in itself inspire affection or respect; students' attitudes toward individual activists depended on how well these activists measured up on other yardsticks—how good their grades were, to what extent they sided with students rather than teachers, and how sincere they were.

Scholars who have studied adolescents in various societies have been impressed by the strength of young people's attachments to their peer groups and the tendency of young people to conform with peer norms rather than the values of adult authorities. The peer group norms of high school students do not appear out of thin air, however; they represent students' adaptations to the probable futures conferred on them by their schools.[30]

---

29. ZGQNB, November 18, 1965, p. 2.

30. For example, James S. Coleman found that the bases of prestige in American high schools were those activities—athletics and extracurricular organizations—which were seen as oriented toward the students themselves; "good grades" and studiousness were seen as "acquiescence and conformity to adult constraints" and as such had little prestige (*The Adolescent Society*, p. 172). Coleman does not explain, however, that American teenagers could afford to invest their energies in sports and dating because their fate was not as dependent on their high school records as it would have been in some other countries, notably China. In the United States there are a multitude of colleges and universities varying in character and selectivity, and aside from college attendance, there are several alternative routes (entrepreneurship, family businesses, promotion through corporate ranks) to career success. Moreover, extracurricular involvements did not detract from—but actually en-

The impact of the wider economic and social context on student peer group norms is clear when we compare the three different types of high schools in Chinese cities: private, specialized, and regular. Because private-school students faced almost certain failure after graduation, they rejected the official values of the school and created a delinquent counter culture that was both anti-academic and anti-political. Conversely, students at specialized senior high schools were assured good job placements after graduation, so they wholeheartedly embraced official values; their peer norms supported academic and especially political achievement. Finally, students at regular competitive high schools were offered a good chance for a successful future, but there were no guarantees. Therefore they developed peer group norms that helped them hedge their bets. These norms—respect for academic achievement, orientation toward peers rather than authorities, and sincerity in speech and behavior—represented their adaptations to the competitive school situation. All students cared about winning the approval of their classmates as well as preparing for a successful future; but it was difficult for those who pursued a political activist strategy to achieve popularity by conforming with peer-group norms.

Academic Achievement and Political Achievement

The striking importance of good academic grades in the urban student culture was demonstrated by all respondents. When asked to describe any fellow-student—whether a friend, a class president, or a League activist—they almost always began by saying how good the person's grades were. And the majority, when questioned about what type of student was the most admired, described a person with excellent academic grades and a friendly manner.

The academic achiever had more prestige than the political achiever. As Yao said, "Usually people would think more highly of a student with good grades than one with good politics." And political activists were evaluated according to their intellectual abilities. As Jiang expressed it, "If they don't have good study grades, then the students don't respect

---

hanced—an American graduate's attractiveness in the eyes of most college admissions officers. Studies of student peer norms that analyze the impact of post-graduation career opportunities include Stinchcombe, *Rebellion in a High School,* and Hargreaves, *Social Relations in a Secondary School.*

them." To be an effective leader, an activist had to win students' respect by academic achievement.

Whether or not activists had high grades depended largely on the type of person recruited by teachers and school authorities to be student leaders. In Jiang's senior-1 class, the class president (Jiang himself), the League branch secretary, and the class study officer were the top three students academically; the class director that year paid a great deal of attention to academics and de-emphasized class background.

The more common pattern was for activists to have mediocre or poor grades. Many academic achievers were prevented from entering the League or playing a political leadership role because their bourgeois family origin was held against them. Some of the students who adopted an activist strategy looked upon it as a way of compensating for their lack of intellectual success. Once a student embarked on the activist route, its heavy demands—attending meetings, keeping up with national political trends, doing thought work with students—prevented him or her from spending much time reviewing lessons. For all these reasons, activists were seldom at the top of their classes, and sometimes were at the bottom. (In Gao's class there were only three League members, and all three were repeating the year because of academic failure.)

Students respected academic excellence because of several factors in the high school environment. First, academic achievement was valued highly by most teachers and parents. Although parental values no doubt varied with class background, expressions of admiration for intellectual prowess were not limited to respondents of bourgeois background; even the few respondents of working-class origin respected academic ability. There have been indications in the Chinese press that parental attitudes toward education—even the attitudes of peasants—continue to be very traditional.[31] Despite the regime's efforts to use the school for political transformation and popularization of practical skills, academic learning continues to be perceived by parents and teachers as the central task of the school, and those who excel in it have the most prestige.

A second reason for the popularity of academic achievers was that

31. RMRB, August 25, 1964, SCMP, 3299, pp. 16-17; *Nanfang ribao*, December 11, 1964, SCMP, 3377, p. 23; *Nanfang ribao*, February 22, 1965, SCMP, 3240, p. 18; HQ, 13 (1965), p. 35.

students viewed academic competition as a fair contest. Unlike political activism, in which an ascribed characteristic (family class background) gave some people an advantage and others a disadvantage, academic success was seen as being based entirely on individual achievement. For Jiang, and other students as well, academic success was more legitimate than political prominence because it was *earned*: "I didn't have many League friends because I didn't think very highly of most of them. They became League members not because of their own effort. Good study grades show your own effort, but the League members became League members just because of their background and political performance."

Third, whereas the standards for political recognition were subjective and imprecise, judgments of academic excellence were seen as unambiguous. Because Chinese pedagogy has traditionally paid scant attention to original thinking and still relies on rote learning, the standards of academic success were particularly clear. You achieved academic success by getting excellent grades in your courses, and you got good grades in your courses by memorizing the material and giving the correct answers. You couldn't pretend to know the answer or get a good grade by playing up to the teacher. In contrast, you could win a reputation as a political activist by fakery and flattery. Political evaluations were made by student activists and teachers together, whereas academic ones were made by teachers alone. Students were more confident of the objectivity of their teachers than of their classmates.

Fourth, while there was a zero-sum element in all high school competition (because university places were apportioned to localities), the mutually destructive character of competition was more overt in political competition than in academic competition. Proving one's activism required criticizing particular collegues to the teacher and in criticism sessions; to make yourself look good, you had to make certain others looked bad. The costs to other students of one person's academic success were not nearly so direct; one student's good grades would indirectly lower everyone else's chances for success, but they did not threaten specific people.

The impact of the differences between academic and political competition on student norms is brought into vivid focus by considering the popularity of student athletes. Sports stars were almost as respected as valedictorians, and were even more popular. Peng compared the two:

> Athletes were admired. If you had a special skill or talent, people would admire you. The most admired people were those good in study,

next were those good in sports, and third were those good in cultural activities. Usually the athletes had more friends and were more popular because they were usually more open-minded, easier to get along with. Studious people were usually quieter, spoke out less, and thus had somewhat fewer friends.

If the popularity of athletes was due in part due to their temperament—they were described as "relaxed (*suibian*), without any airs, and easy to get along with"—it was also owing to certain special characteristics of sports activity. Athletic excellence was clearly earned by an individual's "special skill or talent."[32] No one could "fake" a track record or a winning basket.[33] And although the athletic superiority of one student might prevent another from making the school team, athletic activity—unlike political activism—did not directly harm other students.

But athletic activity was even more socially approved than academic activity because besides not hurting others it actually benefited them. Whereas good grades and League membership were purely individual matters, students collectively rooted for their class and school athletic teams to win. An individual player's contribution to the team's victory brought glory to all the students, even those cheering on the sidelines. (The differences between political, academic, and athletic-cultural activities are discussed at length in Chapter Six.) Outstanding athletic ability was the best way—even better than the academic route—for a student to reconcile the conflicting pressures of popularity, ambition, and duty. One respondent, a swimmer, was welcomed warmly by her fellow-students with a poster over the school gate every time she returned from a meet, and she was sought after by the top university in her province as well.

Activists Caught Between Teachers and Classmates

Playing the activist role required a student to chart a course between the expectations of school authorities and those of fellow-students. Ac-

32. Of course although physical strength and agility are largely the results of individual training, other athletic traits—height or weight, for example—are inherited rather than achieved.

33. Students also respected individuals who demonstrated their physical prowess in manual labor, where the standards of accomplishment were as obvious and unambiguous as they were in sports. Students who were weak or inept in work felt ashamed in front of their classmates. For example, Gao confessed that he used to hide a pile of thin towels on his shoulder under his shirt so that he could carry a heavier load.

tivists were often confronted by situations—criticism sessions and reporting to the teacher, in particular—in which they could either fulfill their official obligations or help their classmates, but not do both. Many activists were unpopular because in such situations they turned their back on their peers, choosing instead to please the teacher.

Chinese students did not expect their classmates to flout or ignore the demands of school authorities. They accepted a certain degree of striving for university places and city jobs as necessary and legitimate, but they condemned people who tried *too hard* to please the authorities. Students with good grades were respected, but the "grinds" were derided. Academic achievement was admired, but conspicuous effort was ridiculed.[34] The kids in Shi's gang were popular because they received top grades with apparent ease: "We were lazy but very intelligent. We could get high grades by just listening well in class. We always crammed at the last minute for exams. Those other students who worked so hard at their studies—we called them fools, because if you have to study so hard, you can't be very smart."

Similarly, students rejected individuals who were *too* active. Activists who discredited their classmates before teachers too often, in too exaggerated a fashion, or with too much relish, were condemned as traitors.

The only activists who managed to win peer-group popularity were those who found ways to demonstrate loyalty to their classmates. One effective method was to warn students before you criticized them. Yang said that his friend, the class president, informed his friends in advance that he would have to bring up their shortcomings in a meeting; his friends understood that it was "just part of his job."

Another technique for handling the cross-pressures of leadership roles was to let students know that when you met with the teacher, you would protect them. As Peng, a former class president, said, "Sometimes the class director would ask me about a certain person, and I would just give an ambiguous and vague answer." Peng also won his classmates' affection by refusing to report minor deviance: "I would obey school rules whenever matters of principle were involved. But in small matters, I would bend toward my classmates." Because he was worried about alienating his classmates, Peng was reluctant to report

34. James S. Coleman found that even in the most scholastically oriented high school he studied, the group norm was to get good grades without appearing to make an effort to do so. "Academic Achievement and the Structure of Competition," p. 375.

even a fight he had witnessed: "My classmates were very surprised that I hadn't told on them; they expect a class president to report this kind of thing. So afterwards they always liked me and cooperated with me because they knew I was on their side."

Another former class president, Jiang, tried to arbitrate fights and not involve the teacher.

> If I saw two students having a quarrel, I would talk with them and find out the story, then decide who was right and who was wrong, and advise them about how to resolve it. They would usually listen to me if I was sincere (*zhen xin cheng yi*); they wouldn't listen if I put on official airs. . . . I told the class director only the most serious things and I never told tales. My classmates knew that—they can tell if you're sincere or if you tell tales.

Even when they made adjustments to show students that they were on their side, many political activists found the cross-pressures of their position unbearable. Like a noncommissioned officer, factory foreman, production team head, or any basic level leader, they were very susceptible to informal group pressure and felt torn between their duties to higher authorities and their loyalties to the group.[35] Peng complained that one student taunted him no matter how lenient he was: "In junior-2, as class president, I volunteered the class to be responsible for digging an air raid shelter for the school, a job nobody liked to do. Shi publicly teased me in the playground . . . saying that I was trying to establish myself by making the class do hard labor."

Some students—especially the "natural" peer group leaders who were acutely sensitive to their classmates' opinions—found the pressures so intolerable that they resigned their offices and shifted to an academic strategy:

> A good friend of mine was class president in senior-1 and senior-2 but quit in the beginning of senior-3 because he wanted more time to

35. "The noncom finds himself in a conflict situation involving official responsibility to his officer on one hand and unofficial allegiance to the other enlisted men on the other hand. It is probably easier for the noncom to give way to the internal social pressure of the enlisted group and to avoid conflict with his officers by diplomacy and outward obedience than to accept the official point of view and be in continuous conflict with his social group." Stouffer and others, *The American Soldier,* pp. 409-410. This type of adjustment by local Chinese cadres produces distortion in the implementation of policy (down) and the communication of information about local conditions (up). See Bernstein, "Cadre and Peasant Behavior Under Conditions of Insecurity and Deprivation," pp. 365-399.

study for graduation examinations and entrance examinations, and also because he felt caught in the middle as class president. He was chosen class president because he had the ability to persuade people, but he didn't like the pressure of the job. He had to mobilize students, and they resented this and didn't cooperate. Then the class director and Youth League would criticize him. He felt forced to scold and force students and he didn't like to, but if he didn't then the League would get on his back. Sometimes he would get so frustrated that he would lose his temper in front of the students.

A person highly sensitive to student opinion and therefore distressed by the cross-pressures of the activist role, was, ironically, the type of person who probably would have made the best student leader. When popular and prestigious students were recruited as activists and filled class and League positions, students followed and emulated the activists, and the class functioned well.[36] Luo described one such leader: "The class president in junior-2 was a boy League member. He was respected by the students, had good grades, and was the son of a cadre. He didn't separate himself from the students and worked together with them, so even when they were criticized by him, they still accepted it and trusted him."

But more often, the class lacked social cohesiveness because power and popularity required separate roles.[37] The activists had power delegated to them by the Party and school authorities, but not popularity. Some well-liked students who ventured down the activist path found their popularity eroded. And many other popular individuals did not serve as activists either because they did not want to jeopardize their friendships or because they were screened out. Many "natural" leaders were prevented from entering the Youth League or holding class office by established activists who were jealous of their social influence.

In some school classes there was fierce antagonism between political activists and peer group leaders. In the struggle between political power and social power, the activists often prevailed. For example, An, one of

36. In his landmark study of Bennington College, *Personality and Social Change: Attitude Formation in a Student Community,* Theodore M. Newcomb found that the socializing power of the peer group was strengthened by the congruence of progressive attitudes, institutional prestige, and personal popularity.

37. "In high cohesive groups leadership and popularity tend to form an integrated role complex, while in low cohesive groups leadership and popularity are segmentalized roles." Theodorson, "The Relationship Between Leadership and Popularity Roles in Small Groups," p. 67.

the most popular boys in his class, found the Youth League members ganging up on him:

> When my name was put forward in the election for Five Good Students, it caused a big debate in the class meeting. The League members opposed my election because they said I wasn't good enough in politics. I finally got so angry that I went up to the blackboard and erased my name, withdrawing myself from the election. . . . By senior-3 my friends and I gave up arguing with the class director and the Youth League majority because it was useless.

In other instances, those like Li who had a social following triumphed. Li was so popular that he received the most votes in class officer elections, but he declined to serve as president, preferring instead the position of sports and culture officer because it was less political (and less likely to alienate him from his fellow-students). When he was continually "mistreated" by the League branch secretary, he mobilized his supporters: "My friends decided to help me. We organized other students in the class to write small character posters criticizing the secretary. It worked, and afterwards the secretary's manner was much nicer, especially to me."

Sometimes those with social influence could strike a bargain with the holders of political power, who needed students' cooperation in order to satisfy the demands of their superiors. Li evolved this type of mutually beneficial relationship with his class director: "Although the class director didn't particularly like us, he realized that we had considerable power among the students; so he had to listen to us and give us special consideration." Shi was treated with similar deference by his class president: "He had to be friendly to us because he had to rely on our gang to handle all the non-political activities in the class, like cultural competitions, drawing posters, etc."

Sometimes, however, tension between a popular group and an activist one led to a fight. There was such an incident in Shi's class. His gang of popular boys was constantly tormented by the Youth League branch secretary, who would report to the teacher every minor instance of mischief—such as sleeping on the job during labor or talking in school meetings. Once when Shi and five others were caught gambling for biscuits and sweets, the activist labeled their behavior a serious crime, and charged them with participation in illegal activities. Shi believed that the fellow picked on him because he was the ringleader of the leading crowd in the class. For six years they had been in the same class, and for at least the final three years, Shi had been forced to defer to the superior political power of this activist. There was no way for him to retaliate without risking his future. He suppressed his anger until right after graduation:

> After we had taken the university entrance examination, the class went out to the countryside to work for a while, and we finally beat up the League secretary—in front of the class director and the dean! There was nothing the school authorities could do about it because the examinations were done, the conduct comments were already written, and we had our graduation certificates in our hands.

Relations between activists and other students rarely erupted into open conflict, but in many classes there was a clear separation between those with social influence and those with political power. Because the activists were seen as beholden to adult authorities, they had difficulty winning popularity with their peers. The only activists who endeared themselves to their classmates were those who dealt with the cross-pressures of their role by bending toward the students.

Sincerity and Hypocrisy

Students distinguished between two categories of activists: those who were sincerely committed to the revolution and those who were hypocrites. As Huang summarized the distinction: "One kind was those who were truly loyal to Mao Zedong and the Party. The other kind were people who exploited the opportunity (*zuan kongzi*) to join the Youth League and accumulate political capital."

Students were acutely aware of the political pressures in Chinese society in general, and in the school environment in particular. In meetings, criticism sessions, and even in everyday social discourse, people had to speak as if they were doubt-free supporters of the current political line to protect themselves from political stigmatization and professional demotion. And because career prospects depended to such a large extent on authorities' judgments of an individual's political character, people were constantly tempted to promote themselves through politics. These pressures produced a lot of what people in China call "empty talk" (*kong hua*)—unexamined, even false, statements made in order to go along with or rise up in the system.

Ironically, the pressures generated by the communist regime's political efforts to transform Chinese society have heightened people's appreciation of the traditional virtues of honesty, sincerity, and loyalty.[38] Where the air was filled with "empty talk," people put a premium on speaking the truth, on honestly saying what they believed. Where people were rewarded for presenting themselves as political zealots, those who admitted their doubts were admired. And where one person's political success was accomplished at another person's expense, people who stood by their colleagues were esteemed.

Students did not expect anyone to be devoid of individual self-interest or calculation, but they asked that people pursue individual career goals in a manner which did not betray their classmates or their integrity. Some respondents abstained from politics in the belief that it was impossible to resolve this predicament, that no one could pursue a political route to success without being corrupted.[39] But others felt that although it was difficult, it was possible for some people to maintain their moral commitments while becoming activists.

The expressions used to describe these good activists came directly from the traditional Confucian lexicon. They were described as "sincere" (*zhencheng*) or "sincere in belief and intention" (*zhen xin cheng yi*). Their public statements were "honest" (*laoshi*).[40] They were "genuine" (*zhenzheng*) activists, acting on the basis of real belief. The term most frequently used by respondents to differentiate the activists worthy of respect was *yiqi*, a traditional moral category translated as "a sense of honor." The term combines the notions of loyalty and righteousness. An individual with *yiqi* balanced personal loyalties (to friends, the family, the village) with more transcendent commitments (to the Party, the nation, the revolution) while maintaining personal integrity. Only this kind of activist earned students' respect. The word frequently used by respondents to mean "respect," *xinfu,* joins the ideas of trust and admiration. In other words, before one could respect an activist, one must have trust in his or her authenticity and loyalty.

38. This point is made by Michel Oksenberg, "Getting Ahead and Along in Communist China," pp. 323-324.

39. "For many, the pursuit of power and wealth appear to have become antithetical to the pursuit of respect," Oksenberg wrote *(ibid.)*. But Oksenberg does not discuss the people who attempted to combine these objectives. In high schools some students were able to achieve both political power and peer respect.

40. Li Erzhong, "A Talk on Being Honest," ZGQN, No. 3-4 (February 5, 1962), SCMM, 304, pp. 6-9. And "Be an Honest Person, Speak Honestly, Manage Affairs Honestly," ZGQN, No. 4 (February 16, 1964), pp. 12-13.

Almost all the activists described as sincere were from good family backgrounds and were senior members of the Youth League. A large number of the sincere activists were from cadre families. Tang said, "The children of cadres are not hypocritical activists but genuine activists. . . . They have a sense of honor." She also noted that the sincere activists, who were the core League members of cadre origin "didn't trust the new activists and thought they were hypocritical."

Activists of excellent class background were viewed as sincere because of the "natural redness" assumption and because their political style was more relaxed than that of activists without background credentials. Students with outstanding class background who established themselves as activists very early were relatively confident of a successful future. Therefore they could afford to use a strategy that reconciled ambition and peer respect: they did not have to report every trivial mistake of a classmate to the teacher, and did not have to exaggerate their public criticism of others. Thus they were less likely to hurt other students and more likely to be perceived by them as loyal, honest, and genuinely committed to the revolutionary cause.

"Flocking around these real activists," said Luo, were the hypocritical activists who "patted the horse's rump, tried to perform well in campaigns, and actively sought responsibility; these people usually had poor relationships with ordinary students, but were close to the class director and the real activists." Even respondents who were themselves politically active described some activists as devious and insincere. The students who talked the most about politics and were the most aggressive in meetings were viewed as phonies with the gift of gab.[41]

The expression used to describe this kind of activist was *xiangyuan*, translated as "hypocritical," but with the connotation of moral betrayal.[42] The current meaning of this traditional term is one who feigns an enthusiasm for revolutionary goals in order to promote himself.

41. Apparently people tend to equate quietness with honesty. One article criticized this view and reminded readers that the person who speaks infrequently may be only the "agreeable person (*laohao ren*) of the old society" rather than the "honest person of the revolution"; restraint may be motivated by "looking after one's own skin" (*ming zhe bao shen*) and by "overcaution" (*jinxiao shenwei*) rather than by sincere commitment. On the other hand, speaking a lot may be motivated by sincerity, or may just mean that a person is "glib" (*youzui huashe*), has "fancy words and an insinuating appearance" (*qiaoyan lingse*), and "believes one thing while saying another thing" (*xin kou bu yi*). The only way to tell an honest person is to look beyond "superficial appearances." "Are People Who Don't Say Much Honest People?," ZGQN, No. 12 (June 16, 1964), p. 32.

42. The author is grateful to Thomas P. Metzger for identifying themes of sincerity and hypocrisy that emerged from the interviews. The notion of moral hypocrisy (*xiangyuan*) is discussed in his book *Escape from Predicament*.

Most students had internalized the regime's ideology to the extent that its values—of selflessness and serving the people—had a certain sanctity to them. They were morally repelled by people who profaned these values by exploiting them for self-promotion. Their voices rose with moral outrage when they talked about the activists who made a big show of their own altruism and attacked others for selfishness when they themselves were out for personal gain.

With very few exceptions, the activists condemned by students as phonies were the less confident ones: new Youth League members or aspirants to membership, those who lacked good background credentials or a record of academic achievement. Perhaps projecting their own calculations onto the motivations of others, students assumed that someone from a non-proletarian family who behaved actively must have ulterior motives.

Students of good family origin encouraged the notion that non-proletarian activists might appear enthusiastic on the surface but had not undergone a real conversion to the revolutionary cause. They employed a pun to the effect that in college admissions policy, the stress on political behavior (*zhongzai biaoxian*) had become stress on superficial appearance (*zhongzai biaomian*).[43]

The stereotype of the hypocritical activist was most strongly held, however, by people from non-proletarian families. Students with bad or middle-range family class labels condemned as hypocritical the political transformations of their friends of similar background who "turned active." They felt betrayed by them. Moreover, they could see the element of calculation in the actions of those who had been close to them, whereas they had no basis for doubting the public images of good-background, established activists who were socially distant from them. Leaders need to limit access to information about themselves if their "mask" of altruism and public service is not to be questioned. The individual who has risen from the ranks—the "upstart"—is in a difficult position "since a great deal is known about him and his antecedents and he cannot achieve the mystery required for leadership."[44] Because students remained in the same school class for three years or more and often lived in the same neighborhood, they were quite familiar with one another and likely to be skeptical of sudden changes in political behavior, especially if their family situations were similar.

43. White, *The Politics of Class and Class Origin*, p. 24.
44. F. G. Bailey, *Gifts and Poison*, p. 293.

New activists without the security of good background credentials or good grades were also more likely to behave in ways that roused the anger of their peers. A person who is upwardly mobile, striving to join a higher-status reference group, always tends to "overconform" to the norms of that group out of social insecurity.[45] What was at stake for the aspiring Chinese activist was not just social acceptance but a future career. In order to impress the League power-holders and class director with their political zeal, insecure new activists tended to go overboard, and their excessively eager behavior was interpreted as hypocritical. Individuals of bad family origin who were attempting to become politically active knew that they were at a clear disadvantage. They were vulnerable on two counts: no matter what they did, people would suspect they were insincere because it was so widely assumed that those of non-proletarian origin were "naturally" apolitical or hostile to socialism; and their rivals could always attack them in class terms—for example, by denouncing their "bourgeois" selfishness. Therefore they had to try harder to prove themselves politically. Ironically, these conspicuous efforts appeared to others as hypocrisy.

AT ARM'S LENGTH

In all the high school classes described by respondents there was a social separation between political activists and other students. The clique structure of the classes reflected this separation. A typical class was that of Xu:

> There were three cliques in my class, the playful and naughty (*tiaopi*) group, the studious group, and the League activist group. The activist group was the most separate. Ordinary students were friendly with the members of the activist group only when they themselves wanted to join the League. The naughty group didn't like the activists because they were always trying to keep them quiet and control them. The academic group didn't like the activists because they didn't have good grades.

Even when students respected activists and felt no strong resentment of them, they tended to keep their distance. Chen said: "Although the Youth League members in my class tended to flock together, there was no resentment of them on the part of non-League members. Everybody was aware of who were the activists and League members. We

45. Peter Blau, "Social Mobility and Interpersonal Relations," p. 293.

wouldn't exclude activists, although there was a certain subtle gap between us and them." Although overt antagonism was rare, students still preferred not to mix with activists. School authorities tried to foster friendships between non-active and active students. Chen explained why: "It was a good thing in the eyes of the teacher if an ordinary student became close friends with League members and activists because it showed that you were trying to be progressive." But, he said, there were few "real" friendships across this political line, and "most of the students who hung around with the League members were people who hoped to become League members themselves."

This gap between activists and their classmates can be explained, in part, by the different interests and schedules of the two groups. Wu noted that they spent their time in different activities: "Activists always had meetings, while the ordinary kids just hung around." Not only did League activists have to spend a lot of their time in meetings, but these meetings—like all League affairs—were secret and could not be discussed with nonmembers. Peng said that as a result, "every League member had a kind of mysterious aura around him. . . . League members never showed their cards to people, nobody ever knew what they were aiming at. They claimed to have different ways of working which were unknown to ordinary students, which had to be kept confidential. They looked mysterious. Even when the members were chatting casually with other students, whenever people asked about the League, they would immediately turn silent."

The world of the activist was so separate that when someone entered it, he or she inevitably became estranged from non-active friends. Zhou recalled a friendship that ended this way: "Even though I had nothing against him, because he didn't tell tales on me or criticize me, I just felt that I couldn't talk with him anymore."

The cleavage was sometimes reinforced by regional differences. In several of the Guangdong schools attended by respondents, the dominant activists were the children of Northern cadres assigned to work in South China. Local students described school conflicts in regional rather than political terms—they talked about "the Northerners" rather than "the activists" or "the Youth League members." There were few friendships between Cantonese and Northerners because of language and cultural differences, and because the local students resented the Northern carpetbaggers who had come South to make their political fortunes.

The social distance between activists and their classmates was widened by both sides. Wu observed that they had a mutual interest in avoiding one another: "It was almost impossible for activists and non-activists to hang around together as friends. The non-activists feared being reported and the activists feared bad connections." As noted earlier, students who had already achieved political prominence were at best ambivalent about cultivating new activists. Activists also worried about being tainted by association with students who were politically backward. Because people were judged by the company they kept, there was a risk involved in appearing too socially comfortable with political unreliables.[46] It was safer to spend your time with other activists. For an activist, another danger of allowing ordinary students to become familiar with you was that they might begin to question your public image. Just as non-active students had to worry about revealing their weaknesses to activists, the activists wanted to hide their flaws from others. If their classmates knew too much about them, their position of moral authority could be eroded.

Therefore, although there were some potential benefits to an activist in associating with ordinary students—such as obtaining information on student attitudes and receiving help in academic coursework ("activists seldom hung around with non-active students unless they were bad in their studies," said Luo), such associations could also jeopardize an activist's position. Only the most secure activists—those who were confident of their prominence, their political inviolability, their future opportunities, and their peers' esteem—would want to form close relations with non-active students.

Such relations were even riskier from the non-activists' point of view. Activists, as respondents often said, had the power to determine your fate. If they criticized you publicly or to the teacher, it could mean bad conduct comments, which in turn could lead to a rural work assignment. Even if you respected individual activists, An said, "you had to be careful with them because they had the power to struggle against you. . . . It was better to keep them at arm's length."

Of course, becoming friendly with an activist could sometimes work to your advantage. When students adopted a political strategy and aspired to Youth League membership, they had to become backbone elements and ingratiate themselves with established activists.[47] League

46. Oksenberg, "Getting Ahead and Along in Communist China," p. 341.
47. Sometimes this entailed doing an activist's mischief in exchange for Youth League admission. An article on League cadres described how one cadre took advantage of patronage to wage a personal vendetta. The League officer was angry at a student who had criticized

aspirants had to spend many hours in conversation with their introducer. Respondents who had rejected the political option labeled these relationships between new and old activists "not real friendship" and "mutual use" (*huxiang liyong*). They condemned aspiring activists for "running to the heat and clinging to the power" (*guyan fushi*), a traditional expression that means associating with important people in the hope that their power and influence will rub off. Although these relationships with established activists certainly were instrumental, they were not necessarily calculated consciously. Rather, they were a natural concomitant of social mobility, easing the social strains for the individual moving upward.[48]

There also were secondary advantages to political contestants who got close to senior activists. The established activists would not only sponsor you for League membership, but would also give the class director a good impression of you. As Yang said: "It was always good to be close to the activists and League members because it would be easier to get into the League, and the activists would say good things about you to the class director, whose evaluation of your conduct determined your future." The patronage of a senior activist with high political credibility could also protect you from the attacks of people who were trying to prove their political zeal.

Activists could share with you one of their most valuable resources, information on political trends. In a place like China, where careers depend on adherence to the political line and where the line frequently shifts, advance knowledge of national political developments is at a premium.[49] The well-connected activist who was privy to internal directives and, even more valuable, to political gossip, had control of a crucial resource.[50] Activists often "leaked" political news to their

---

him in a wall poster. He got another student to write a poster against his critic by promising to recommend the student for Youth League admission. *Singdao ribao* (Hong Kong), November 30 1966.

48. Blau, "Social Mobility and Interpersonal Relations," p. 294, notes that if an upwardly mobile person stays friends with members of his former group, he is constantly reminded of his mobility; if he associates largely with companions in his new group, then he can forget the ascent.

49. "Where persons are deprived of knowledge of what is likely to happen to them, and where they are uninformed about how to 'make out' in a situation where making out may mean psychological survival, information itself becomes a crucial good, and he who can dispense it finds himself in a favorable position in the economic and social exchange systems." Goffman, *Asylums*, p. 286.

50. During the Cultural Revolution, when the political world became particularly dangerous and unpredictable, a Red Guard who had good connections with top leadership circles could turn special information into political power. Tang said: "The higher the father's

friends. Jiang, a former class president, said that his friends benefited because he "had to talk with the class director a lot and could always tell my friends the inside dope." Even a non-activist like Luo saw the benefits: "The advantage of being friendly with activists was that you might get information on things before others did."

There were other minor advantages of an activist's patronage. Because Youth League members and class officers consulted with the class director on classroom seat assignments, they could arrange to place you near your pals. And when activists participated in arranging periodic stints of manual labor, they could assign you to preferred locations or jobs. Although the class usually labored together, sometimes it was dispersed among different work units; and in that case the student labor officer would determine one's placement. Luo said: "During the busy season and in summer we had to stay in the countryside for anywhere from ten days to a month, so if you were [a Cantonese] assigned to a Hakka area, you would go crazy for a month. If you were friendly with the labor officer, he would assign you to a Cantonese area." And in Guo's class, "The activists arranged for themselves to work at a film factory where the work was interesting, while other students had to do uninteresting manual labor."

Despite these favors to be gained by getting close to an activist, most students preferred to keep their distance. For students who were not attempting to make a name for themselves politically and who were just trying to preserve a clean political reputation, the risks of association with activists outweighed the potential benefits. Because the standards for evaluating political character were so vague and subjective, students who lacked a sense of political confidence felt safer away from the scrutiny of activists. If you said or did something that could be construed as "bourgeois" or "counter-revolutionary," the activists could not be trusted to keep it to themselves. They were likely to bring it up in a meeting or report it to a teacher, and to exaggerate the seriousness of your "crime." Even an offhand remark could get you into trouble. One

---

position, the more powerful was the student in the Red Guard organization, because higher-level cadres could get the news and directives faster and their children could act faster than others in the right direction. For example, this is how a Red Guard leader would emerge. A student got information from his father that something was up in Peking. He quickly wrote a wall poster with unconventional contents. Everybody criticized his views, but he stood firm on his ground. Later his view was affirmed by the Party center, and so he won and was acclaimed by everybody as a daring hero."

former League activist, Fang, explained why ordinary students avoided activists:

> League members listen to the school authorities, the upper level, so most ordinary students were not willing to go around with them or reveal their thoughts to them. They would prefer not to let League members hear even ordinary remarks. . . . For example, there was a girl whose father was a professor and rather wealthy. One day she was chatting about clothes, saying something about buttons that were 12 cents apiece. A League member overheard her and said it showed her bourgeois thought. The member brought it up in class meeting, and the girl had to do a self-criticism.

The way to protect yourself against this kind of criticism—which could mar your political record and ruin your chances for university admission—was to keep activists at arm's length.

It was difficult, however, for ordinary students to escape supervision from activists. Students who needed political "help" sometimes were assigned seats next to activists.[51] Activists were supposed to talk frequently with them as part of their "thought work." And, Gao complained, "they knew how to get information out of you even though you didn't want to tell them." One respondent, Lin, who attended a boarding school, found the round-the-clock presence of activists so "restrictive" that in senior-2 he returned to his home to live.

When students had to be around activists, they watched their tongues. They were particularly careful not to antagonize the activist or discuss political topics. In Gao's words:

> When I was introduced to a League member, my first reaction was to speak carefully, to avoid politics, and to try to speak less and talk about harmless, small things. When activists approached me, I would just ignore them until they went away or just answer with as few words

---

51. One short story, "New Deskmate," ZXS, November 1957, pp. 19-21, describes the reaction of the author upon learning that he has been assigned to share a classroom desk with an activist, Xu Qiuping, rather than his friend, Li Wenhua: "Why didn't I want to sit with Xu? Everybody knew she liked to pick on others. Ever since she was elected League branch head she had thought of herself as a big official. Look what a nobody I am—she would even pick on Li Wenhua and pick out a whole truckload of faults: being preoccupied with one's own studies, incorrect attitude toward helping others, not uniting with female classmates, etc. . . . Just because of these opinions of hers, Li's application to join the Youth League was not approved. How could I take such a petty bureaucrat sitting with me and pushing me around?" The story goes on to tell how the author was helped by his new deskmate and came to appreciate her as a true friend.

as I could. It was a bad thing to offend them because they could talk to
the class director and get you bad conduct comments. Nobody would
dare argue with them, unless he was a good element too. Ordinary
students didn't criticize activists because they would remember it in
their hearts and make trouble for you when you did something wrong.

Guo said that friends changed the subject of conversation when they
saw an activist approaching. Xi said that although "there wasn't a big
division between the League and most ordinary students, you didn't
want to let the League members hear your personal talk because they
might tell tales."

Respondents who were former League activists were aware of the
constraint in their conversations with classmates. Fang said that after
she joined the League, her friends were no longer willing to discuss
their families with her. Yu expressed regret at the way her role as an
activist made it impossible for students to talk freely, as they had done
before she joined the League. Ding said that if your grades were good
and you "weren't too proud," your friends would continue going
around with you after you joined the Youth League, but she added,
"Some of these friends weren't willing to talk about politics with me
after I joined the League."

To counteract this tendency of students to hide their thoughts from
activists, the practice of "heart-to-heart talks" was established in all
Chinese high schools. League members were supposed to approach
students, inquire into their personal problems, and "help" them become more progressive. The goal was for students to resolve their
doubts and reform their ideas by opening their hearts to activists. In the
competitive school environment, students found this practice personally
threatening. There were complaints that the heart-to-heart talk relationship was unequal, patronizing, and condescending. Girls were
often assigned to talk with boys, and boys with girls, probably because
the competitive tensions between members of the same sex were too
strong.[52]

According to the respondents, you could withhold your ideas from
activists even when they approached you for heart-to-heart talks if you
learned to maintain your detachment. You had to pretend to be recep-
tive and acquiescent. Deng explained: "The only thing to do when the
activists approach you for heart-to-heart talks is to let them keep talk-

52. Whyte, *Small Groups and Political Rituals in China*, p. 123.

ing. You should speak as little as possible so you won't give them clues for criticizing you." Xi said that he too "just listened and was passive and pleasant and tried to get it over with."

Another regime effort to bring activists and their fellow-students closer together was even less successful. In 1965 there was a campaign in almost all high schools to create friendships between activists and non-activists called Red Pairs (*yi dui hong*). All activist students were paired with non-activist peers; the activist was supposed to help his or her partner become more progressive. Pairs were urged to spend most of their time together and were assigned to share a classroom desk in some schools. At the end of one semester, the class met to evaluate and compare (*pingbi*) the progress made by each couple, and to praise the pairs that had become the most red. The campaign was a failure. According to respondents, it did not generate any new friendships or change anyone's attitudes. Ordinary students managed to maintain their psychic distance by outward compliance.

Despite the articles and short stories urging greater intimacy between the student activists and their classmates, and despite special regime efforts like heart-to-heart talks and Red Pairs, the separation between the two groups of students persisted. For both activists and non-activists—but particularly for the latter, who were trying to be politically inconspicuous—the risks of such intimacy far outweighed the potential benefits. Many activists were unpopular and had low prestige among their peers, but even when students respected activists, they preferred to avoid them. They saw activists as politically powerful and beholden to adult authorities; revealing themselves to activists could imperil their career prospects. There was a fundamental conflict of interest between the students pursuing the political route to success and those who hoped to get ahead through academic and professional skill; and this conflict, though particularly acute among high school students poised at the brink of adult careers, did not disappear after graduation.[53]

53. Along with the cleavages caused by Red Guard factionalism, the division between political activists and non-activists remains. According to Bernstein, (*Up to the Mountains,* pp. 126-127), among youths sent-down to the countryside, non-activists tend to avoid activists. The estrangement of activists and their colleagues is so widespread, in work units as well as in schools, that the issue has been taken up by the official press. In 1980, Chinese Youth asked in poetic language why activists were respected by outsiders but not by the members of their own units: "Why do the flowers inside the wall smell sweet only to those outside the wall?" ZGQN, No. 2 (February 1980), pp. 12-13.

5

THE HAVEN OF FRIENDSHIP

What impact did the political pressures and competitive conflicts of the Chinese urban high school have on student friendships? The matter of friendship is a highly political one in the Chinese context. The Communist Party leadership, though it does not criticize the concept of friendship per se, gives priority to group loyalties and political principle. According to the universalistic ethic of "comradeship," one is supposed to care for all of society, not just for a few friends. Friendships are suspect because they pull people away from the collective. I expected to find that under the influence of the communists' universalistic, collectivist ethic there had been a flattening out of degrees of interpersonal relations and a weakening of the emotional intensity of friendship ties.[1] Ezra F. Vogel, in his important article "From Friendship to Comradeship," has argued that friendship relations among Chinese have indeed been weakened—not because of political principle and overriding loyalty to the collective, but because of the political risks of confiding in a friend.[2]

My research indicates that in fact friendship bonds between urban high school students were very strong. Individuals sought out friends who were like themselves in respect to age, sex, class background, native region, and style of political participation. After friends decided they could trust one another, they confided even their unorthodox political opinions. Loyalty to friends often prevailed over official political standards when the two conflicted—as they did in mutual criticism sessions.

The previous chapter focused on the divisiveness and interpersonal

1. Ai-li Chin, unpublished paper, 1972; and Richard H. Solomon, "Mao's Effort to Reintegrate the Chinese Polity," p. 339.
2. Vogel, "From Friendship to Comradeship," pp. 407-421.

tension generated by the competition for career opportunities, and by political competition in particular. This chapter analyzes the bonds between students, the friendship relations of trust and loyalty. Like all patterns of social interaction, they cannot be viewed in isolation; they can be understood only as individual behavioral responses to the organizational context in which people must operate. Friendships were formed by students as a haven, a "protective environment" from the political pressures of school life.[3] These pressures did not erode friendship between students but instead heightened their perceived need for the emotional support of a friend. Friendship relations persisted not *despite* the political pressures in the Chinese system, but rather *because* they helped people adapt to these very pressures.

THE OFFICIAL VIEW OF FRIENDSHIP

The official Chinese attitude toward friendship was that it detracted from a person's commitment to the revolutionary enterprise. Excessive concern with personal relationships was seen as a manifestation of bourgeois selfishness. Friendship was viewed as harmful because it reinforced political deviance rather than fostering reform.[4] In his frequently quoted essay "Combat Liberalism," Mao Zedong warned of the dangers of putting personal relations, including friendship, ahead of political principle. One type of liberalism, he said, was "To let things slide for the sake of peace and friendship when a person has clearly gone wrong, and refrain from principled argument because he is an old acquaintance, a fellow townsman, a schoolmate, a close friend, a loved one, an old colleague or old subordinate. Or to touch the matter lightly instead of going into it thoroughly, so as to keep on good terms."[5] This

---

3. In 1975, Gordon Bennett interviewed 37 adults who had lived in the PRC, and found that friendship relations were strong because they were used as "safety valves" or "havens." Bennett, "China's Mass Campaigns and Social Control," pp. 135-136. The concept of "protective environment" was proposed by Ada W. Finifter in her study of friendship patterns in the work groups of American auto workers, "The Friendship Group as a Protective Environment for Political Deviants." Eric R. Wolf notes that friendship can "provide emotional release and catharsis from the strains and pressures of role-playing" in "Kinship, Friendship, and Patron-Client Relations," p. 11.

4. The Chinese were correct in assuming that friendship would enable individuals to resist pressures to conform. In S. E. Asch's famous experiment on the effect of group pressure upon individual judgment, the presence of a single ally provided sufficient support to enable a person to withstand group pressure and make a correct judgment. For a discussion of the political implications of Asch's findings, see Moore, *Injustice*, p. 93.

5. Mao Zedong, "Combat Liberalism," p. 31.

message was the major reference point for many articles on friendship in Chinese youth periodicals.

The Chinese press never attacked friendship per se. A teacher-training textbook noted that adolescents have a particularly strong need for friendships.[6] A 1964 article on friendship acknowledged that "all people like friendship."[7] It said, however, that friendship must be redefined to harmonize with political imperatives. Friends must not allow themselves to become estranged from the collective, to "build a wall around themselves and separate themselves from their environment." The article reminded students that "a revolutionary definitely should not be concerned about only a few people. The music of friendship should not be played only to a few people." It admonished youth not to fall in with someone who was a bad political influence, a "class enemy who puts on the mask of friendship to . . . carry out his tricks and conspiracies." The best kind of friendship is one in which a proletarian helps a member of the bourgeoisie "conquer his errors, reforms him."[8] Friendships should be based upon shared commitments to political principle.

A person's commitment to the official values of the regime was measured by his or her willingness to criticize a friend's political mistakes. The plots of short stories in Chinese magazines often revolved around the hurt feelings produced when friends criticized one another; the stories always concluded with the hero's realization that the friend who criticized him was not an enemy but a true friend.[9] Friends must staunchly defend political standards in private as well as in public: "When a person is frustrated and has some discontents, he wants to find a friend to grumble to. The friend listens to your grumbling, sympathizes with your complaints, and begins to grumble with you himself. This makes you feel nice and comfortable. But is this the warmth of friendship? No, this is not warmth. This is intoxication, this is poisoning."[10] By commiserating with discontented friends, you helped them believe that their complaints were reasonable and thereby reinforced their political alienation, whereas a true friend would try to bring them back into the fold.

6. *Jiaoyuxue* (Pedagogy), p. 74.
7. "Friendship and Warmth", ZGQN, No. 2, 1964, pp. 21-22.
8. *Ibid.*
9. Examples are in ZXS, October 1954, pp. 43-47, and October 1955, pp. 60-61.
10. "Friendship and Warmth," ZGQN, pp. 21-22.

THE RISKS OF FRIENDSHIP

In the high school environment, where students were required to supervise one another as well as compete with one another for career opportunities, friendship was a risky proposition.[11] All the respondents were aware of the political risks of friendship. They described several ways in which friendship could sully a student's political reputation and thereby diminish his or her chances for a successful future.

First, when you confided in a friend, you risked having your friend expose you in public criticism or to the authorities. Respondent Chen was reluctant to reveal himself to a friend for this reason:

> True, intimate friendship was impossible in school because everyone was hesitant to share confidences, especially about family matters, for fear of being reported and getting into trouble. Older people tended to have more political problems than students who have been educated in the new society. So what would happen if my father said that the Communist Party was not as good as the Kuomintang in some respect, and if I told someone that my father had said that? It would probably lead to trouble for me and my family. So I was just friendly with everyone in the same degree.

Establishing intimacy always involves mutual disclosure of information that could be damaging. Even in societies less politicized than China, friends have many opportunities to harm one another by revealing such information.[12] In this sense, there is always an element of risk in friendship. The risk of exposure is particularly great in the Chinese setting, because opportunities are distributed according to evaluations of political virture. A confession of political doubt or an irreverent political joke shared with a friend, if revealed and represented as a sign of bad political character, could not only embarrass you but damage your career prospects as well.

Students recognized that the pressures of political competition could

11. Andrew J. Watson argues that friendship is uninhibited among ordinary workers and peasants because the pressures of political life and the risks of friendship are not as great as those "at higher social levels and among some people with authority or with social aspirations" ("A Revolution to Touch Men's Souls," p. 327.) Urban high school students certainly fall within the latter category, where the risks and pressures are great, but the risks strengthen rather than weaken friendships.

12. Kurth, "Friendships and Friendly Relations," p. 162.

force even the most trustworthy friend to turn against them. Luo's family, for example, warned her that telling friends about family matters "might be all right in ordinary times, but when the crucial moment comes, people are bound to use your weakness against you." The theme of betrayal by friends runs through the accounts of many respondents. Through personal experience or observation of others, they learned how a person could be driven by personal ambition to trade on a friend's confidences.

Another risk of friendship was guilt by association. As Yang explained: "Friendship is difficult because if your friend has a political problem, it could reflect on you and hurt you. It can be a lot of hassle (*mafan*). If your friend is criticized, then people will criticize you for being friends with him and will get suspicious, saying "what are the two of you plotting?' " Associating with a person under political suspicion could force you into a moral predicament, because you would be expected to criticize your wayward friend. Should you violate the trust of friendship by speaking out, or raise questions about your own political commitments by keeping quiet? As Yang said, "If you become friends with someone who likes to fight, then you get criticized for not helping him by stopping him from fighting. If your friend gets into serious trouble, then they ask you why you didn't report him." By becoming publicly linked with a friend, you *doubled* the risk of slips of the tongue and other political mistakes. This made the price of friendship prohibitive for some security-conscious students.[13]

The costs could be raised even higher if a friendship were labeled part of a "clique" (*xiao jituan*). A clique was understood to be a social group, as small as two friends, that operates counter to the aims of the collective. The standards for distinguishing a clique from a non-threatening relationship were vague and imprecise. Therefore, since any friendship might be criticized as a clique, the safest approach was not to form a friendship at all.[14] Class background was often used as the

13. All students, including both those who were confident and those who were reconciled to failure, had to worry about whether their talk or actions would make trouble for their friends. If you thought you might come under political suspicion, you would best serve your friend by staying away from—or at least not being seen with—him or her.

14. Samuel L. Popkin has made this point about ambiguous standards for judging relationships in his work on communism and village politics in Vietnam. He argues, for example, that because any relationship between a man and a woman can come under political attack as illicit romance, people have to avoid being seen with members of the opposite sex. (Personal communication, June 1979.)

factor distinguishing a clique from a harmless friendship. As Peng said, "When two bad elements hung around too much, people criticized them as forming cliques." Therefore, the worse your class background label, the the greater your fear of being accused of forming cliques. As Lin explained:

> Chairman Mao and the Communist Party said that friendships were less important and could stand in the way of devotion to organizations like the Youth League and the Party. But it's still all right to be friends if both people have good background. If one person has good background and one bad background, then [the friendship] sometimes was criticized, mainly because of the possibility that the bad background person might influence the good background friend. But the worst thing, in the Party's view, is two classmates with bad backgrounds becoming close friends. So you have to think about this. If you hang around all the time with a close friend, then your classmates might be suspicious.

Whereas good background students and others who were confident of their career prospects felt relatively free to make friends, the risks of friendship were much greater for the politically vulnerable. They were more likely to be accused of forming cliques and less politically adept at negotiating the perilous path between private and public discourse. The more unorthodox the attitudes of their family members, the more they had to worry about revealing these attitudes to friends.[15] And the more politically suspect they were, the more likely it was that friends who needed to make political reputations would have to renounce them.

These risks, however, did not discourage most students from making friends. The pressures of political competition had two contradictory effects on friendship patterns. On the one hand, the concern for political security did lead some students to limit intimacy. Four of the thirty-one respondents said they had no close friend, but as Chen put it, "were just friendly with everyone in the same degree." They maintained casual, comparatively superficial relationships with a number of pals—what Chinese students called "ordinary friends" (*yibande pengyou*) and

---

15. Also, all other things being equal, the larger the family, the greater the risks of friendship. Luo's father had ten siblings and her mother had twelve. They all gathered at her house every Sunday. With so many relatives whose words and actions could reflect badly on her, she worried about discussing her family with friends.

what Vogel would call "comrades."[16] These relationships were safer than friendship but less fulfilling. Ordinary friends gave up the rewards of mutual revelation in order to avoid its risks. The four respondents who had not chosen friendship expressed regret at what they had lost, but said they felt the choice had been forced upon them by the high school environment.

Five other respondents did have close friends, but exercised some restraint in the relationship. Some friends were more like comrades in that, as Vogel described it, there was "an implicit comrades' agreement that they will not say anything that would create in the other a conflict about whether or not he should reveal something."[17] For example, as class president, Peng was aware of a tension between official obligations and loyalty to his friend. Therefore, he said, when his friend expressed discontent, he "warned" him to keep quiet. An's best friend was in a similar situation because his mother served as principal of the school they attended:

> After the Great Leap Forward, when the economy was so bad, my friend and I would discuss how dissatisfied we were with China's lack of progress. But what we criticized was how the policies were implemented, not the policies themselves. It was the people who implemented the policies who were to blame, we thought, and we often discussed this together. But when one day I started to blame the Communist Party, my friend stopped me. He told me I shouldn't say such things because if a campaign came and his mother asked him about it, he would have to tell his mother what I had said. This would put him in a difficult position. So in order to avoid a conflict of conscience, my friend asked me not to say such things to him. From then on we continued to criticize individual cadres but never the Party itself.

Two other respondents, Guo and Huang, did not confront the special problems of official roles, but nonetheless preferred to hide their deepest thoughts even from their closest friends. Huang said: "The only true and best discussions were those inside the family, where you could really express yourself. In school you must hold something back from even your best friends."

16. Vogel, "From Friendship to Comradeship." Kurth, in "Friendship and Friendly Relations," labels relationships which are characterized by less commitment, risk, extensiveness, and intimacy than friendship as "friendly relations."
17. Vogel, "From Friendship to Comradeship," p. 414.

The tendency to confide in family members rather than friends was revealed in a story Peng told. A classmate who was caught trying to escape to Hong Kong was held under guard in the school. As class president, Peng was responsible for bringing food to the culprit:

> One day when I brought the meal, he pleaded with me to take a note to the fellow who had tried to escape with him but had not been caught. He looked so miserable and helpless that I did it. Afterward I realized I had committed a crime by helping an escapee. I was scared and confused. I didn't know what to do. My feelings were very complicated. Having promised to help my classmate I felt I should honor my words, but on the other hand I felt guilty about committing a crime. I talked with my uncle about it. He was stunned and ordered me to confess to the school about it immediately, before anyone found out. I did, and surprisingly, the school didn't punish me and kept the whole thing quiet.

When asked why he had turned to his uncle instead of his best friend, Peng said: "Because it was such a serious matter. Almost criminal. The consequences could be very serious, and I was afraid of a slip of the tongue. I felt it was safer to talk about such a serious matter with someone in the family rather than with a friend." Even though he described his best friend as an ideal friend—"frank, sincere, and able to share mutual trust"—when he was in political jeopardy he felt he could rely more on his family than on his friends.

The political pressures in the Chinese milieu raised the risks of friendship but also increased the need for it. The great majority of respondents (27) had close friends, and all but five of them said they could tell anything to these friends. The respondents who had found close friends (called "good friends," or *hao pengyou*, by Chinese students) were no less aware of the risks of friendship than students who did not have close friends. But recognition of the pressures of political competition not only made students wary of one another but also made them crave the relief of intimacy. Because students, in order to protect their political reputations, always had to be on their guard and present a good "face," they felt a need for one person with whom they could relax and be themselves. Even this desire was considered deviant according to official political morality. In a system that expects so much of its members, almost everyone becomes a deviant to some extent; at least, many feel like deviants. This self-perception of deviance intensifies people's need for a "protective environment," the safe haven of friendship—a place where they can reveal their doubts and failures without fear of being condemned or reported.[18]

A GOOD FRIEND

The threats to friendship in the high school setting increased students' attachments to their good friends, and the risks of friendship made students put a premium on the loyalty and trust they found only with such friends. Our respondents said that it was hard to find a true friendship in China, but once found, it was a deep relationship.[19]

The first ingredient in a good friendship was openness. Jiang's definition of the difference between good and ordinary friends, which was echoed by many other respondents, was that "with good friends you can talk about anything, even politics." Because you could not risk political talk with ordinary friends, conversation with them was limited to "superficial and harmless things." Peng added that you would never dare get into an argument with an ordinary friend. Jiang explained: "With good friends you discuss things a lot and with ordinary friends you just do things together." A good friend was someone with whom students could share their innermost thoughts, even to the point of revealing the thoughts which they had previously confided only to their diaries. Several respondents said that they communicated personal feelings to their friends in the traditional fashion, by reading and writing notes in the margins of one another's diaries.

One theme that emerged from interview accounts of friendship was "speaking the truth." Students were constantly aware of the incentives to speak and act falsely in order to protect their future prospects. Because they felt the strain of pretending—to school authorities, to activists, and to ordinary classmates—they sought out a good friend to whom they could speak the truth. For example, on the eve of graduation, when everyone had to declare a desire to be sent down to the countryside, you

    18. Finifter, "The Friendship Group."
    19. Solomon ("Mao's Effort to Reintegrate the Chinese Polity," p. 299), found that young Chinese, educated after 1949, were more pessimistic about finding friends than were the older respondents. The majority of his 32 young respondents agreed with the statement, "It is an unfortunate thing that during one's life it is so difficult to find true friends with whom one can share thoughts and feelings deep in one's heart."

could confess your reluctance about accepting this assignment only with a good friend. Most respondents had only one close friend, because openness and truth-speaking were impossible to achieve in larger groups. An said, "It's best to have just one close friend. When there are three or more people together you can't talk about everything." The novelist Ding Ling, after having been under almost constant attack by the Communist Party since 1949, spoke out in 1979 and recalled a saying that expressed the same idea as a principle of Chinese social life: "When there are only two persons, they talk frankly. When there are three, they tell jokes, and when there are four, they speak falsehood."[20]

The second element in good friendship was trust: students spoke freely only to friends who could be trusted not to betray them. The determination of trust was based on a student's judgment about whether the potential friend felt a stronger allegiance to personal friends or to the Communist Party. If you fell under a political cloud, would this person turn against you, abandon you, or stand by you even at risk to his or her own political reputation? As Deng said: "When one made friends one had to consider whether the person was able or not to go through a trial. When a campaign came, the authorities would make friends tell about each other's thoughts and feelings. So you had to be careful about a person's thought, family background, and behavior when making friends." Students did not expect their friends to be totally lacking in self-interest or political commitment, but they looked for friends who could balance these concerns with friendship loyalties. Our respondent An described his ideal friend as a person who "courageously commits himself and then lives up to the commitment without selling out."

Students had a highly romantic ideal of friendship.[21] The refugee respondents spoke lovingly of the good friends they had left behind in China. Most of them still felt bound to their friends and corresponded with them because, as Guo said, "friends are forever, even though they may be parted." In contrast to other social relations which were based on instrumentalism, friendship was described as a purely expressive

---

20. *New York Times,* June 7, 1979, p. 2.
21. In traditional China there was a sentimental, almost romantic, view of friendship, which was due to the emotional release it provided from restrictive hierarchical role relations. For the traditional Chinese perspective on friendship, see Pye, *The Spirit of Chinese Politics,* pp. 102-103; Solomon, *Mao's Revolution,* pp. 123-124; and Lang, *Chinese Family and Society,* pp. 324-327.

relationship.[22] In a system like that in China, where people's life chances depend in large part on official judgments of their attitudes and behavior, people are forced to calculate the risks of their social actions. Constant worries about who you are seen with and what you say lead students to crave one relationship that is untainted by self-protective calculations. Respondents often contrasted the "mutual use" of other relationships with the pure affection of friendship. Chinese in Taiwan and Malaya were found to view friends as sources of material support.[23] In contrast, students from the People's Republic looked upon their friends as sources of emotional support.

CHOOSING A FRIEND

Most students chose good friends who were like themselves: people of the same age, sex, family class background, native region, and political orientation. This tendency is not unique to China, of course. In societies characterized by instrumental friendship relations, people must cultivate ties with persons who can provide practical assistance, with those who are older, more affluent, or better connected than themselves. But where expressive friendships prevail, people seek out friends who are like themselves because the more they share, the greater their mutual understanding. In China, where the risks of confiding in a friend were especially severe, friendship choice was motivated by a desire for security as well as for empathy. Before you revealed yourself to a friend, you had to be able to predict how that person would behave; you had to be sure that he or she would not betray you. Zhou said: "In schools people think carefully about what kind of person an individual is, what background he has, and what way he has treated you before deciding to be friends with him." It was easier to predict the behavior of a person who had been shaped by life experiences similar to your own.

---

22. Eric R. Wolf distinguishes two kinds of friendship: expressive (or emotional) friendship, in which each person "satisfies some emotional need" in the other; and instrumental friendship, in which the striving for "access to resources" is central to the relationship ("Kinship, Friendship, and Patron-Client Relations," pp. 10-12).

23. Grichting, *The Value System in Taiwan*, p. 291; and Pye, *Guerilla Communism in Malaya*, p. 149. Although in China the expressive side of friendship predominated, people were not reluctant to use friendship relations (*guanxi*) for gaining access to scarce goods, facilitating their childrens' careers, and so on.

Age

Almost all the respondents had chosen friends of the same age. Of the twenty-seven respondents who had a good friend, only two had picked someone considerably older or younger than themselves.[24] This research finding is in large part due to the lack of opportunity for meeting students of other ages. The students of each class, who were approximately the same age, spent almost the entire school day together and were kept together as a class throughout the three years of junior or senior high school (some key schools which provided education at both the junior high and senior high level kept the classes together for as many as five or six years). According to the respondents, students rarely settled into a close friendship in junior high school. They were still too "immature" for real friendship, they said, and the pressures of political competition were not yet so acute that students needed to seek refuge in friendship. When they finally formed close friendships, they chose their friends only after long, careful acquaintanceship. Therefore it was almost inevitable that friends would be members of the same class and approximately of the same age.[25] Even when a class contained a few individuals several years older than the norm—such as rural youths whose schooling had been interrupted because their families could not afford the tuition or needed their labor power, or Army veterans returning to school, or those who had been forced by illness to drop out— this principle applied. As Yang said, "The older students felt more at ease (*tandelai*) with each other." Guo said that he always picked a friend of the same age because the younger ones were too frivolous and the older ones too sophisticated.

Sex

Throughout the high school years there was a social separation of boys and girls. Only one of the twenty-seven respondents with close

24. One exception, Liu, became friends with someone two years ahead of him because he was a "big wheel," prominent throughout the school. He met his friend through school extracurricular activities—the radio club and the Young Pioneer school committee. The other exception, Xi, chose two older friends because he felt he could talk more freely with them than with classmates in the same class.

25. Grichting found in Taiwan that younger people and people with more education chose friends closer in age. (*The Value System in Taiwan*, p. 282).

friends had made friends across sex lines.[26] Although many respondents were eager to gossip about one or two notorious love affairs
between students (or between a teacher and a student), as a rule there
was little contact between the sexes. This was, in part, a result of the
official prohibition of student romance.[27] Tang said:

> Boys and girls can talk together openly only if it's based on poli-
> tics—for example, League members talking with classmates who want
> to join. If there is other contact between the sexes this is marked in your
> conduct comment as romance. So boys and girls don't even greet one
> another if they meet, and don't dare to borrow things from one another
> because they are afraid of being criticized for having a romance.

Once again, the problem of vague and subjective standards for evaluating behavior—it was difficult for the authorities to distinguish between
innocent contact and wicked romance—led security-conscious students
to abstain from all actions that might be misconstrued as political
deviations. Only students who were doomed to failure (those who attended private schools) or were confident of success (cadres' children in
particular) dared to engage in conspicuous flirtation or even friendship
with members of the opposite sex.[28]

These patterns of avoidance have non-political roots as well. When
young adolescents begin to notice sexual differences, they express their
embarassment in shyness or antagonism toward those of the other sex.
One female respondent described relations between boys and girls in
junior high: "In junior-1 boys and girls were assigned to share desks.
They drew a line between them and the one who went over the line got
punched. By junior-2 there was no line, but we seldom talked to the
boys, otherwise we would be laughed at."

26. Because the proportion of female students shrunk every year, it became progressively
more difficult for girls to find same-sex friends. For example, Deng, the daughter of a
landlord, had to make friends with boys, because in her school (located in a rural county seat
in Guangdong Province) there were only seven girls left in her fifty-student class by senior-3.
Most of the students' parents were poor peasants, and the one other girl with bad family
background was acting very progressive in an effort to win acceptance as an activist. Deng
said, "Even though we came from similar backgrounds, I could not go with her." Therefore
she had no choice but to find a friend of similar background and political style from among the
boys.
27. Romance was prohibited by school rules. For the rationale for this regulation, see
"Do Not Fall in Love Too Early," ZXS, April 1956, pp. 64-66.
28. During the Cultural Revolution, when the rules of the opportunity game were
suspended and there was no supervision of behavior by school authorities, relations between
boys and girls were much freer.

An educational journal advised teachers to organize folk dancing and other activities to mix boys and girls in order to overcome the antagonism between them.[29] The traditional taboo on physical contact between males and females (*nan nu shou shoubujin*) nevertheless was strongly adhered to by adolescents anxious about their sexual identity. In senior high, students began to engage in flirtations, but only with tentative expressions of affection such as anonymous love letters, shy admiration from afar, and tantalizingly brief encounters in school groups. Girls were willing to confess their infatuations to their close friends, but boys were embarrassed to admit their romantic interests even to one another. One male respondent said: "In high school boys and girls are very separate. If you dared to have a romance, you wouldn't tell anyone about it because romance was considered a disgusting (*taoyan*) rather than a glorious thing."

Class Background

In a school environment characterized by political competition, students looked primarily at political criteria when selecting their friends. As Jiang said: "In China the first prerequisite for friendship is political position and class background. When you're looking for a friend, you have to settle this first, and then you can fit together your interests, and so on." Class background was the most important consideration, especially in senior high, when students become increasingly anxious about their futures, and especially after 1963, when national policy was expressed in the slogan "never forget class struggle." "The most important requirement for friendship is class standpoint (*jieji lichang*)," said Lin. Students felt that intimacy was possible only with someone of similar background. As Jiang said: "A person with the same class background is in the same position as you, and since he is in the same position, then you have more to talk about and share . . . the same standpoint on things . . . a common language." Students assumed that political attitudes were influenced by family background. Moreover, because the authorities' treatment of students varied according to their class backgrounds, students of similar class labels were in the same

29. *Shanghai jiaoyu* (Shanghai Education), May 1957, p. 11.

situation vis-à-vis the internal dynamics of the school.[30] Deng said, "The school treated students of different background so differently that students of different background would naturally turn away from each other."

Students from bad class backgrounds, who were very worried about the political risks of friendship, were especially mistrustful of those blessed with better class status. For example, Lin, the son of a professor condemned as a rightist in 1957, rejected the son of a high-ranking Air Force officer who sought him out as a friend. This boy was rebelling against his family by expressing politically backward ideas; he told Lin about the conflicts in his family and criticized government policy. But, as Lin said, "Although I liked him a lot, I could never get close to him because our class backgrounds were too far apart." Instead, Lin chose a friend whose father had worked for the Kuomintang: "We were closer because both of us had bad class background."

Although class background was particularly salient to those of bad class background, students from middle-range backgrounds also felt it was safer to choose friends with backgrounds like their own. Gao explained why: "I needed a friend who was bourgeois class, but not a very bad element. My background wasn't very bad, so if I hung around with a very bad element, I would be dragged along. . . . I didn't want to hang around with good background classmates—not because they had irritating characteristics or behaviors, but because I was afraid they would tell on me." Even the fortunate ones of good class origin tended to form friendships among themselves.[31]

It was not always easy for students to identify their classmates' class background. People in all societies give signals to one another through external appearances. Clues like dress style are important in the getting-acquainted process, when people meet and decide whether or not to initiate further contact.[32] Dress clues, however, were more difficult to

30. For example, students of bad background were the only ones required to give a public report on their family history; the children of cadres were given special tutoring sessions and called to special meetings; and, as He, an activist respondent of good family origin, admitted: "Political power in the school was given only to students with good class background. Students with bad background were completely powerless."

31. The children of cadres were separated into several groups according to differences in family environment and personal style. The children of military officers tended to keep to themselves (or associate only with the children of high-level cadres), whereas the children of middle-level officials in the provincial, municipal, or county governments felt they had something in common with the children of intellectuals.

32. See Suttles, "Friendship as a Social Institution," pp. 129-131, and Goffman, *The Presentation of Self in Everyday Life,* pp. 22-30.

discern in China where everyone wore much the same clothes—plain trousers and shirts, conforming to the norms of simplicity, utility, and comfort (as well as availability and political inconspicuousness). Therefore Chinese students became adept at noticing small but significant differences in dress and possessions. Overseas Chinese students, whose income and access to consumer goods were enhanced by remittances from relatives living abroad, dressed slightly better than others, and those from wealthy families always had better shoes. Peasant youth wore traditional black garb until senior high school, when they started to dress like everyone else. The children of cadres, especially those of high rank and from the military, wore the old uniforms of relatives. Some of them were chauffeured to school in official cars. Those from affluent bourgeois and cadre families had nice bicycles.

Differences in dialect and diction also signaled different class backgrounds. Peasants had a "clumsy" but "straightforward" manner of speaking and often used vulgar expressions. The children of army officers and cadres "spoke in a commanding tone." A student who spoke Mandarin outside of class (with the exception of the top key schools, most schools used the local dialect as the medium of instruction and taught Mandarin as a second language) was assumed to be the child of a non-local cadre.

There were also differences in demeanor that reinforced students' stereotypes of people from various family origins. Urban respondents spoke patronizingly of the peasant "country bumpkins" (*tubaozi*) who were coarse, clumsy, and had a "sense of inferiority." The sons and daughters of officials, especially high-ranking ones, were attractive (because, respondents explained, the cadres marry the prettiest women), and had a manner of natural superiority—they had either a quietly proprietary air or an overbearing, arrogant manner. Some students resented them, but all deferred to them.[33] Students from affluent bourgeois or capitalist families also were attractive. And although they

---

33. A fictional account of student life in a 1920s rural school describes a similar pattern of social deference to youths with powerful parents: "The boys from the landowner-and-official class were always the leaders, and whether they were in the classroom or in the playground it always appeared that all authority and privilege belonged to them alone; only they could give orders and make suggestions. As for the other boys, some of them stood to one side and said nothing, as if afraid to challenge the authority of the leaders; others displayed an attitude of obedience by which they hoped to share in the advantages and pleasures of their more powerful classmates. This attitude might be called inborn; there was no doubt about its existence, for it was evident in every nod and smile." Yeh Sheng-tao, *Schoolmaster Ni Huan-chih*, p. 88.

sometimes put on airs, the poise, beauty, and cultural refinement—
particularly of the daughters from such families—won them considerable popularity. Even though the Communist Party had stripped these
old wealthy families of their political status and continued to discriminate against their offspring, bourgeois youth were still able to command
respect from many of their classmates.

Native Region

Often reinforcing the class background basis of friendship choice
were the regional differences among students in a high school class.
Individuals from the same province, who spoke the same dialect, were
naturally drawn to one another and found it easier to develop understanding and trust. In China, regional stereotypes are even more
powerful than class stereotypes. Northerners scorn the "slyness" and
"political backwardness" of Southerners, and Southerners deride the
"bluntness" and "stupidity" of Northerners. In many high school
classes, there was a small minority of students from another province
whose parents were bourgeois experts or cadres assigned to special
work. When such minority status coincided with cadre background, it
reinforced in them a sense of regional and class superiority. For example, in some key schools in Canton, as many as one-third of a class were
the children of Northern cadres and military officers. Their military
uniforms, Mandarin speech, and commanding manner set them apart;
they clustered together and rarely befriended the Cantonese. The Cantonese, who are known for their strong feelings of regional chauvinism,
mocked the "dumb clumsiness" of their Northern classmates among
themselves. Nevertheless they deferred to these powerful outsiders
(Luo reported that they shifted from Cantonese to Mandarin when a
Northern classmate joined a conversation). When there were a large
number of Cantonese students at a school in another province—even
though their parents may have been technical specialists and not cadres—they tended to stick together and ridicule the locals.

While regional origin was a salient factor in friendship choice, class
background was even more salient. If non-locals did not share the same
class background, class background considerations prevailed over re-

gional ties.[34] For example, in the Jiangsu Province school attended by Jiang, a Cantonese, there were only a small number of non-native students and their family backgrounds were dissimilar; therefore they all chose local friends rather than risk friendship across class lines.

Political Orientation

In order to maximize empathy and security, students looked for friends whose political style was like their own. Activists and non-activists were almost never friends. The only time they became close was when one of them wanted to gain admission to the YCL; and these relationships were labeled, by activists and non-activists alike, as pacts of "mutual use" rather than genuine friendship. As Guo said (quoting the traditional philosopher Xun Zi), "Birds of a feather flock together" (*wu yi lei zhu*). Yao compared this pattern to the one found in Hong Kong: "In Hong Kong financial differences keep people from being friends, but in the Mainland, political consciousness is the most important thing for friendship." Class background was, however, an even more powerful influence on friendship choice than political consciousness. Students sought out friends of like mind, but different background, only when the pool of classmates from the same background was so small that they could not find a friend there.[35]

Underlying this pattern of selecting friends on the basis of political criteria—class background and level of activism—were two opposing types of political risks. On the one hand, students wanted to avoid being publicly linked with those whose family origin or political reputation would make them targets of suspicion; such an association might raise doubts about their own political reliability. Because of this risk of guilt by association, students tended to snub those with bad background and the politically backward.[36] But on the other hand, the risk of betrayal

34. Interviews with two peasant respondents indicate that in rural schools, village and clan ties were more important than class background in determining friendship choice.

35. Another option was to find a friend of the same background, but of different sex, age, or native region.

36. "There are still people who are reluctant to come into contact with youths born of families of exploiting classes. They fear that others might say their 'stand is unstable' and that they have 'confused the line.'" ZGQN, September 1, 1965, SCMM, No. 495, p. 37.

led students to avoid those of good origin and the activists, who would put the Party ahead of their friends, and to confide instead in the non-activists of middle-range or bad family origin. There was some danger that someone of bad background might attack a friend in a desperate attempt to demonstrate political regeneration; but according to the respondents, most people of bad origin could be counted on to remain politically inconspicuous. And even if a friend with a bad background or bad political label exposed you, the damage to your own political reputation was minimized because such a person had low credibility. Ironically, in a system where people are supposed to reveal their innermost beliefs and doubts to the politically most committed, in actuality people instead confide in those who are labeled backward. As a result, the politically deviant become the ones to hear the most complaints and reports of abuses, which no doubt reinforce their own disaffection from the system.

Classmates and Friends

Classmate (*tongxue*) ties have always been very important in Chinese culture, as a basis for adult economic and political alliances, as well as for friendship sentiments.[37] Given the risks of friendship in contemporary China, however, students might be expected to make friends outside their school class. The dangers of friendship could be minimized by finding a friend from another class or another school who, unlike your own classmates, was not in direct competition with you.[38] However, only two of our twenty-seven respondents with good friends had gone outside their classes to find them.[39] One of them, Xi, explained the logic of his choice: "You have to be careful with friends in the same class because they might take what you tell them and report it to the League members or the class director. But if you have good friends outside the class you don't have to worry about that and can talk more freely with them." Gao, who had never been able to find a close friend, spent most

37. Nathan, *Peking Politics, 1918-1923,* p. 53.
38. Morris Wills found that Peking University students usually became friends with students in different departments or different classes ("Peking University," unpublished manuscript.) And in Whyte's case study of a high school student, it is shown that students sought out friends from other classes. (*Small Groups and Political Rituals,* p. 125).
39. Liu's choice of a friend two years ahead of him was based on his high status in the school, while Xi's choice of friends in other classes was based on the fact that he "felt more free with them than with students in the class."

of his time with ordinary friends from other schools (fellow-musicians with whom he played Western classical music, an activity considered deviant in the Chinese context) because "school friends may tell tales on you while friends outside school would never do that."

Although few respondents went outside their classes for friends, many of them acknowledged the advisability of such a strategy for maximizing individual security. It would not guarantee that you escaped supervision, Tang said, because the League branches in both classes would be suspicious of such a friendship; but, she said, "if you have a friend from another class, the supervision is less direct and there is less political pressure." When the respondents were asked why most students still made friends within the class, they offered two reasons, which Jiang summarized articulately. The first was this:

> Everyone in China usually makes friends with people outside their work units because when campaigns come, people in the same unit have to reveal their co-workers' actions and what they have talked about. This means that it would be dangerous to express dissatisfaction with people in the same unit because they may have to tell the authorities during campaign time. But it is different when you are a student in school. There were no campaigns that took high school students as targets, and the high school situation is different from a work unit, because after graduation students are scattered all over and don't have contact again. In work units people work together for year after year. So it isn't important to look for a friend outside your class in high school.

Other respondents agreed that although the pressures of political competition were considerable in high schools, they were not as severe as those in adult organizations.[40] The school pressures were sufficient to motivate students to seek a friend for support in coping with them, but not so great that friendship within the class was impossible.

A second reason why students made friends within the class was the lack of opportunity to become acquainted with other people. Whereas adults maintained strong ties with relatives, neighbors, old school pals, and people outside the workplace, as Jiang said, "students in school

---

40. One might have predicted the opposite: a more competitive atmosphere in schools than in urban work units. In schools, the students' futures are clearly determined by the evaluations of school authorities; in factories and offices there is little occupational mobility, and work-unit authorities have little autonomous power to promote or fire employees or to alter their wages.

have no chance to become familiar with students from other classes or schools; you're always together with students from your class." The organization of the school limited the occasions for students to become acquainted with one another.[41] The students in a class remained together in the same classroom for the entire day; only at lunchtime and before and after school did students get a chance to mix with their peers from other classes. In the key schools that provided boarding facilities, dormitory living did not encourage friendships across class lines (although within a class, boarding students tended to be friends with other boarders and commuting day students with other commuters). Dormitory arrangements varied—anywhere from four to thirty students might share a room—but roommates were always from the same class. Moreover, boarding students spent so little time in the dormitory in the evenings—because they did their homework in classroom study halls— that they seldom became close friends with their roommates. Students got to know schoolmates from other classes through participation in athletic, cultural, or political extracurricular activities, but such acquaintances rarely grew into close friendships. Moreover, by the time students reached high school age, there was little opportunity for neighborhood-based friendships. Those who attended key schools often had to travel long distances across the city; the boarding students returned home only on weekends, and even day students were at school until late in the afternoon. Although school activities were so demanding that they left students little time for making neighborhood pals, classmates whose homes were nearby sometimes became good friends. They filled their walks to and from school with conversation, which flowed more freely outside the school grounds. Also, because housing was often assigned by work units, residential neighborhoods tended to be socially homogeneous, so that neighbor-classmate friends were likely to have similar family backgrounds.

ESTABLISHING TRUST

How did students decide whether they could trust potential friends? In China, the decision was based on a perception of shared deviance. Because of its very demanding official morality, the Chinese system

41. See Hargreaves, *Social Relations in a Secondary School,* p. 6, and Lacey, *Hightown Grammar,* pp. 73-82.

turns many individuals into deviants. For example, in regard to volunteering for rural transfer, students were expected to be totally altruistic, to make their pledge to go to the countryside with genuine enthusiasm. The loss of personal opportunity and the dreariness of rural life were never officially acknowledged. Therefore individuals who felt any reluctance to go were likely to be ashamed of their own feelings; they had internalized enough of the official morality to deplore their own inability to purge themselves of self-interest. Self-perceived deviants are strongly motivated to develop friendships.[42] They need to validate their ideas with a sympathetic peer, and to ease their anxiety about their deviant position.

Trust would begin to be established when one student revealed to a potential friend an attitude or behavior that was unorthodox. Such disclosure encouraged the other student to do the same. They would discover that they could trust one another enough to drop their public faces and expose their true selves. The more they opened up to one another, admitting things that would harm them if they became publicly known, the stronger became their bond. Their knowledge of one another's deviance—the fact that each of them "had something" on the other—committed them to the relationship.[43]

The test of trustworthiness was some sign of nonconformity. Before friendship could be established acquaintances moved cautiously, feeling out the other person while not revealing any of their own nonconformist side. Joseph Novak (better known as novelist Jerzy Kosinski) described the identical process in the Soviet Union: "We walked into a restaurant asking each other tricky questions. Finally the 'test of sincerity' was over and we were fast friends."[44] Sometimes a student decided to trust someone after observing him or her engaging in behavior which demonstrated loyalty to peers rather than to authorities—for example, declining to report classmates for fighting or complaining. Anyone who was

42. Finifter, ("The Friendship Group," p. xi) points out that perceiving one's own deviance "leads to social insecurity, cognitive dissonance, and a need for opinion evaluation, all of which motivate affiliative behavior."

43. Kurth says, "Once an individual has shared intimate knowledge with another, he generally feels he has little to lose by revealing more" ("Friendship and Friendly Relations," pp. 140-141). Suttles ("Friendship as a Social Institution," p. 119), describes friends who have "violated the rules of public propriety" to one another as similar to "partners in crime," who are "bound together."

44. Novak, *No Third Path*, p. 106.

so discreet, who would not use the failings of others for self-promotion, could be trusted as a friend.[45]

But for most respondents, it was something that a friend told them which proved trustworthiness. As Guo said, "I would share confidences only when a friend opened up and shared confidences first." An decided he could rely on his friend, the son of the school principal, after they had been acquainted for several years, when the boy told him in advance that the school janitor and a student were about to be struggled against as reactionaries: "This was a very serious thing, and since he told me about it, it showed that he trusted me. I decided that if he could trust me with such a big thing then I certainly could trust him." Other friendships were forged in the anxious atmosphere generated by the pressure to volunteer for rural assignments. For example, Deng and a classmate had known one another since junior middle school, but they opened up to one another only in senior-3:

> That boy had known me for many years although we had never been close. . . . One day after school he suggested that we walk home together because he had something to ask me. I had no idea what he wanted to talk about. I figured it must be something to do with our studies. Then on the way home he asked me what I hoped to do after graduation. Before I could decide how to answer he said that he was very unhappy because he didn't want to be sent to the countryside. That is how our friendship started.

Often trust was established through mutual revelations about families. Many city students had family secrets—such as an aunt living in Taiwan, a father who read foreign books, some old jewelry or new plastic kitchenware sent from relatives overseas—which could make them the focus of political suspicion in school. Therefore, talking about their

---

45. For example, Luo became a bosom friend (*zhixin pengyou*) of the female class president after observing the tact and discretion with which she handled a scholarship application from a boy of very bad family origin. The class director told the class president that this boy was ineligible for financial aid because his father had been executed by the People's Liberation Army during the Revolution, a story not known by the other students in the class (except for Luo, whose father worked with the boy's mother in a factory). Luo found it extraordinary that although such a dramatic family history was a good topic for student gossip, the class president kept it entirely to herself. This story indicates that although officially, students from reactionary families—even those with parents in labor camps—were supposed to be eligible for scholarship aid, in some schools the administrators were reluctant to show benevolence to such students.

family situation or inviting a classmate home to meet their family were signs that they desired close friendship and could be trusted as friends. When respondents were asked how their close friendships were different from ordinary friendships, they often replied that they visited the homes of close friends and knew their families well. Only with good friends would they dare bridge the gap between their home lives and their school lives.

Once trust was established, good friends no longer had to pretend. They could relax and share deviant opinions and activities. For example, Yao and his best friend listened together to Voice of America broadcasts. Guo and his friend both loved traditional Chinese philosophy and spent many happy hours together analyzing Mencius. Girls revealed their romantic crushes to their close friends. Students complained about teachers and agonized over the uncertain future with close friends. Almost all of the twenty-seven respondents who had close friends had confided to them plans to escape to Hong Kong, the ultimate revelation of political deviance: if the information were leaked, their escape plans would be foiled, they would be punished, and they would forever be under a black cloud of political suspicion.

Students who were aware of the discrepancy between their own attitudes and the official prescriptions had a strong need for friends. On the other hand, Jiang remarked, "Of course everyone needs a good friend, but if you are sure of the rightness of your ideas and life, then friends don't really matter that much." Most students were not that confident, and the solace and support they received from their friends enabled them to resist pressures to conform to official values.[46] In this way student friendships reinforced deviance and weakened the social control of the school. In a situation characterized by risk and uncertainty, students—even those who wanted to serve the revolution—needed to "hedge their bets," to limit their emotional commitment to political goals. Friendship enabled students to reserve something of themselves from the clutch of institutions, to keep some distance between themselves and that with which others assumed they should be identified.[47]

46. Finifter notes, "Much experimental evidence indicates that subjects in friendship groups are better able to resist pressures for conformity than subjects alone or subjects receiving support from strangers" ("The Friendship Group," p. 20).

47. Goffman, *Asylums,* pp. 319-320.

FRIENDSHIP AND CRITICISM

One way in which friendship eased pressures to conform with official standards was in mutual criticism. All students had to participate in group criticism in small-group discussions and class meetings. They were expected to criticize themselves and their classmates for any deviant thoughts or actions, regardless of friendship sentiments. But because of the steep emotional and career costs of being publicly criticized, friends were loath to criticize one another, and friendship involved an implicit agreement to minimize the costs of public criticism for one another. The requirements of criticism could put a severe strain on friendships, because people known to be friends were singled out and required to comment on one another's behavior. For example, in Deng's class, during the last term before graduation, Youth League activists and the class director questioned students about their friends' true feelings about assignment to the rural areas. (Apparently not even the authorities believed that the public declarations of enthusiasm for rural transfer were authentic).

Therefore in choosing friends and determining trustworthiness, students kept in mind the pressures of mutual criticism. They tried to pick friends who wouldn't put them in a tough spot by actions that attracted criticism, and before they confided in a friend they considered, as Deng said, "whether or not the person would be able to go through trials for you."

If friends were assigned to different small groups they considered themselves lucky, because they faced only the relatively remote possibility that one of them would become the target of criticism in a class or school meeting (only the more serious errors were dealt with at these levels). If friends were members of the same small group, they were expected to speak up and criticize one another in small group discussions held every week or so.[48] Respondents said they adjusted by mentioning only "small things" and "minor mistakes." They never made "serious political criticism" of close friends. To do so would, as An said, "announce the end of the friendship," or in Guo's words, "turn a friend into an enemy." This norm of mutual protection led to a ritualization of the criticism process, and thus weakened the power of that process to reform student behavior.

48. In some schools small-group criticism sessions were held only irregularly but at least once a term, during the summing-up period at the end of every term.

When students became the target of criticism in larger public meetings, their friends tried to remain silent. Public defense was foolhardy. Guo said, "You can't defend someone being criticized because it would reflect on you; you would then be considered as guilty as the target himself." No one expected a friend to go that far to prove his or her loyalty. If friends were forced to take a public position, they first discussed it privately with the target. For example, Shi was criticized in a school meeting for snatching fruit from a production brigade during a labor stint. He said:

> My friends had to criticize me. They had to say that since they were my friends they would try to help me improve in the future. But they came up to me privately before the meeting to tell me that they would have to speak up and to make sure that I understood—because they didn't want to hurt me or upset me. Therefore when they stood up to criticize me in the meeting I wasn't surprised.

By warning a friend in advance, it was possible to reaffirm the friendship tie while conforming to the formal demands of the institution.

Friendship was also a source of emotional support for the individual who underwent the ordeal of public criticism. For example, when Huang was made the object of a series of criticism meetings, his friend consoled him: "My friend was a big help to me in my difficult time. He encouraged me to bear the ordeal and tried to convince me that after it was over everything would be all right." Students were unwilling to show sympathy to ordinary friends who became the target of criticism because they didn't want to "get involved." (Xi was so fearful that he even saw a possibility that the target might report a classmate's show of sympathy in a last-ditch attempt to redeem himself.) But the mark of a *close* friend was his or her willingness to support you even when you were ostracized by the rest of the class. Even so, there were limits beyond which students would not go to protect their friends. As An put it, "My friend and I were absolutely loyal to one another. If I was a Kuomintang agent, then my friend would report me to the authorities, but up to that point we would stand by one another."

POLITICAL COMPETITION AND THE MORALITY OF FRIENDSHIP

The pressures of political competition in Chinese high schools strengthened rather than weakened friendships between students. Instead of throwing themselves heart and soul into the public political arena, young people invested much of their emotion in the private world of friendship. The complex dynamics of this privatization were the result of several features of the Chinese system, which distributed opportunities according to judgments of political virtue.

Since people had internalized the official moral creed, many of them felt like deviants when they could not satisfy its stringent demands. Because the official morality did not recognize the legitimacy of any self-interest, people were ashamed of their ambitions and were constantly on guard lest their "selfishness" be discovered by others. Therefore people sought out trustworthy friends with whom they could validate their beliefs and express their true identities. Pledges of friendship increased people's self-perceptions of deviance, because actions taken to protect friends (such as not reporting political errors, or keeping criticism to a superficial level) were officially considered transgressions. Thus, once a friendship was made, the mutual commitment to the relationship grew increasingly intense because the friends needed one another, for emotional support and mutual protection, more and more.

Friendship commitments were also strengthened because people's futures depended in large part on the authorities' evaluations of their thoughts and behavior. This made friendship risky but all the more cherished. Everyone recognized that a person could enhance his or her career prospects by renouncing a friend. Therefore if someone chose you as a friend even though he or she could gain greater advantage by associating with the politically powerful, if someone walked proudly alongside you even though the association might result in taint, if someone refused to betray your confidence even when he or she could benefit from doing so, then you loved that person with a deep appreciation and fierce loyalty. The risks (and temptations) of political competition made people acutely sensitive to two dualities of social life: the hypocrisy-sincerity dimension, manifested in the relations between activists and nonactivists (see Chapter Four); and the perfidy-loyalty dimension, manifested in friendship relations. Under a system in which anyone can gain career advantage by betraying a friend, loyalty to friends becomes more highly valued. When people see others all around them being forced to cultivate instrumental relationships, the expressive quality of friendship is made more vivid: people contrast pure friendship with corrupt, "mutual-use" alliances.

In a system like the Chinese one, where there is no autonomous economic realm and the political realm is the arena of career competition, politics loses much of its romance and people channel their emotions into private life. Foreign observers, influenced by their own societies, in which individuals compete in the economic sphere and express their moral sentiments in the political sphere, may see excitement and romance in Chinese politics. But the Chinese themselves are more aware of the careerism in political life. Most Chinese citizens found it difficult to express their more passionate emotions in political life, so they confined them to the private world of friends and family.

Yet because people in China genuinely revered the official political values, this retreat into the private haven of friendship, although consoling, was not ultimately satisfying. People yearned to overcome the tension between friendship loyalties and political beliefs.[49] This tension was transcended only during the Cultural Revolution when, students said, they found "ideal" friendship. In An's words, "There was no conflict of interest and we all had the same ideals (*yiqi*)." The Red Guards were fighting both to protect their friends and to realize the noble values of the revolution. Politics regained its romance, and the private morality of friendship and the public morality of politics merged in a way that was not possible before or after, when politics was dominated by career competition.

49. For example, in a letter to the editor one student asked, "Does it violate the principle of justice (*yi*) to expose a friend's mistakes?" ZGQN, May 1, 1965, p. 28.

6

COOPERATION AND COMPETITION

City high schools in China were characterized by a complex mix of cooperation and competition. Although the goal of educational socialization was to inculcate collectivism and cooperation, the regime's recruitment policies instead promoted academic and political competition among students. An opportunity structure characterized by limited opportunities, high stakes, monolithic distribution, and apportionment by localities created a contest between classmates; and because career opportunities were assigned according to both political and academic performance in school, students had to compete with one another politically as well as academically. The limits on cooperation, the extent of competition and the differences between political and academic competition become comprehensible when we analyze the impact of recruitment policies on student society.

THE OFFICIAL VIEW OF COOPERATION
AND COMPETITION

Chinese communist writings condemned the pursuit of individual self-interest and competition between individuals. But communist theorists did not believe that people were inherently selfish; they were supposed to be malleable, capable of being molded into collectivists rather than individualists.[1] The communists viewed moralities as the expressions of different economic systems: individualism was bourgeois, collectivism was proletarian. Competition was condemned as the linchpin of the capitalist system. The "capitalist law of free competition" was said to mean that "whoever is strongest in competition can climb to 'the top of the pagoda'" whereas "whoever competes and doesn't make it falls

1. Munro, *The Concept of Man in Contemporary China*, esp. pp. 57-83 and 175-176.

down deservedly and ought to work for 'a few grains of millet.'"[2] Although under capitalism there may be some cooperation among the oppressed members of the working class, "the relations within the exploiting class . . . are dominated by the ideology of extremely selfish individualism, of benefiting oneself at the expense of others." In general, the social relations of capitalism were thought to be distorted by zero-sum competition: "As Lenin said, they were infected by the psychology of 'if you are not going to take things from others, then others will take from you' as early as they were nursed by their mothers. The life view of the exploiting class is 'if you do not try to benefit yourself, then the sky and the earth will kill you' and 'to build one's happiness upon others' sorrow.' "[3]

In contrast, schools in a socialist society like China's were supposed to teach students to cooperate rather than compete, and to replace individualistic orientations with collectivist ones. Teachers were told to make every student a "collectivist." A collectivist "puts the interest of the collective before his individual interest, treats his comrades and the collective with the spirit of 'I am for everybody and everybody is for me' and 'sacrifice oneself for the group.' "[4] Although students were supposed to strive for individual achievement, their motives were supposed to be altruistic; the goal was not their own career success but service to the people and the country. In every aspect of school life cooperation should prevail over competition; as one slogan put it, "friendship first, competition second" (*youyi diyi bisai dier*). Textbook lessons and magazine short stories constantly reiterated the message. Of course, special remolding efforts might be expected to be required for the older generation raised in the pre-1949 society, but theoretically young people raised under socialism would show more spontaneous collectivism. In fact, not only the lag in family socialization practices but also the incentives for individual competition created by communist policies themselves sustained individual competition among youth; and this

2. Fang O, "Let the Bell of Educational Revolution Ring Throughout the Land," HQ, No. 2 (February 1, 1976), SCMM, Nos. 859-860, p. 79.
3. Guo Sheng, "On Collectivism and Collective Education," p. 60. The premise of moral relativism has had some influence on Chinese dissidents, who criticize the new Party elite for exploiting socialist ideology to maintain its class privileges; they advocate "fair competition" as a counter-ideology to challenge the power of the Party. See Shirk, "Going Against the Tide," pp. 82-114, and Li Yizhe, "Concerning Socialist Democracy," pp. 110-149.
4. *Jiaoyuxue* (Pedagogy), p. 248. This collectivist model of education was incorporated by the Chinese from Soviet pedagogy. See Bowen, *Soviet Education;* Bronfenbrenner, *Two Worlds of Childhood;* and Weaver, *Lenin's Grandchildren.*

situation forced the regime to try to counteract competition with exhortations through the media and in the classrooms.

Many educational experts who study schools in the United States have a preference for cooperation over competition as strong as that of any Chinese pedagogue. They believe that face-to-face competition—based on the constant evaluation of accomplishments and individual responsibility for failure—is destructive to students' sense of self-worth.[5] They also cite social-psychological research findings to the effect that cooperative problem-solving is more productive than competition.[6] They argue that the "failure" of American education can be laid to academic competition: it "turns off" students and encourages them to direct their energies toward tangential activities like athletics, which are cooperative.[7] Some attribute academic competition to capitalism, to the capitalist elite's use of schools to perpetuate class inequality.[8]

School competition cannot be blamed on capitalism, however, because it is found in socialist as well as capitalist states. In both China and the United States the structure of teaching and learning is more competitive than cooperative, because in both countries the educational system is used to sort students and assign them to adult roles. This sorting process requires the evaluation of individuals, and to the extent that desirable opportunities are limited, it puts students in competition with one another. As scholars of American education have noted, institutions of higher learning and employers want to know how well

5. Dreeben, *On What is Learned in School,* p. 50; and Coleman, *The Adolescent Society,* pp. 318-319.

6. Mintz, "Non-Adaptive Group Behavior," *Journal of Abnormal and Social Psychology,* No. 48 (1954), pp. 341-349; Grossack, "Some Effects of Cooperation and Competition upon Small Group Behavior," *Journal of Abnormal and Social Psychology,* No. 49 (1954), pp.341-348; Thomas, "Effects of Facilitative Role Interdependence on Group Functioning," *Human Relations,* No. 10 (1957), pp. 347-366; Berkowitz, "Group Standards, Cohesiveness, and Productivity," *Human Relations,* No. 7 (1954), pp. 509-519; Haythorn, "Influence of Individual Members on the Characteristics of Small Groups," *Journal of Abnormal and Social Psychology,* No. 48 (1953), pp. 276-284; Fouriezos, Hutt and Guetzkow, "Measurement of Self-Oriented Needs in Discussion Groups," *Journal of Abnormal and Social Psychology,* No. 45 (1950), pp. 682-690; all cited in Roberts, *Scene of the Battle,* p. 192; and Deutsch, "The Effects of Cooperation and Competition," p. 478.

7. Coleman, "Academic Achievement and the Structure of Competition," pp. 367-387; Coleman, *The Adolescent Society;* and Roberts, *Scene of the Battle.* The presumption of natural cooperation has no empirical basis. Students in American schools pay more attention to social life than to academic study because the career stakes are not as high as they have been in Chinese schools. The difference in career incentives explains why the Chinese, who are thought by many to be *more* naturally collectivist than Westerners, would be more academically competitive than American students.

8. Bowles and Gintis, *Schooling in Capitalist America.*

each person can do, and they demand that the school provide grades in order to find out.[9] Therefore teachers are forced to be judges as well as teachers.[10]

Chinese educational experts have shown a recognition that the structure as well as the content of schooling influences student behavior. They have reminded teachers that textbook lessons on cooperation will be ignored unless they are experienced in daily life, and that students would learn collectivism only if they were organized collectively with a clear group goal.[11] Despite this pedagogical realism, there was a clear disjunction between the official morality of cooperation and the actual structure of competition in Chinese high schools.

COOPERATION IN LABOR, ATHLETICS, AND PERFORMANCE

My research shows that a student's decision to compete or to cooperate depended on the costs and benefits accruing to each mode in various school activities. Students cooperated in some areas of school life and competed in others. My respondents indicated that they enjoyed cooperative activities more than competitive ones; they had assimilated the official anti-competitive ethic and also felt that cooperation put fewer strains on their relations with classmates. Although the student peer group favored cooperation, the structure and incentives of academic study and political activism made cooperation in these realms very difficult, if not impossible. Cooperation prevailed only in labor and in athletic and cultural activities, where three conditions were satisfied: there was a clear group goal, there was inter-group competition, and the costs of helping others were low.

Manual labor, in particular, was included in the curriculum by Chinese policymakers for the explicit purpose of instilling "a spirit of collectivism."[12] The interviews indicate that the leadership's expecta-

9. Dreeben, *On What is Learned in School*, p. 70.
10. Coleman, *The Adolescent Society*, p. 323.
11. Guo Sheng, "On Collectivism and Collective Education," p. 66, and "Discussing Collectivism and Collectivist Education," *Jiaoyu wenti mantan* (Introductory Discussions on Educational Problems) (Beijing Chuban She, 1957), pp. 65-70.
12. Guo Renchuan, *Jiaoyuxue jiben wenti jianghua* (Lectures on Basic Problems in Pedagogy), (Hangzhou: Zhejiang Renmin Chuban She, 1956), pp. 50-56, quoted in Ridley, Godwin, and Doolin, *The Making of a Model Citizen in Communist China*, p. 62. One pedagogical expert asserted that labor was more conducive than study to teaching cooperation. "For example, it is difficult to induce a perspective of acquiring good results in study when the collectivity is newly formed. But if we begin by posing a labor perspective of

tion was correct: students worked together most cooperatively during labor, when they were cleaning school buildings and cultivating vegetable plots on campus, and even more when they went into the countryside every term to help the peasants plant or harvest. As Deng said, "When we did labor, people's relations were particularly good, even between boys and girls and between people of different backgrounds." Athletic and cultural activities had a similar unifying effect. As Chen recalled:

> My class showed a lot of group spirit when we organized the school sports meet in senior-3. Our whole class was mobilized and worked really hard, with a division of labor so that everyone got involved, not only those who competed in the meet. Some did designing, others paper-cutting, the girls made paper flowers, and others marked scores on the blackboard. Everyone, not only those who could do great things, got involved. We used all our free time to prepare. We really felt united and had great spirit when we were working on the meet.

Cooperation was effective in these activities because—in vivid contrast to academic work, which was assigned to and graded according to individuals—there was a clear group goal. In sports and cultural activities each class (or the entire school) constituted a "team," whose purpose was, for example, to win basketball games or to present a program of songs and dances. The group objective was also apparent in labor. Although there was no standard rule of labor organization (sometimes each class worked as a unit, and at other times students were scattered among peasant work groups), the most common pattern was to assign each small group (usually the same classroom small group used for political discussion) a section to work on. Each group aimed to harvest (or seed or weed) as much as it could—a clear goal that encouraged a cooperative work style.[13] The advantages of a division of labor

---

'beautifying our learning environment,' and organize students for cleaning and hygiene activities, then students will act together to accomplish the goal easily. Students are able to see the fruits of their labor: the well-polished desks, chairs, blackboard, glass window panes, floor, walls, the nice and meaningful decorations, and the clean and beautiful hallways and gardens" (Guo Sheng, "On Collectivism and Collective Education," p. 75). For the other objectives of labor education see Shirk, "Work Experience in Chinese Education," pp. 7-13.

13. "The fifty students in the junior-3 number 2 class are now as united as the strands of a rope, caring for one another in every regard. But before they participated in labor in the workshop, they were not at all this way.... The units and sections cooperated well among themselves. Everybody realized that any troublemaking, quarreling, or irresponsible work

were evident to all. Therefore, Deng said, "the group would divide the tasks among the members according to their special abilities so that the group could win. We thought more of group than of individual interest." And for the annual school sports day or Olympics, each class assigned its athletes to various events in order to maximize its points. In cultural presentations, some students performed while others worked backstage and the rest applauded from the audience.

Cooperation, as well as group identification and cohesiveness, were enhanced by intergroup competitions. Routine relations among small group members were at best polite and sometimes acrimonious because of mutual criticism.[14] But "during small-group labor competitions there is more mutual help and generally closer relations," according to Jiang and other respondents. Competition between groups made manual labor stints exciting. If the winning group harvested 100 bushels of tomatoes yesterday, then every group wanted to pick 110 bushels today. As Jiang said, "Generally students like to win individual competitions in study, but they prefer to win group competitions in sports and labor." Sports were described by respondents as "the most exciting activity in school. . . . Everyone got excited about them except a few bookworms." All the non-athletes attended the games to cheer on their classmates. When discussing labor and sports competitions, Shi described their impact on group solidarity: "My class cared most about competition between classes. Individual competition becomes important later on in life, but in school, group feeling and group competition matters most."

In the heat of a contest, group loyalties sometimes turned into group chauvinism; as Chinese pedagogues put it, "collective pride can turn into narrow sectarian feelings (*xiaozongpai qingxu*) and selfish departmentalism (*benweizhuyi*)."[15] Peng described an incident in which friendly rivalry became unfriendly:

---

attitude would affect the completing of the whole workshop's production assignment." Li Wen, "Every Labor Flower is Blooming Red," ZXS, March 1959, pp. 6-8.

14. There is no evidence from the interviews that the small group had become a "psychological substitute" for friendship, as Vogel thought it had ("From Friendship to Comradeship," p. 421).

15. Guo Sheng, "On Collectivism and Collective Education," p. 83. An example of a fictional lesson on group chauvinism is Zhang Tianyi, "They and We," *Wenxue* (Literature), Book I (Beijing, Renmin Chuban She, 1955, reprinted December 1956), pp. 308-317. Students at prestigious key schools, as Xi said, "felt proud of being students in those schools and looked down on students in ordinary schools." One of the most prominent high schools in Canton celebrated its long and glorious history with a reunion on its founding day every year until the Cultural Revolution; young alumni living in Hong Kong still keep up the tradition.

The class cultural and sports competitions were very exciting. They helped improve class cooperation in a short time. During the competitions, the students were very united; we would all go to the playground as a group. Sometimes the competitions created conflicts between classes. Once my class had a volleyball game with another class. Each class had one referee. The two referees had different opinions on a call, and got so aroused that the two classes almost got into a fight. I had to pull people away from one another. The two classes didn't talk to each other for a while, but gradually the fight was forgotten.

On the one hand, school authorities used intergroup competitions to motivate students to work harder and "to nourish a sense of identification with the collective."[16] On the other, however, they criticized excessive loyalty to the group.

Group competitions in labor and sports (cultural contests were rarer) effectively promoted cooperation and cohesiveness because these competitions, unlike political ones, were based on clear standards that were intrinsic to the activity itself.[17] In both activities comparisons between groups were obvious. During labor stints, Peng said, "There was a big chart in the commune on which the work of each class was marked by red flags, the more flags for the more work done. Everyone looked at the chart and the best classes were praised in the labor bulletin. It was very exciting." It was easy to tell which group harvested the most vegetables or scored the most points in the basketball game. Because the standards were objective, the contest was viewed as fair by all participants. Moreover, physical strength and agility, which were tested in these contests, were widely respected by students.

Teamwork in labor, sports, and cultural activities was not based on a total absence of individual self-interest. Certainly, compared with good grades and proven activism in the Youth League, a student's showing in these tangential activities was of minor importance for his or her future. Nevertheless, the best workers received good conduct comments, and the top athletes or musicians stood a chance, albeit a remote one, of being recruited by specialized colleges. High schools tried to play down the element of individual competition in athletics (in An's school, "when they announced the winners of a sports meet, they read out the year and class of the winners rather than the winners' individual

16. RMJY, October 1953, p. 51.
17. Coleman, *The Adolescent Society,* p. 319.

names"); but individual work activists were elected by the class after every stint of agricultural labor. The significance of this designation was lessened because so many students—almost half the class—were named labor activists every term. Nevertheless, in the highly competitive high school environment, being a labor activist could tip the scales toward university admission rather than permanent rural assignment.

Why, then, did students cooperate in labor and extracurricular activities rather than trying to outshine one another? Their sociability and idealism led them to prefer cooperation to competition, and in these activities they could be helpful without sacrificing any personal interests; they had nothing to lose, and something to gain. Team players were rewarded in sports and dancing and in manual labor as well. The teachers who observed and evaluated students during labor and the students who chose labor activists looked for cooperation and group spirit. As Peng said, "It wasn't how much you carried or harvested, because when you are working in a group, it is impossible for anyone to tell how much each individual has accomplished. It was the labor viewpoint—cooperation, enthusiasm, and so on—that was the important thing." Given these incentives, cooperation enhanced a student's career prospects and brought peer group approval as well.

THE LIMITS TO ACADEMIC COOPERATION

There was less cooperation in academic study than in these other arenas. Study was organized individually, with no collective goal; the stakes also were higher—university selection was in large part based on academic records. Furthermore, the structure of educational selection and job assignment placed classmates in direct, face-to-face competition with one another. If intellectual ability had been evaluated only on the basis of the national entrance examination, then academic competition would have been diffused. But because course grades as well as entrance examination scores were considered, academic competition was direct, constant, and zero-sum. It was impossible to increase the number of college places, they were allocated to each locality, the locus of competition was within the class, and the relative standing of classmates was important. There was only one class valedictorian, and even second-place might not be good enough for the student with lacklustre political credentials to get into a top university. Therefore many students could not afford to devote much effort to helping others in their coursework, even though helpfulness was valued by peer group norms. As Deng said, "Even though there was a good atmosphere during group labor competitions, individual competition is still more important. Being the top student in the national examination or in a school examination is entirely different from a small group winning a competition within the class."

Many students did, nevertheless, help one another in their studies. Approximately half the respondents frequently studied with friends, and an even larger number said that students were willing to help when they were asked. Chen pointed out, "People would wait until they were approached for help, rather than volunteering their time." But according to Tang, "Students were always very willing to help one another with study, even if they were not close friends [and] even when they hadn't finished their own work." Shi said that he liked studying with a group of friends because "You can ask them questions and save time."

Study cooperation was most efficient for students at the middle or bottom of the class, who received more help than they had to give. But a student's decision to cooperate did not depend solely on whether the balance of aid was in his or her favor. The peer group norms approving helpfulness and the simple enjoyment of social rather than isolated studying often led students to cooperate even if they had to give more help than they received. They would not cooperate if the costs were too high, however, so they tended to study with others of approximately equal ability.

For students at the head of their classes, the costs of cooperation were steep; they usually studied alone. Those who needed to compensate for political liabilities with outstanding academic records felt the competition keenly. Although helping others might earn them popularity—and if noticed by the class director, praise for their unselfishness—they felt they could not risk taking time away from their own work. The brainiest students were put in a tight spot right before midterm and final examinations: just when they wanted to cram by themselves, they were deluged with questions from panicky classmates. Tang said, "I had no time for my own study the day before examinations because I was so busy answering the questions of my classmates." Jiang's compromise was to answer questions, "but not if it took all day." The trial implementation in some key schools during 1964-1965 of "open book" examinations, in which students were permitted to consult with one another, also put academic achievers in a bind. Chen described his strategy this way: "When we had open book examinations, I preferred to hide myself and not appear until I had finished my own work, because a lot of classmates would ask me for help and gave me no time to do my own work." Because of this type of behavior, the top students were often the objects of social censure.[18] For example, Deng described the boy with the highest grades in her class: "He was very selfish and impatient with people who asked him questions. He was only concerned with himself."

Study cooperation was constrained not only by the structure of competition in school but also by the school's institutional ambivalence toward academic cooperation—an ambivalence that was communicated to students. Deng said, "Teachers encouraged mutual help in study but they also urged us to do independent thinking and be original." In Zhang's eyes, the contradiction was that "teachers encouraged students to study together but always warned us not to copy from one another." Because schools were required to evaluate students on an individual basis, certain rules of fairness were needed. Cooperation during tests and examinations was labeled "cheating" and prohibited by school rules and the copying of homework assignments was forbidden by teachers. There was a logical inconsistency between the socialization goal of cooperation and the rules against cheating, an inconsistency that was recognized but not resolved by Mao Zedong.[19] Students were praised for lending a hand to a classmate in labor, but punished for sharing answers when working on academic assignments.[20] Therefore although media differentiated between good kinds of study cooperation (reviewing lessons together, tutoring) and bad

18. There is a cartoon ridiculing top students who hide their papers to avoid helping others in ZXS, January 1956, p. 9.

19. During 1973-1974, student radicals defended cheating as being in line with Mao's ideas on education. In one case, a student monitor argued that the rules against cheating taught self-reliance: "When building the 10,000 ton ship, why didn't the working people of our country simply buy one from abroad and copy it to the last detail?" Those who had been caught cheating responded, "By comparing answers we can correct our mistakes and acquire comprehension. . . . And those who built the ship had countless discussions and comparing of answers." RMRB, October 19, 1973, SCMP, 5488, pp. 1-3; RMRB, December 1, 1973, SCMP, 5517, pp. 10-15. A letter from a junior high school student asked, "Isn't it also a kind of achievement to obtain knowledge by asking others what we did not know before?" RMRB, January 10, 1974, SCMP, 5547, pp. 87-88.

20. "The irony of cheating *in school* is that the same kinds of acts are considered morally acceptable and even commmendable in other situations. It is praiseworthy for one friend to assist another in distress, or for a parent to help a child; and if one lacks the information to do a job, the resourceful thing is to look it up. In effect, many school activities called cheating are the customary forms of support and assistance in the family and among friends." Dreeben, *On What is Learned in School*, p. 68.

kinds (copying homework, cheating in examinations), the teachers, who had to evaluate students as individuals and had to monitor the "honesty" of academic work, seldom initiated any cooperative academic efforts at all.[21] They gave lectures on the moral superiority of cooperation, but did little to facilitate it.

The rules against cheating and the sanctions against them—ranging from a grade of zero on the test, to public criticism, to a disciplinary mark on one's permanent record, or even to expulsion—were effective. Because even the mildest punishment could damage an ambitious student's chances for a successful career, he or she would cheat only if completely confident that the cheating partner and nearby observers would not report it. But the rules also shaped the ethics of students. As An said: "We didn't copy because the principal was very strict about it, and also because it wasn't respected by students. Those who copied homework were looked down on. Your dignity ought to make you want to do it yourself."

According to the respondents, many teachers were lax in enforcing these rules (probably because they worried that cheating cases would reflect poorly on them and damage their own careers). But even if teachers took a lenient attitude toward cheating, students considered it "shameful" (*bu guangzai*). Copying homework was a much less serious crime than cheating, because daily homework assignments were less crucial to evaluation. Therefore, a request from a friend to copy homework would sometimes make students risk discovery and forget their scruples; but cheating on examinations was much rarer.

The only classes described by respondents as characterized by institutionalized cheating (almost everyone participated and those who refused to assist others were ostracized) were found at the junior high school level or at private schools. Almost half the respondents said, as Xu did, "There was a lot of cheating in my junior high class, but none in my senior high class." The younger students were more willing to cheat because, as several respondents said, junior high classes were more united than senior high classes. The students were too young to be anxious about careers and there was less "conflict of interest" among them. Moreover, the moral injunction against cheating had not yet been

---

21. For examples of good and bad study cooperation, see the short stories "New Deskmate," ZXS, November 1957, pp. 19-21, and "Advancing Shoulder to Shoulder," ZXS, April 1959, pp. 46-51.

completely assimilated by students. As Yao said, "In junior high we all took cheating very lightly, but in senior high it was extremely serious." In private schools like Wu's, "cheating was a fashion." Because private school students were reconciled to failure, the sanctions against cheating were ineffective: "Cheating was a frequent topic in class meetings, but no one really cared, not even the teachers. Even three teachers in the examination hall couldn't keep us from cheating." Cheating was institutionalized only when the peer group norm of helpfulness prevailed over the competitive structure of schools—in other words, when the competition for opportunities was either in the remote future (as it was for junior high students) or practically a lost cause (as it was for students in private schools).[22]

THE LIMITS TO POLITICAL COOPERATION

One goal of school socialization was to inculcate the ethic of helping other people. Frequent press articles praised good deeds by students.[23] Class directors organized mutual help ventures. Tang recalled an example: "In senior-2 the son of a worker complained to the class director that he needed to see a doctor and had no money. The class director asked the students in the class to volunteer assistance. We all donated money." And Chen remembered, "If a classmate was sick, the class director organized the class to send representatives to visit him, take him some fruit and food, and help him in his studies." Students earnestly supported this mutual help ethic. All respondents reported frequent instances of visiting sick classmates, washing and mending clothes for one another, lending course notes to fellow-students who had missed a class, donating money or labor to students with family problems, sharing special food brought from home, taking someone else's turn at cleaning the classroom or dormitory room, and lending books. Most

22. This explanation for cheating is supported by Hargreaves' finding that cheating was rare in the highest track of the British secondary school, but was the norm in the lower tracks. (*Social Relations in a Secondary School*, p. 29).

23. The following examples were reported in ZXS: (Donating cotton shoes and woolen socks to a boy in winter), March 1953, p. 57; (doing a peasant girl's farm work so she could do her school homework), June 1953, p. 55; (loaning used textbooks to a younger student) March 1957, p. 16; (copying class notes for a sick classmate), April 1955, p. 63; (anonymous washing lunch boxes for others), March 1957, p. 16; (making the bed for a new student), September 1957, p. 9; (girls mending clothes and washing linen for the boys), January 1958, p. 60; (giving savings to a classmate for his school fee instead of buying a new harmonica for oneself), January 1958, p. 42.

good deeds were spontaneously initiated by students, although they earned them commendations as good samaritans from the teachers. For example, Deng said: "A boy in my senior high class had a mother who died and he had to take care of his family with a lot of younger brothers and sisters. A few of us [girls] went to his house and helped him take care of the children, wash the clothes, etc. Later this became known in the class, and the class director praised us and mobilized the whole class to help."

This type of mutual help increased positive feelings among fellow-students and eased the interpersonal tensions in the class. Many respondents, when asked to compare social relations in China and Hong Kong, pointed to mutual help as the source of better relations in China. Peng reported: "There is a lot of mutual help in the Mainland. In the Mainland personal relationships are much better than in Hong Kong; people there have much more 'humanity' (*renqingwei*) and are willing to help other people for nothing."

Young people were happy to do favors for one another because helpfulness earned them the approval of both their classmates and the school authorities. There was a fortunate coincidence of informal peer norms and official values in regard to mutual help. Jiang explained: "There is a lot of mutual help in China because there is a lot of propaganda about it; China is so poor that people need to help one another; and people don't have complicated thinking and really believe in mutual help."

However, the structure of political competition in schools put constraints on the forms and extent of mutual help. Students had to consider how giving or receiving help would affect their relative political standing in the class. For one thing, as Luo pointed out, political activists were not eager to help someone who might eclipse them:

> An activist would help you only when it didn't affect his personal interests. For example, he would teach you something in study. That was all right because he would be praised as being helpful to students, and also because what you gained from the knowledge wouldn't make him lose anything. But for other things, like helping you put up the wall newspaper, then he wouldn't do it even though he knew his help would be important for the job. Because if he helped and the paper got praised by the class director, then the person responsible for the job would gain a better image from the class director, which meant the other person's image would be decreased relatively.

Moreover, from the perspective of recipients, mutual help sometimes appeared to be a hostile act designed to make them look bad. The "gift" of help had both competitive and cooperative meanings.[24] Receiving help could be humiliating, especially if the recipient was unable to reciprocate, as well as damaging to one's image in the eyes of the authorities. For example, when An and his friend tried to tutor a classmate whose difficult home situation (a poor, disorderly family living in a house with no lights) was causing him to fail in several subjects, the boy "didn't like their coming so often because he felt constrained by them and felt that it implied a loss of dignity for him. He felt that they were coming to manage him more than to help him and he resented it."

In 1964-1965, when there was a campaign to put Mao Zedong Thought into practice and to emulate the self-sacrifice of the political model Lei Feng, mutual help became more competitive than cooperative. According to the respondents, aspiring activists rushed around washing everyone's clothes, and giving away their shoes and other possessions. The activists monopolized the opportunities for helpfulness so aggressively that their classmates were prevented from demonstrating their own altruism. When the official incentives for helpfulness were increased, an act such as washing a fellow student's clothes, which students had once viewed as motivated primarily by real amicability and only secondarily by careerism, was redefined by the students as a self-interested, hostile act.

The mutually destructive character and ascriptive element of political competition also interfered with cooperation and cohesiveness. To prove their political enthusiasm, activists had to criticize others and renounce politically unreliable friends. The attempts of some students to build a good political reputation damaged the reputations of other students. It was difficult for mutual help to overcome the divisions produced by political competition: the "losers" were too resentful to offer a hand in aid to those who had won at their expense, and the "winners" were reluctant to risk their hard-won reputations by showing benevolence toward the politically suspect. Of course, in Mao Zedong's view, genuine group solidarity and cooperation was never to be achieved on the basis of artificial harmony; only open, principled

24. Bailey, *Gifts and Poison,* pp. 23-24.

criticism of people with mistaken ideas could produce true unity.[25] But when political struggle was fueled by students' ambitions for scarce opportunities, it was destructive of group cohesiveness.

The ascriptive element in political competition made mutual help even more problematic after 1963, when class background credentials were emphasized in selection, and during the final years of senior high school, when students grew increasingly anxious about their futures. Students were reluctant to reach out to one another across class lines: those with bad background resented the disparagement of good background classmates and refused to help them; those with good background believed that their bad background classmates were obligated to do favors for them; and those of good or middle-range background did not dare help bad background classmates for fear of being labeled "wavering elements." According to Jiang and other respondents, there was a contradiction between mutual help and class struggle.[26]

> Communists say that you must have mutual help, serve the people and sacrifice self for others, put other people ahead of yourself (*xian ren hou ji*). Of course, if this really worked China would be an ideal society. But in reality it doesn't work because of the idea of class struggle. The idea of class line and class struggle is in contradiction with the idea of "put other people ahead of yourself." This is because according to the class line, one class—the proletariat—is *not* supposed to give way to other classes; it is supposed to struggle with the other classes and try to keep its dominant position. If classes are supposed to be struggling, how are people from different classes going to behave according to the principle of "put other people ahead of yourself"? It clearly is a contradiction. And class struggle comes first.

25. "If we cast aside this weapon of criticism and self-criticism and deal with things by way of the rotten attitude of selfism (liberalism, *ziyouzhuyi*); if we only want things to be nice and tranquil on the surface, if we knowingly don't face up to problems, if we don't want to open our mouths, if we don't firmly struggle with the influence of all sorts of unproletarian thinking, this is just unprincipled solidarity. . . . If in relations among comrades differences of opinion are not discussed then these differences cannot be done away with, it will be difficult to avoid mutual suspicion, doubt, and even displeasure; the distance in thinking will become greater and greater, and ultimately even this sort of superficial peace and harmony (*hehao*) will be difficult to maintain. This sort of relationship between comrades naturally cannot be good, and there can hardly be any talk about so-called solidarity." Ying Lin, *Piping he ziwo piping shi women de wuqi* (Criticism and Self-Criticism is Our Weapon) (Beijing: Gongren Chuban She, 1956), pp. 19-20, quoted in Solomon, "Mao's Effort to Reintegrate the Chinese Polity," p. 329.

26. Also see Ridley, Godwin, and Doolin, *The Making of a Model Citizen in Communist China*, pp. 198-199.

Students yearned to reconcile their desire to show kindness to their peers and their need to compete with them. They were frustrated by the disjunction between the communist morality of selflessness, in which they believed, and the very limited amount of mutual help permitted by the political competition that characterized school life.

The attempts of school authorities to increase cooperation between classmates through political group competitions were largely unsuccessful. In most schools, there were Five (or Four) Good Class contests, in which teachers and student officers chose the classes most outstanding in thought, conduct, study, health, and unity, and presented them with red flags. The contest roused students in some classes to make special efforts to clean the classroom and arrive promptly at school, but most classes took an apathetic attitude toward it. According to our respondents, compared to inter-class sports competitions, "the school considered Four Good Class competitions more important, but we didn't care much about them."

These political group competitions did not spark much student interest because many of the behaviors expected of a Five Good Class, such as heart-to-heart talks and strict mutual criticism, were seen as threatening to students, especially to those who were trying to be politically inconspicuous. And because the standards for selection were vague and subjective, there was no clear objective (such as scoring more goals or picking more tomatoes) for which the group could strive. Moreover, Five Good Class competitions, like inter-class competitions in classroom cleanliness or punctuality, smacked too much of doing the teachers' bidding—they were obvious devices to spur student effort without offering significant individual incentives to the winners. When a class won such a competition, it might enhance its class director's career, but it was unlikely to have any impact on the career chances of the students. Therefore, as Shi said, although students liked winning Five Good Class competitions and tried to act a bit better because of them, they were generally not enthusiastic about them, and were particularly uninterested in them in senior high school.

INDIVIDUAL COMPETITIONS IN STUDY AND POLITICS

In contrast to such group contests, individual competitions arranged by the school to encourage student achievement were welcomed. Young people threw themselves wholeheartedly into contests for the best study grades or Five Good Student contests, because winning these competitions brought real mobility rewards.

These individual competitions were regularly held by high school teachers even though they were officially frowned upon because of their alleged deleterious effect on the health and attitudes of students.[27] Political competition was somewhat less distasteful ideologically, because contestants were judged on their collectivist spirit. But the use of interpersonal competition to motivate academic achievement presented a more serious doctrinal problem: there was a contradiction between the values of individual intellectual achievement and collectivist self-sacrifice.[28]

This contradiction put teachers and school administrators in a difficult position: how could they satisfy the Party leadership's desire for high levels of intellectual achievement (particularly in technical fields) and yet inculcate selfless collectivism as well? Because their own career incentives emphasized the academic success of their students (promotions and raises were given to teachers and administrators whose students excelled in national examinations and university admissions), and because most of them had a professional bias toward the intellectual rather than the political side of schooling, they used study competitions despite the ideological issues they raised. During the 1960-1963 period, when the national policy line was to raise educational quality, the teachers were encouraged to hold academic contests (mathematics and

27. For example, "Study Competitions Should Stop," RMJY, August 1953, p. 4. One article in a pedagogical journal stated explicitly, "We object to holding competitions in students' studies (the handling of knowledge) and in their thought education (the progress in thought and consciousness)." It said competition was effective only in the realm of discipline, which was "only a matter of habitual training" and could therefore be accomplished by simple behavioral reinforcement techniques such as competitions. Guo Sheng, "On Collectivism and Collective Education," pp. 80-81. One teachers' training textbook claimed that cooperation motivated academic achievement better than did competition: "education for collectivism in school should be a motivating force to raise students' quality of study." *Jiaoyuxue* (Pedagogy), p. 249.

28. Several Western analysts have remarked upon the emphasis on individual achievement motivation in the socialization of Chinese children. John W. Lewis rated the story themes and games in kindergarten teachers' manuals according to David McClelland's scale of competitiveness and individuality, and found that "the Kiangsu manuals reveal a highly sophisticated program of training conducive to individual achievement motivation." He concluded that although this early socialization might suit the Chinese goal of rapid economic development, it clashed with the prescribed mass line style of work, which was supposed to be "non-competitive, collectivist, and selfless." Lewis, "Party Cadres in Communist China," pp. 425-430. Ridley, Godwin, and Doolin, in *The Making of a Model Citizen,* also saw a contradiction between socialization themes of individual achievement and themes of self-sacrifice for others (p. 196).

essay-writing competitions were held from the local to the national level up to 1964). Even after 1964, however, when the national policy was to de-emphasize academic achievement and pay more attention to political remolding, most teachers continued to hold study competitions in their classes.

In some schools study competitions were highly organized. In Yang's key school:

> Every term there were competitions in mathematics, physics, chemistry, and Russian, with the students of each year competing with one another. The top ten winners of each competition were given prizes—certificates and books. Their names were posted on the year's bulletin board. Prizes and certificates were given in the different subject classes by the head of that subject's teaching group. Students who won were very proud.

But in most schools, especially after 1963, there were few organized schoolwide contests, and teachers tended to publicize interpersonal comparisons within each class instead. The teachers handled these study competitions in various ways. Some announced the top students' names or displayed the best examination papers on the bulletin board. Such a method could be characterized (and justified to higher authorities) as emulation of models rather than competition (although they were much the same thing). Other teachers publicized the grades of all students, as in Jiang's class: "The two or three best examination papers in each subject were posted on the class bulletin board. The teacher also read out everyone's exam grades so as to encourage us to study harder."

An's teachers found a way to make the comparison even more obvious:

> Everyone's grades in every course were posted every term. Although there were no class rankings, the grades were written in different colors: 5 in red, 4 in pink, 3 in blue, 2 in black. So it was easy to see and really made us want to do better. Most of my grades were usually pink. The main thing was not to get any black, but I felt a little ashamed when sometimes I got a blue mark. Girls with bad grades would sometimes cry, but boys with bad grades would pretend that they didn't care at all.

In two respondents' classes, the teacher posted only the top few grades, but kept a chart of all students' grades on his desk and allowed anyone to examine it. In He's class the class director posted everyone's final grades and put little red flags beside the names of those with the most outstanding records. A few teachers ranked students, as in Deng's class:

> All midterm and final grades were posted on the class bulletin board, and at the end of the first term in senior-1 all our averages in politics, Chinese, and mathematics were averaged together and ranked. The top three of the year were praised by the school, but the class rankings were also posted. This was supposed to encourage us to study harder. My grades were pretty high, but those with bad grades felt very embarrassed about everyone seeing how badly they had done.

Sometimes teachers tried to encourage special efforts in a particular subject through competition. Luo's class director was also the mathematics teacher: "He liked to give short 15-minute tests and then mark the names of the five people who got the best grades in a small notebook. At the end of the term the class director would use his own money to buy presents for the top five of the term. In junior-1 my friend was better than me, but starting from junior-2 I was better and I could see that my friend envied me."

The publicizing of grades and rankings had its intended effect, according to respondents: "The students with bad grades wanted to improve because having your poor grades read out was embarrassing, those with good grades wanted to get even higher ones, and the top students were determined to stay on top." From time to time, key schools organized study grade competitions between classes, but these group competitions made students study more intensively on their own rather than together. Jiang asserted, "The class with the most competitive feeling between individuals is also a class that feels competitive with other classes and usually shows up well compared to other classes."[29]

Organized political competitions took the form of Three Good Student (in junior high) and Five Good Student (in senior high) contests held every term. The winners were supposed to be the all-round best students in the class: Three Good Students had to be good in political

---

29. This was because academic study was not organized as an interdependent activity. There were very few ways in which competitive students could interfere with the academic efforts of others. For an analysis of how competition decreases productivity in interdependent bureaucratic activities, see Blau, "Cooperation and Competition in a Bureaucracy," pp. 530-535.

thought, study, and physical fitness, and Five Good Students had to be good in those three respects as well as in labor and political performance. Before 1963, school authorities emphasized academic excellence, and after 1963 they stressed political activism. Although the selection of winners was made by the students in each class—the nominations came out of small group discussions and the election was held in class meetings—the respondents reported that the class directors influenced the outcome through their "suggestions." The winners had to be approved by the school authorities; very few names were turned down, although the authorities downgraded some from Five Good to Four or Three Good. Prizes—usually certificates, stationery, and books of Mao's writings—were presented to the winners at an all-school meeting, and the winners' names were displayed on a big red banner.

When it was an award for political activism, the Three or Five Good Student designation simply ratified the outcome of a more diffuse process of political competition. Respondents said they could usually predict who would win. Although these contests made political competition more explicit—winning was noted in one's permanent record and would enhance one's career prospects—they did not stimulate as much student interest as academic competition. The winners were "respected," but when Yang was chosen, he felt "good about it but not *too* proud about it." According to An, "Students didn't feel that winning Three or Five Good Student competitions was that glorious. Winning those competitions was actually more important to teachers than to students." Several respondents noted that being a Five Good Student was "nothing special"—as many as 10 to 15 people were chosen from each class each term, and an even larger number were selected to attend local meetings of people given the official designation of "activists." Being admitted into the Youth League had a greater long-term significance for one's future than winning such contests.

Individual academic and political contests did not create competition between students—the structure of opportunities and institutional incentives were responsible for that—but they did reinforce it. These contests ran counter to the official anticompetitive messages that were directed at students. The authorities might begin an event with a little lecture about the evils of competition—Deng recalled that "during all the competitions the principal would remind us, 'Down with individual championism and up with collective heroism' (*fandui geren jinbiao zhuyi tichang jiti yingxiong*)—but the competitive realities were evident to students.[30] Of course, theoretically, when a student won such a contest it could be interpreted as an expression of collectivist spirit, a class victory rather than an individual one. This perspective was sometimes present, especially in municipal, all-school, or all-year competitions. For example, when Yang won second prize in the senior-3 Russian competition, he said, "My friends were happy for me because it was the class's pride to have such an outstanding student, and it was a personal glory for me too." But students usually viewed these competitions as contests between individuals rather than class representatives, especially because they were most commonly held within the class arena. Students recognized that the contestants were playing more for their own futures than for the glory of the group.

ACADEMIC COMPETITION AND
POLITICAL COMPETITION

Although both academic and political competition, fueled by student ambitions to gain scarce career opportunities, limited cooperation in schools, academic competition was less socially divisive than political competition. Any individual competition creates strain within a group: when the group is differentiated and rewards conferred on some but not on others, it is difficult to integrate the winners and the losers.[31] But some types of competition are more threatening to group cohesiveness than other types. A comparison of academic and political competition among Chinese students reveals the structural differences that explain the different effect of the two competitions on social relations.

In contrast with political competition, academic competition was viewed by students (and their parents as well) as fair. There were several structural features of academic competition that contributed to its greater legitimacy. First, the *standards* for success in the academic contest were *clear and objective*. The learning style of Chinese schools was old-fashioned and rigid; homework assignments and examinations

---

30. The disjunction between the actual structure of competition and the official value on selflessness is illustrated in a short story about an 800-meter race, "Two Champions," ZGQN, No. 10 (1958), p. 22.

31. Parsons, "The School Class as a Social System," pp. 446-447. Also see Blau, "Cooperation and Competition in a Bureaucracy."

tested students' ability to recall information and analyze material in a prescribed fashion. There was little ambiguity about what constituted a good or a bad piece of work. This is not to say that there was no room at all for subjective evaluations. Respondents had some complaints about teacher favoritism in grading practices. But generally speaking, students felt that the standards for evaluating academic work were more objective than those used for judging political activism.

All the standards of activism were behavioral—for example, how enthusiastically students responded to political directives, what they said in criticism sessions and political meetings, whether they volunteered for unpleasant tasks—because the only way to judge "thought" was to evaluate behavior. Eager behavior was often a genuine expression of personal commitment, but it could also be "faked" for opportunistic reasons. It was difficult to distinguish the sincere activists from the false ones, and there was considerable leeway for arbitrary judgments on the part of authorities.

In academic work it was much harder to "fake" knowledge, and there were rules against cheating to guarantee that tests evaluated actual knowledge (not just the ability to pass notes without being observed by the teacher). In the political realm, the screening process was more subjective and problematical. It was always possible for someone to obtain a good conduct comment or gain admission to the Youth League by playing up to the teacher (and established activists) and "acting" active. Tang, comparing academic and political competition, said: "Academic competition was the only valid kind of competition because no one can pretend well enough to win. It really judges people's true accomplishments."

A second reason why academic competition was less socially divisive than political competition was that the *judges* of academic competition were all adult authorities who stood *outside the social organization of the class.* Whenever a student was disgruntled about an examination grade, he or she could blame the teacher. A teacher who was a "tough grader" could have an integrating effect on the class, uniting students in opposition to a common villain.

Political competition was more divisive because activism was evaluated by peers as well as by adult authorities. This power of established student activists was a wedge between them and their classmates. They were supposed to be their classmates' friends and helpers as well as their judges, an impossible combination of roles. Security-conscious students decided that the safest strategy was to keep these activists, who had the power to ruin their career prospects, at arm's length.

All things being equal, the type of individual competition least destructive of group cohesiveness is one in which winning and losing are intrinsic to the activity. For example, in a footrace, no judge is necessary because the winners are determined by the race itself.[32] If a judge is necessary, then social divisiveness is minimized if the standards for determining winners and losers are clear and objective and if the judge is an authority figure outside the group; this was the case in academic competition. The type of competition most destructive of social unity is one in which the standards are vague and subjective and the judges are members of the group, as in political competition.

The third feature of academic competition which made it more legitimate than political competition was its *standards* for success, which were *based on achievement rather than ascription*. In most modern societies, academic competition is viewed as fair and intellectual success is highly regarded because people believe it is *earned* by achievement. This widespread valuation of achievement provides the "glue" that holds society together despite the strains of competition. Even the losers accept the legitimacy of the contest, telling themselves that they deserved to lose because they weren't smart enough or didn't work hard enough (and perhaps their children will do better).[33] People believe the contest is fair and based entirely on achievement despite research findings which show a high correlation between family background and educational attainment. When Mao Zedong tried to convince people that academic competition was unfair because bourgeois youth had the advantages of family resources and home socialization, he was unsuccessful. Even Chinese peasants and their children believed that a contest based on academic achievement provided equality of opportunity—that "everyone was equal before marks."[34]

The authorities relied on class background labels in political recruit-

---

32. Coleman, *The Adolescent Society*, p. 319.
33. Parsons, "The School Class as a Social System," pp. 446-447, and Prewitt, "Schooling, Stratification, Equality," pp. 97-99, 106-107. Parsons reminds us that for academic competition to be accepted as fair, it "is crucial that the distribution of abilities, though correlated with family status, clearly does not coincide with it."
34. This belief was the target of radical criticism during 1973-1974. Zhu Yan, "The Far-reaching Significance of Reforming the System of Enrolling College Students," HQ, No. 8 (August 1, 1973), SCMM, 758, p. 9; RMRB, August 22, 1973, SCMP, 5473, p. 140; also Gao Gang, "Enrollment of Students for Institutions of Higher Learning," GMRB, July 15, 1974; SCMP, 5662, p. 187. Chinese culture probably played a role in enhancing the legitimacy of rewards for intellectual attainment.

ment for two reasons: they wanted to compensate for pre-1949 class inequalities, and they needed a clue other than superficial behavior for distinguishing political virtue. But the injection of the class background criterion into political competition diminished the legitimacy of the contest and generated social conflict among students. Because individuals from cadre, army, worker, and peasant families were given special treatment, the competition appeared unfair. The unfortunate students born to non-proletarian parents felt that the game was rigged against them. As some of them argued during the Cultural Revolution, it was unfair to equate political commitment with the accident of birth: "Who constitutes the backbone? This can't be decided in the fetus. We do not recognize any right that cannot be attained through individual effort."[35]

The emphasis on family background not only made students view political competition as unfair but also turned students of different backgrounds against one another. They resented each other as well as the system. As Jiang said, "It was like two friends, one who gets in trouble and blames the other for his trouble; he blames his failure on his friend's success because his friend got in the way of his success." Social hostilities were exacerbated by the requirement that all activists draw a clear "class line." As a result, students from non-proletarian families were criticized publicly and their company was scorned by politically ambitious classmates. These class resentments interfered with social cooperation and erupted into Red Guard factionalism during the Cultural Revolution.

Finally, academic competition was less divisive than political competition because it was less mutually destructive. Since students were in direct competition for limited post-graduation opportunities, both contests had a zero-sum character. Even in academic study, when one student got a high grade, in mathematics for example, it decreased the general probability of another student's chances of getting into a university. But the structure of political competition was more direct. Political activism was defined by actions that were costly to particular students; the activist had to select a particular person whose chances for college admission he or she was going to down-grade through criticism.[36] Criticism was central to the political life of the class and everyone was

35. "Origin Theory," *Zhongxue wen ge bao* (Middle School Cultural Revolution News) (Beijing, February 1967), in White, *The Politics of Class and Class Origin*, p. 81.

36. The author is grateful to Arthur L. Stinchcombe, who in personal correspondence helped her clarify the distinction between "zero-sum-ness" and focusing on a single victim.

expected to participate. Students developed peer group norms of criticizing only minor shortcomings in order to minimize the divisiveness of the criticism process. But aspiring activists had to violate these norms: in order to make themselves look good, they had to make certain others look bad. The necessity of choosing a specific victim made political competition seem to participants to be more threatening and divisive than academic competition.

All efforts to win recognition in social, academic, or political activities enhanced an individual student's chances for a good future, but they had different costs for other students. Social involvements—in athletic, cultural, or school Student Association activities—were harmless to other students and even benefited them. Success in academic study affected the relative standing of all other students in the class. Political activism not only affected the relative standing of others, but also directly hurt certain other students by revealing their political mistakes. This helps explain why cooperation prevailed in social activities, and was sometimes present in academic study, but was almost never possible in political activism. The structural features of academic and political competition that affected social cohesiveness are summarized below:

Academic Competition	*Political Competition*
Clear, objective standards	Vague, subjective standards
Adult judges	Peer and adult judges
Achievement based standards	Ascriptive and achievement-based standards
General zero-sum effect	Zero-sum with specific victim

How could Chinese schools discourage competition and foster cooperation between students? The concluding chapter will answer this question by considering the dilemmas of policy-making in a society which distributes opportunities to individuals largely on the basis of political virtue.

7

VIRTUE, OPPORTUNITY, AND BEHAVIOR

As this study has shown, the behavior of students in urban high schools was characterized by a complex mixture of unity and conflict, of cooperation and competition. The Communist Party leadership had succeeded in motivating students to strive for intellectual and political achievement, to participate in political discussions and in assigned periods of manual labor, and to accept the values of revolutionary commitment, public service, and collectivism. But it had been unsuccessful in using the schools to transform social relations to fit the Maoist vision. This failure stemmed not from the persistence of traditional attitudes and modes of action but from the impact of virtuocratic recruitment policies on school incentives. Students tried to maximize their career opportunities without betraying their fellow students or their own sense of self-respect. Depending on their comparative advantages—such as intellectual aptitude or class background—they decided whether to pursue the academic or the political route to success. Even those who decided to concentrate their energies on academic study had to make sure that they would be viewed as politically acceptable.

The interests of political activists and other students were in conflict: activists wanted to demonstrate their zeal and monopolize the rewards of political status, whereas non-activists wanted only to keep a clean political record. The behavior of activists, most notably their criticizing of classmates in public and to teachers, created costs for other students who therefore tried to keep them at arm's length. Because of the career rewards for political activism, the Youth League attracted opportunists as well as those sincerely committed to revolutionary goals. Students were cautious in dealing with all activists, whether they regarded them as sincere or phony.

But the political pressures that made students cautious did not weaken friendship ties, as might have been expected; rather they intensified the need for friendship. Students had internalized the official moral creed, and many of them felt like deviants because they could not satisfy its stringent demands. The pressures of political competition and the self-perception of deviance led them to seek out a friend with whom they could validate their beliefs and express their true selves. Thus, virtuocracy generated privatism as well as social conflict.

Although friendship ties and peer group norms of mutual support had a unifying effect on the class, they did not prevent competition from prevailing over cooperation in the two central spheres of school life, academic study and political activity. Students willingly cooperated in athletic, cultural, and work activities because they provided a collective goal and group competition and did not require a sacrifice of individual advantage. But in study and in politics, which were evaluated on an individual basis, students had to worry about staying ahead of their peers and thus could not afford to help them. Political competition was more socially divisive than academic competition for several reasons: its standards were vague and subjective, it was judged by peers as well as by adult authorities, it was based on ascription (family background) as well as achievement, and it required mutually destructive actions.

The policies governing the supply of educational and occupational opportunities for high school graduates and the criteria for assigning graduates to these opportunities established the rules of the game in school and thereby shaped student behavior. An opportunity structure characterized by limited opportunities, high stakes, monolithic distribution, and apportionment by localities put students into face-to-face competition with one another for limited goods in one high-stakes game, with no alternative avenues to success.

The style of that competition and its effects on social relations were the result of recruitment policies which selected graduates according to political virtue (or "redness") as well as academic achievement and class background. Although the relative emphasis given to these three criteria shifted from year to year, none was ever totally abandoned, which meant that students always had to be concerned about all three. All students had to engage in political competition, if only for self-defense, to avoid political opprobrium.

When students graduated from high school they had to devise new strategies to cope with the specific incentive structures of their college or work organizations. Future research on how Chinese behavior (and behavior in other socialist systems) is shaped by the incentive structure of particular adult organizations should consider the variables identified by this study of schools: the availability of rewards, the rewards and penalties for success and failure, the control of distribution decisions, the apportionment of rewards to organizations, the ties between individual rewards and collective effort, the fungibility of occupational and political achievement, the prevailing definition of political virtue, and the relationship of achievement and ascriptive criteria.[1] Many adult organizations in China did, however, resemble schools in that they rewarded individuals in part according to political virtue. Therefore I would expect to find in such organizations avoidance between activists and their colleagues, the use of friendship as a haven, and socially divisive political competition similar to that found in schools. Still, whenever the specific rules are changed or people move from one organization to another, there is likely to be a lag as people learn how to adapt to the new situation. A fruitful approach to studying the influence of school socialization on adult behavior would be to examine how students modify their school-learned strategies when they attempt to use them in a new setting.

THE CULTURAL REVOLUTION AND THE DECLINE OF VIRTUOCRACY

This study has focused on how people adapt to institutional incentives rather than on how they attempt to change them. In an authoritarian system, people have little chance to rewrite the rules of the game. At the elite level, however, there is a feedback loop from citizen behavior to policy. Chinese Party leaders recognized that behavior in schools and adult organizations was not what they had wanted it to be. Chinese magazine short stories and articles have criticized all the behavioral "problems" revealed in refugee interviews. But seeing the problems and knowing how to solve them are two very different things.

Mao Zedong created the Cultural Revolution in 1966 to revive the flagging revolutionary spirit and stem the tide toward Soviet-style privilege, bureaucratism, and competition. His strategy was to purify the virtuocracy and purge it of the meritocratic and feodocratic features which had to come to infect it. Many of the students described in this book, who were torn between their political ideals on the one hand and their friendship loyalties and personal ambitions on the other, re-

---

1. For an excellent analysis of the impact of security of employment and evaluation practices on patterns of cooperation and competition in two bureaucratic work groups, see Blau, "Cooperation and Competition in a Bureaucracy," pp. 530-535.

sponded enthusiastically to Mao's Cultural Revolution call, seeing in the Red Guard movement a chance to merge their private and public concerns. They could fight to realize revolutionary values, protect their friends, and change the rules of the game which, they felt, had put them at an unfair disadvantage in the competition for careers.

The Cultural Revolution cure, however, did more social damage than the revisionist tendencies it was designed to eradicate. The changes in the opportunity structure—an expansion of primary and secondary education combined with a constriction of higher education and urban jobs—made competition more intense than ever. The separation of selection from school performance promoted lack of discipline rather than an interest in learning for its own sake. The elimination of all non-political criteria for selection and promotion, rather than inspiring new revolutionary commitments, worsened the problems of opportunism, fakery and sycophancy, and instead of creating more equality of opportunity, worked to the advantage of political elites who could use "the back door."

The penetration of politics into every corner of social and economic life destroyed people's trust of one another and of their leaders. All actions were evaluated in political terms. Peasants who sold more grain to the state, workers who volunteered to work overtime, rural cadres who constructed terraced fields like those of the well-publicized model village, Dazhai, even if they were impractical in their locales, were praised as "red"; anyone who did not join in these campaigns or who questioned their logic or justice was condemned as "white." People felt intense pressure to conform because the Cultural Revolution had widened the gap between rewards and penalties. A person deemed morally excellent could now be catapulted to a high leadership position overnight; someone accused of political sins could be stripped of power, browbeaten and sometimes physically abused in struggle meetings, and then sent to do hard labor. Everyday life became a minefield of risks; one never knew when a colleague might seek personal protection by making a pre-emptive attack on you. With political tension raised to a higher pitch, the methods people had formerly used to adapt to political competition no longer worked, and many people suffered from anxiety.[2]

2. The devastating social and psychological effects of the Cultural Revolution are vividly depicted in two collections of short stories: Lu Xinhua and others, *The Wounded*, and Chen Jo-hsi, *The Execution of Mayor Yin*.

Political cynicism resulted from the increasingly widespread practice of political favoritism. The elimination of all objective standards of merit or birth and the dominance of vague, subjective virtuocratic standards facilitated the efforts of leaders to build personal factions. Even officials who made an earnest effort to promote the truly virtuous tended to promote their relatives and friends because one could detect sincerity and insincerity only in those one was familiar with. The more leaders used their appointment powers to promote personal supporters, the more virtuous behavior seemed to people merely a guise for self interest.

The rhetoric of factional struggles at the top levels of leadership deepened public cynicism. Political competitors assume the mantle of the public interest in all systems, but in a virtuocratic state like China this tendency is more pronounced. Chinese politicians assailed their rivals not only for their bad policy positions but for their moral wickedness as well. Shrill attacks on the motives and attitudes of Liu Shaoqi, Deng Xiaoping, Lin Biao, Chen Boda, Jiang Qing, and many other top-ranking leaders, who were purged from office in rapid-fire succession, were so inconsistent and unconvincing that people became highly skeptical. Revolutionary moral categories lost their meaning as leaders hurled them at one another in overblown rhetoric. Citizens came to believe that their national leaders used virtuocratic claims as a hypocritical cover for ambition.

By the mid-1960s virtuocracy in China was eroding, because of its divisive social effects and because the difficulty of applying virtuocratic selection standards increased the use of meritocratic and feodocratic criteria. The extreme pursuit of virtuocracy during the Cultural Revolution accelerated this process, so that by 1976 citizens were estranged not only from one another but also from their leaders. They believed that at national as well as local levels, it was not really virtue that was rewarded but the ability to ingratiate oneself with a powerful patron. The virtuocratic foundation for the legitimacy of the communist regime was severely damaged.

With the decline of virtuocracy came dissent (along with the more common reaction of privatistic retreat). Those who risked punishment by speaking out were like the members of revolutionary movements—visionaries, people who had nothing to lose, or those who could tolerate risks. In China, the majority of 1970s dissidents were the 1960s graduates of the high schools portrayed in this study; they were disillusioned by the failure of the Cultural Revolution and approached middle age with only the dismal future of more rural work or urban unemployment or underemployment before them. Some of the most vocal were those who had been politically criticized in past campaigns and who knew that despite official rehabilitation, they would never be able to erase the stigma of unreliability. A few of the best-known leaders were the children of high-ranking cadres whose radical opposition to the system appeared to be motivated by contempt for their parents' hypocrisy.[3] Reacting to what they perceived as the moral degeneration of the virtuocracy, the dissidents pleaded for fairer standards for promotion and for a tolerance of ideological diversity; their career frustrations and political critique merged under the banner of democracy.[4]

The weakening of political legitimacy caused by the Cultural Revolution is a dramatic example of the inherent instability of virtuocracy. When a revolutionary elite attempts the total moral transformation of society by making virtue the basis for selection and promotion, it sets in motion a process which will inevitably lead to meritocracy or feodocracy. The vague and subjective standards, peer judges, and mutual destructiveness that characterize virtuocracies make it possible for people to succeed through opportunism, fakery, or sycophancy. Political competition on such virtuocratic grounds generates social mistrust and conflict. Those who seek to demonstrate their moral superiority are avoided by those who want only to hide their doubts from scrutiny. The element of falseness enters into social relations. The losers resent the "virtuocrats" who win through obsequiousness and dissembling. Many sincerely committed people are frustrated by the failure of the authorities to recognize their moral rectitude.

The growth of privatism also contributes to the decline of virtuocracy. In a non-virtuocratic system with an autonomous economic sphere, most of the hustling for careers takes place in business, and people can express their moral identities in politics. But in a monolithic virtuocratic state, like China, the competition for careers permeates the political sphere, polluting it with conniving and opportunism. The contamination of political life by careerism detracts from the emotional

3. For example, see the profile of Wei Jingsheng, convicted in a Chinese court for counter-revolutionary activity in October 1979, in *The New York Times,* October 20, 1979.

4. During the Cultural Revolution, the anti-individualistic ideology of the movement was in tension with the individual ambition that motivated many student Red Guards. The democratic ideology of the 1978-1980 opposition is much more congruent with the individualistic concerns of youth.

and moral hold of politics; people channel their moral sentiments from public life into the private world of friendship and family. This tendency toward privatism is reinforced by the leadership's efforts to instill the regime's very demanding morality in every aspect of the lives of its citizens. People who cannot satisfy the regime's high standards—those who have even faint doubts about the purity of the leaders' motives or of their own—are made to feel like deviants, and deviants have a strong need to seek validation and solace from friends or family.

The moral claims of virtuocratic elites make them highly susceptible to popular doubts about their purity. Members of virtuocratic elites who are visibly striving to attain power and who pass their privileges down to their children are vulnerable to questions about their sincerity. After years of factional struggles waged by character assasination and Manichean rhetoric, which reveal to ordinary people the sordid side of palace politics, citizens can no longer accept the leaders' "masks" of altruism.

The ambiguity of virtuocratic standards fosters the application of meritocratic and ascriptive tests which are comparatively clear and simple. But the injection of ascriptive criteria into virtuocratic competition intensifies the frustrations of the losers and makes it more difficult to justify the results. Under these conditions it becomes more and more difficult to maintain the reign of virtue. Mao's attempts to revive virtuocracy and purge it of all meritocratic and feodocratic tendencies only increased the alienation of the public from the regime.

It is more possible to sustain enthusiasm in a virtuocratic *movement*, or in a society where only some sectors are virtuocratic while others promote people on the basis of merit or family status, than in a virtuocratic state with monopolistic control. When people are free to move in and out of virtuocratic institutions (like the kibbutz in Israel), self-selection fosters organizational commitment. Highly selective virtuocratic institutions (for example, some religious or military ones) are able to induce particularly deep loyalties.[5] Moreover, virtuocratic movements or institutions which, unlike states, have no access to power or job positions can offer their members only special status or salvation, and therefore attract few opportunists.[6]

---

5. Etzioni, *Modern Organizations*, p. 69; Hirschman, *Exit, Voice, and Loyalty*, pp. 92-96.

6. Virtuocratic movements tend to attract visionaries, those who have nothing to lose (such as members of a criminal counter-culture), or those who are temperamentally less fearful of risk than most people. If such a movement is victorious and is transformed from a

Religious virtuocratic states are less prone to instability than secular ones. Vows of poverty and celibacy provide convincing testimony of the altruism of religious elites. Celibacy makes virtuocratic competition a fairer contest by preventing the inheritance of elite status. Salvation and damnation also provide powerful incentives to deter cheaters.[7] Lacking these safeguards, non-religious virtuocratic states find themselves threatened by social division and the erosion of the moral legitimacy of political authority.

THE MERITOCRATIC BACKLASH

Since Mao Zedong's death, the defeat of the Gang of Four, and the return to power of Deng Xiaoping in 1976, there has been a dramatic shift to meritocracy in China. This shift has been initiated by Deng and the leaders allied with him who believe that virtuocracy produced economic disaster. Productivity suffered because, as the Li Yizhe poster said, "the giving prominence to politics . . . rewarded the lazy and punished the diligent."[8] Internecine political strife and interminable political discussions sapped workers' time and energy and interfered with production.[9] Many of those selected as managers were politically reliable but technically incompetent. Because managers had to worry more about becoming the target of political criticism than about producing economic results, they tended to stress sheer hard work and death-defying spirit rather than careful planning and technical expertise.[10] Multiplying the economic costs of virtuocracy were its social costs, which were borne directly by ordinary citizens. There is today a genuine popular backlash against virtuocracy, which Deng and his allies are encouraging.

Signs of the new meritocracy are everywhere. On a 1980 visit to Sichuan I found factories using academic tests (in mathematics, Chi-

---

crusade into a state, then the vanguard "sect" is likely to be plagued by conflict between its original members and the careerists who join later. Is it preferable to be ruled by visionaries and bandits, or by careerists?

7. The author is grateful to John Gorman for these ideas about religious virtuocracies.

8. Shirk, "Going Against the Tide," p. 94.

9. Unger, *Knowledge and Politics,* p. 273.

10. The often disastrous consequences of the "politics can decide everything" mentality were well publicized by the Chinese press during 1980. The most egregious example was the collapse of an offshore oil rig which killed 72 people.

nese language, politics, and physics and chemistry) to select new workers and assign them to job categories. Technicians and engineers now can move up the ladder of rank and salary according to their performance on special examinations. The 40 percent of workers who received wage increases in 1980 had their skills and knowledge assessed in written and practical examinations designed specifically for each job category.[11] Party cadres have been warned to upgrade their technical skills and may have to pass tests in the future.[12] New Party cadres will "from now on be selected mainly from among graduates of universities and secondary technical schools . . . instead of from among workers and peasants with a little education."[13] More military officers are being recruited through special army schools rather than through the ranks, and demobilized soldiers with no technical expertise are having a harder time finding civilian jobs.

The meritocratic trend is clearest in educational selection, of course. Academic examinations are once again required for admission to secondary schools and universities; oral interview examinations are even used for selecting six-year-olds to attend elite key primary schools. Although applicants are still required to pass a political screening, the examination results are weighed much more heavily. Young university faculty members also are now required to take competency tests in their specialties; those who fail repeatedly will be demoted to teach in secondary schools.

The emphasis on merit rather than virtue is also reflected in the increasing use of piecework pay. Piecework is a way to translate behavior into clear, quantitative measures of performance. By 1980 the rage for piecework had spread beyond the industrial sector: in beauty parlors hairdressers were paid according to the number of heads of hair they cut, and in some hospitals, doctors and nurses were paid according to the number of patients they treated.

The widespread enthusiasm for meritocratic standards stems mainly from their clarity and objectivity. After years of experience with the vague and subjective criteria of virtuocracy, people in China—both elites and ordinary people—feel a strong need for a fairer process of

11. All wage increases are in the form of promotions in wage grade.
12. See Hu Yaobang's speech at the Second National Congress of the Chinese Scientific and Technical Association, BR, No. 15 (April 14, 1980), pp. 13-16.
13. BR, August 11, 1980, p. 7.

distribution. Their experience with the use of political criteria has strengthened their belief in the norm "to each according to his work."[14]

People believe that meritocratic evaluations are fairer than political ones: they measure actual individual achievement, whereas political assessments can be won through family influence or fakery. According to the press many people believe in the procedural norm of equal opportunity: "In the past, gaining admission to a school depended upon a relationship. Now gaining admission to a school depends upon a student's own ability. If our sons and daughters fail the entrance examination, we yield willingly."[15]

The desire for objectivity is particularly strong in work units which are still recovering from the factional fighting of the Cultural Revolution decade. In many offices, shops, and factories there are too many people for too few positions, almost two complete sets of cadres, promoted by the leaders of rival factions, who now have to find some way to coexist in close quarters. Both sides have an interest in a fair distribution method which eliminates the possibility of factional favoritism and provides the basis for reconciliation.[16]

The tendency for virtuocracy to degenerate into favoritism and backdoor deals has caused people to devise meritocratic practices which allow little scope for local authorities to exercise their own judgment. Monthly bonuses are determined by counting the number of pieces produced by each individual (or by each small group) or by adding up the points earned daily by workers for meeting various production targets (such as output, quality, use of materials and energy, and safety). The pieces produced or the points earned are recorded daily in

14. A pattern noted in other socialist systems by W. Wesolowski: "It appears that the objective contradiction of interests implied in the unequal distribution of goods following from the application of the principle 'to each according to his work,' does not arouse such strong tendencies towards the creation of conflicts as the defects in its application." ("The Notions of Strata and Class in Socialist Society," p. 136).

15. Anhwei Provincial Service, June 5, 1978, FBIS, June 12, 1978, p. G2. Another article explains that under the old recommendation system "appraisal by the masses often turned out to be a mere formality," and that in practice the door was closed to the children of ordinary people. "This situation became a source of general dissatisfaction. The new enrollment system provides children of workers and peasants with wide opportunity to take part in examinations for entering college, so they support this way of doing things." ("Enrollment System: A Meaningful Discussion," BR, No. 30 [July 28, 1978], p. 19.)

16. In some organizations there are more than two factions. For example, according to Kraus (talk at the Universities Service Centre, Hong Kong, January 1980), in organizations of artists and writers there are old grudges among the so-called "conservatives" who have recently been rehabilitated. Many of those who were purged in 1966 were responsible for purging their colleagues in the Anti-Rightist Campaign of 1957. Now they all must find some way to get along.

the work group, so the relative standings at the end of the month are clear, unambiguous, and not subject to manipulation by factory leaders.[17] The distrust of local authorities is also reflected in current procedures for university entrance examinations. Examination scores are publicly posted as a protection against favoritism by local officials. And whereas in the past academic promise was measured by a combination of school grades and examination scores, today admissions officers look only at examinations because they no longer trust the validity of school grades.

The renunciation of virtuocracy involves not only a turn to meritocracy but also a redefinition of ascriptive criteria for career distribution. The national leadership has abolished reverse discrimination against people of bad class origin, but rather than totally eliminating ascriptive partiality and making all career contests universal, it has instead institutionalized the practice of work units hiring the children of their own employees. Under the replacement (*dingti*) policy, when an employee retires his or her son or daughter is guaranteed a job in the unit. Employees' offspring are also favored when factories recruit new workers. This kind of ascriptive favoritism turns work units into guild-like institutions in which membership is inherited. It also gives city dwellers a virtual monopoly on the best job positions and closes the city gates to rural dwellers. If these policies of ascriptive exclusivity are sustained, there will be more limitations on social mobility and more inheritance of occupational status in China than in most traditional societies. Although family favoritism runs counter to the meritocratic trend, it is a quick answer to the urban unemployment problem and is popular with city-dwellers. (Factory managers and college presidents are trying to resolve the contradiction by using academic tests to assign new workers to particular jobs; but are still constrained to find jobs of some sort for even the incompetent children of their employees.)

From the standpoint of Deng and his allies, the move away from virtuocracy makes political sense. They have formulated an economic development strategy that relies more on improvements in technology and capital inputs than on mass mobilization of labor. The erosion of popular response to moral appeals means that the mobilization option

17. As one newspaper article said, the advantages of the point system are that it has "clear standards," a "concrete method," and uses "less time for evaluation." RMRB, September 17, 1979.

is now closed to them. The foreign banks and companies whose help China needs to relieve her shortages of investment funds and foreign exchange worry about the reappearance of ideological crusades like the Cultural Revolution and are reassured by the promise of tests for hiring and promoting employees.

The turn to meritocracy also lends Deng the support of the intellectuals, which he needs to carry out the technical modernization of the economy. Under meritocracy there will be an alliance between the academic-technical elite and the political elite, a trend which has been apparent for many years in the Soviet Union.[18] The popular disillusionment with virtuocracy and respect for meritocracy are shown by Deng's recent efforts to get more intellectuals and professionals to join the Party and lend it their prestige. Of course this new emphasis on technical merit threatens Communist Party cadres, most of whom are political generalists with little technical competence. However, virtuocracy had its victims even within the ranks of the political elite. Under the new meritocracy the chances for promotion may be diminished, but so are the risks of becoming the object of political struggle.

There is probably widespread support, both within the Party and among the masses, for abandoning the goals of social transformation. The Maoist vision of a communist utopia was very appealing, but people now seem to feel that it is not worth the price of constant anxiety about being politically attacked by one's classmates or fellow workers. Years of experience with the realities of virtuocratic competition seem to have convinced people that state-led moral crusades are futile. People would prefer that political leaders, instead of extolling a communist future with no scarcity and perfect harmony, discuss how to improve the equity, efficiency, and affluence of the socialist system that actually exists in China today.

Although the moves away from virtuocracy may be popular, in the long run they raise severe problems of legitimation for the leaders of the regime. On the one hand, the meritocratic defense of inequality—that it is based on differences in individual achievement, and is therefore a fair distribution "according to work"—is very persuasive.[19] As the example

18. Parkin, *Class Inequality and Political Order,* p. 152.
19. Newspapers frequently report inspirational stories about individuals who rose overnight from lowly positions to become professors or engineers by showing their talent in meritocratic examinations (for example, GRRB, November 3, 1978, and *Wenhuibao,* January 1, 1980).

of other societies makes clear, under the meritocratic principle of equality of opportunity, those who lose contests tend to blame themselves rather than the rules or the judges. As one Chinese university administrator said to me: "The important thing is that everyone has an equal chance, an equal opportunity to try. Then if someone doesn't succeed, he says, 'that's all right; it was my own fault.'"

On the other hand, it is difficult to legitimate the social division of labor through meritocracy. Whereas in a market society inequalities of income and status are justified by the need to provide incentives for people to prepare for and to fill certain jobs, in a centrally planned economy these inequalities represent the judgments of state leaders about which groups are more deserving (or more politically assertive) than others. And because of the state-controlled, monolithic character of recruitment and promotion, the "hand" is not "hidden" as it is in a market system, and people hold the government directly responsible for unfair and unjust decisions.[20] The government tries to claim that the division of labor is necessary for economic efficiency, and that China is unique because everyone is equally respected even if they do different work ("In our country, people differ only in the kind of work they do, and are not classified into superior and inferior, high and low").[21] The leadership may be able to defend the necessity for inequality, but it will be more difficult for it to persuade people that one particular pattern of distribution is more just than another.

Meritocracy, like virtuocracy, can generate social strains. People in China may believe that meritocracy is less ambiguous or less mutually destructive than virtuocracy, but the translation of meritocratic principles into specific distributive outcomes remains a difficult process. Those who lose the contest may challenge the definition of merit as discriminatory. For example, in 1980 older workers who were illiterate or barely literate objected to the use of written technical tests as a basis for wage increases. They argued that actual work accomplished rather than theoretical knowledge should be the sole criterion for raises. In

---

20. Weber describes the "transparency of the connection between the causes and the consequences of the 'class situation'" in "Class, Status, Party," in *From Max Weber,* p. 184. On this point, also see Parkin, *Class Inequality and Political Order,* pp. 160–165. The concentration in Beijing of petitioners seeking rehabilitation from past political mistreatment illustrates how centralized people perceive power to be.

21. "Guiding Principles of Inner-Party Political Life" (adopted at the Fifth Plenary Session of the Eleventh Chinese Communist Party Central Committee), BR, No. 14 (April 7, 1980), p. 18.

heavy industry, women may oppose piecework because it is biased by the superior physical strength of men.[22] Moreover, so long as competition has a zero-sum character, the winners will be resented by the losers.[23]

An educational system that distributes opportunities on the basis of academic merit is always open to the charge of discrimination, as the example of Western societies has shown. Groups whose children fail examinations can argue that there is no genuine equality of opportunity so long as their children are handicapped by past oppression, linguistic or cultural problems, and inferior school facilities. Although the disadvantaged majority in China—the peasants—whose home environment and educational preparation are obviously inferior to those of city dwellers, as yet show few signs of protest, its political advocates are likely to become more vocal in the future.[24] With educational investment concentrated in urban secondary and higher education, the gap between the availability and quality of urban and rural schools will widen, putting peasant youth at an almost insurmountable disadvantage in the competition for university admission.

Other trends may further heighten perceptions of inequity, especially from the standpoint of the peasants. The feodocratic practice of hiring the children of employees in state factories and offices closes the doors of the city to rural dwellers. Moreover, as the private resources of urban families become more valuable, and the distribution of opportunities becomes less monolithic, the ability to enforce career sanctions declines. Although the rural transfer program is still on the books, it is so unpopular that the regime has cut it back. It is still difficult for those

22. Because of the tensions produced by meritocratic distribution in work organizations, I would predict that the Chinese will eventually begin to reintroduce a modified seniority system. As Adam Smith said when comparing age to the "invisible qualities" of wisdom and virtue, "Age is a plain and palpable quality which admits of no dispute"; *An Inquiry into the Nature and Causes of the Wealth of Nations,* excerpted in *Reflections on Inequality,* ed. Andreski, p. 54.

23. A particularly conflict-laden situation is created by bonuses for overfulfillment of individual production quotas. Although the amount of the bonus is not fixed, and theoretically everyone can earn more if they produce more, the setting of the quota is a zero-sum game. The advanced worker who doubles his quota every month and causes the authorities to raise the quota creates costs for all fellow workers and becomes a social outcast. (See "Why are Advanced Comrades the Object of Satire and Irony?" GRRB, February 22, 1980.)

24. Cadres articulating the peasantry's interests raised some objections to university selection procedures and the system of elite key schools at educational conferences in 1978 (see Shirk, "Educational Reform and Political Backlash," pp. 210–217), and to the plan to lengthen the period of urban schooling at conferences in 1980.

who do not win a university place or a city job to make careers—they must live off their families and find work outside the state sector—but the government's increasing tolerance for small private and collective enterprise in the urban economy makes it easier to survive at the interstices of the system. Money and entrepreneurial talents, resources which were once virtually useless in the state-controlled mobility contest, will be rendered more useful by the possibility of "freelancing." They will come in handy not only for building small city businesses but also for arranging foreign educational opportunities. Individuals are now permitted to make private arrangements for sending their children abroad to study if they have the information, the foreign connections, and the money to do so. No doubt some of those who leave China to study, especially those who go under private rather than official auspices, will never return. The weakening of state control over the distribution of career opportunities makes this exit option a real one for urban high school students, or at least for the small number of them with money and overseas connections. Family resources are also more important in the local competition than they were in the past. Because the Cultural Revolution disrupted school education between 1966 and 1976, the intellectual and cadre families who were able to teach their children at home or hire tutors gave their offspring a distinct edge in the new enrollment system.[25] Academics and officials who bring home foreign books and electronic calculators also are able to enrich the education provided by the schools. And affluent parents whose children fail the regular college entrance examination can now send them to new commuter colleges that enroll anyone who can afford the 50 yuan ($30) annual tuition.[26]

The shift from virtuocracy to meritocracy challenges the Communist Party ruling elite to devise a new basis for political legitimacy. Because citizens no longer find credible the leaders' "masks" of purity, current and future leaders must claim legitimacy on the utilitarian basis of competence. Now that practice is considered the sole criterion of truth,

25. "As the role of school education was drastically weakened, family education and self-study by young people began to assume a role of increased prominence. There is a greater number of college students from intellectual families than those from worker and peasant families because the former have better conditions and environment for learning." "Enrollment System: A Meaningful Discussion," BR, No. 30 (July 28, 1978), p. 18.
26. Xinhua, June 29, 1980, FBIS, July 2, 1980, p. Q3; BR, No. 39 (September 29, 1980), p. 6.

competence is the sole criterion for authority. Deng Xiaoping and his successors must convince people that their policy judgments are technically rational and conducive to the improvement of living standards. But if they fail to deliver on their economic promises, there will be no reason for citizens not to prefer a new leader or even a new system of government. When speculating about the prospects for China's economic success in the next decades, it is important to remember that the basic problem of any large, centrally planned economy is that even with the smartest, most public-spirited officials, it is impossible to effectively manage the huge number of interrelated decisions that must be made.[27] The combination of meritocracy with authoritarian control of the economy legitimates individualism and competition and weakens the ideological basis for unity and loyalty, without providing any of the economic advantages of market systems.

The Party elite is reluctant to abandon its efforts at political transformation. The legitimacy of Party leadership is based in large part on its vanguard role in leading the revolutionary transformation of society and guaranteeing a higher moral quality of life than that found in nonsocialist societies. Therefore although much less is expected in the way of citizen political activism than in the past, people still have to satisfy a minimum level of political acceptability. College (and sometimes job) applicants must undergo a political screening, and candidates for job promotion must have their labor attitude scrutinized. All admissions examinations include a section on politics. If anyone makes a serious political mistake (which is noted in his or her dossier) or expresses deviant political views on an examination, his or her career can still be ruined.[28] Political tests now show whether or not an individual is compliant and conforming—which means being willing to memorize current political formulas and sit through boring political meetings. These political tests have become devices for filtering out the trouble-makers rather than measures of revolutionary enthusiasm.

Because revolutionary enthusiasm is no longer expected of people, it is easier for them to meet regime expectations. When the official morality is less demanding, fewer people feel like deviants. Citizens can compartmentalize their political involvements—politics is something to

---

27. Nove, "The Soviet Economy: Problems and Prospects," pp. 3-13.

28. There still are cases reported in the press of people who cannot get jobs because of political stigma (see ZGQN, October 1979, pp. 20 and 46) and employees who receive low bonuses because they do not speak up in meetings (GRRB, November 27, 1978).

worry about during weekly meetings and when taking an admissions test. Political competition is now a less serious threat to one's social relationships. Of course, more is expected of those who join the Communist Party or the Youth League, but even for them there are new rules and regulations which aim at making political life more regular and less acrimonious.[29] Because political participation is less demanding and less traumatic, and because of the continued existence of tests of political reliability, few people will be motivated to risk active opposition.[30]

With meritocratic values growing more pervasive it will become apparent to everyone, however, that Maoist ideas have become symbols of loyalty rather than guides to action—as Chalmers Johnson has put it, more "totem" than "thought."[31] It will become increasingly difficult to justify tests of political reliability, and ideological appeals for self-sacrifice or active participation rather than mere passive conformity will fall on deaf ears. Whereas in 1963 many people could be stirred by stories about the young martyr Lei Feng, today the leadership's efforts to resuscitate this model of altruism are greeted with laughter.[32] The Chinese leadership is becoming increasingly concerned about the political anomie of the younger generation. The young people who are veterans of the Cultural Revolution, have "a particular aversion to hackneyed political preaching" and have "seen much of the seamy side."[33] And since 1976 the schools have concentrated on the pursuit of

29. For example, the principle of the "three not's" is now supposed to be enforced: "Do not seize on another's shortcoming and blow it up, do not put labels on people, and do not use the big stick. The 'three not's' forbid the willful exaggeration of anyone's mistakes, cooking up charges against him and attacking him politically and organizationally and even persecuting him" "Guiding Principles for Inner-Party Life," BR, No. 14 (April 7, 1980), p. 16.

30. Because Deng has a political stake in appearing to enhance democracy and legality, he may increase the use of secret police methods rather than use more conspicuously heavy-handed methods to suppress dissent. The example of the Soviet Union demonstrates how the combination of legalism and police surveillance can be employed to discourage dissidence.

31. Johnson, "The Failure of Socialism in China," p. 29. In 1980 a group of college students wrote to an American magazine to complain about the "debasing indoctrination" they were still required to undergo: "The school authorities themselves knew that this barrage would not produce the desired effect, and that if they themselves had to go through it, [they] would think of every way possible to escape. But they could hardly be expected to move to abolish such practices." "Letter from a Chinese College," *The New York Review of Books,* September 25, 1980, p. 3.

32. Some people even believe that Lei Feng is a fictional invention of the Party propaganda organ; others say, "He was a loser, who would want to be like him?" See Linda Matthews' story in *The Los Angeles Times,* May 1, 1980.

33. BR, No. 32 (August 11, 1980), pp. 22-23.

educational achievement and advancement rather than teaching students to be committed to the revolutionary cause. As a result, "today's outstanding students [may] become tomorrow's political dissenters."[34] The leadership is worried that it also has raised unrealistic expectations and overextended itself with promises of college and job opportunities and new investments, raises, and bonuses in every sector. It has therefore tried to revive political education and reassert the values of altruism. But the widespread cynicism toward these values makes it difficult for the leaders to substitute moral incentives for more expensive material ones.[35]

If the country's economic performance is disappointing and people's expectations for improvement in their living standard are not met, it will be difficult for Deng and his successors to maintain citizen support. Under virtuocracy, Party leaders could claim that China was superior to other societies because it was more cooperative and more egalitarian. But the turn to meritocracy requires them to confront the issue of China's relative economic backwardness. Today the Gang of Four are convenient scapegoats, but ten or twenty years from now, how will leaders explain why China still lags behind capitalist countries? They are devising an answer which is one part patriotic nationalism and one part social security. On the one hand, they say that China is poor and capitalist countries like America are rich because the greedy imperialist countries exploited countries like China. On the other hand, they posit a tradeoff between prosperity and security, and claim that although people in countries like the United States may be more affluent, they are always "worrying that there won't be enough money" when they get old or if they lose their jobs.[36] The theme of job security will strike a

34. Shanghai City Service, February 25, 1980, FBIS, February 27, 1980, p. 02.

35. The economic basis of virtuocracy is evident today as the regime strains to find the resources to foster and reward merit. Hua Guofeng recently argued the economic necessity of political work: "Since China has a large population and the country is still not rich materially and numerous problems remain to be solved, political and ideological work is therefore all the more important. Work must be done to raise the people's political consciousness through political and ideological work and to encourage them to build the country in the revolutionary spirit of diligence and thrift—that is, to encourage them to display the revolutionary spirit of service to the people and dedication to the emancipation of mankind"; BR, No. 20 (May 19, 1980), p. 8.

36. Speech by Zhang Guangdou, vice-president of Qinghua University, quoted by Fox Butterfield, *The New York Times,* May 11, 1980. These arguments are similar to those used by the Soviet leadership to defend the superiority of the Soviet Union (see Victor Zaslavsky, "Socioeconomic Inequality and Changes in Soviet Ideology," pp. 383-407).

responsive chord with employed urbanites who are acutely aware of the oversupply of labor, but not with high school students who face uncertain employment prospects. In addition to these rationales for backwardness, current and future leaders may seek to enhance their legitimacy with a revival of traditional cultural virtues. It would not be surprising to find Chinese leaders paying more attention to their public images—for example, more newspaper stories about Deng Xiaoping's family life or his loyalty to his friends during the Cultural Revolution.[37] Affection based on traditional morality could help politicians postpone eruptions of serious social discontent.

Nevertheless some people in China will begin to argue that the government, besides being unable to deliver on its economic promises, also doesn't stand for anything anymore. Every stratification system has its own sources of strain. Under virtuocracy people come to distrust one another and their leaders, but under meritocracy there is no vision the leaders can use to inspire their followers and legitimate their own role. In contrast to the political dissidents of the 1970s who reacted to what they perceived as the degeneration of virtuocracy by pleading for meritocracy and democracy, the dissidents of the 1980s and 1990s may express a nostalgia for the days when there was moral idealism in politics. Like current dissidents in the Soviet Union, they may start to complain that the Party no longer gives people anything to believe in.[38] The decline of virtuocracy and rise of meritocracy could create new sects which aim at realizing the original ideals of the revolution, at achieving the Maoist vision of spiritual transformation. In the future Chinese youth may again, as Mao once urged them to do, "go against the tide" to seek the moral reformation of politics.[39]

37. The children of Party leaders martyred during the Cultural Revolution have been publishing memoirs of their fathers which emphasize their traditional moral virtues.

38. Shirk, "Dissent in China and the Soviet Union," pp. 263-268.

39. "If our children's generation go in for revisionism and move towards their opposite, so that although they still nominally have socialism it is in fact capitalism, then our grandsons will certainly rise up in revolt and overthrow their fathers"; Mao Zedong, "Speech to the Tenth Plenum of the Central Committee," p. 72.

METHODOLOGICAL APPENDIX

This study of student behavior in Chinese urban high schools is based primarily on the accounts of refugees interviewed in Hong Kong. Because foreign scholars until recently were not permitted to do field research in China, those scholars who were interested in the effects of communist policies on the lives of Chinese citizens had to develop an alternative methodology of refugee interviewing. Although many studies based on refugee interviews have generated rich insights about Chinese society and have presented articulate explanations of the methodology, each study involves its own particular problems of interpretation.[1] As Alex Inkeles and Raymond Bauer state in their landmark study of Soviet society based entirely on refugee data, "The question of the importance of sample bias can be answered only in the context of the specific type of analysis which is made and the specific inferences which are drawn."[2] Therefore it is important for the reader to understand how the interviews for this study were carried out, how I have used the information provided by them, and the background characteristics of the individuals who were interviewed.

THE INTERVIEWS

Every year thousands of Chinese citizens leave China for the British colony of Hong Kong. Most of them cross the border illegally, coming in small boats or as "freedom swimmers." The flow of young refugees increased after 1969, when millions of urban youth were resettled in the countryside after the Cultural Revolution. Although there were in Hong Kong many potential respondents who had attended high schools in Chinese cities, finding them and overcoming their reluctance to talk about their past was a difficult task. People in China are taught that revealing even apparently harmless information to foreigners may en-

---

1. See especially the methodological appendixes in Whyte, *Small Groups and Political Rituals in China*, pp. 237-263, and Parish and Whyte, *Village and Family in Contemporary China*, pp. 339-351.
2. Inkeles and Bauer, *The Soviet Citizen*, p. 26.

danger the national security. Refugees in Hong Kong also worry that revealing details about their lives in China may jeopardize their futures in Hong Kong, their prospects for immigration to the United States or other countries, or the careers and reputations of their family members who remain in China.

When I began my research during the summer of 1969, I was able to contact a small number of respondents through private relief and welfare organizations that aided recent refugees. When I returned to Hong Kong in 1971, I continued to contact respondents through these agencies, but I came to rely more on the introductions of people I had already interviewed than on the agencies. During the winter of 1978-1979, when I conducted additional interviews in Hong Kong, I relied entirely on informal networks and the personal introductions of previous respondents. Only two of the people I interviewed had been interviewed by other foreign scholars.

The use of personal introductions facilitated the establishment of trust between the interviewer and respondent. A previous respondent, who through interview accounts had already proved his or her trustworthiness to me, vouched for the veracity of the new respondent. The previous respondent also reassured his or her friend, the new respondent, that I was committed to the scholarly norm of confidentiality and would cause the respondent no harm.

Respondents were generally paid the standard fee for participating in interviews. In 1969 and 1971 the customary fee was H.K. $30 (U.S. $5) for a three-hour interview; it increased to H.K. $45 (U.S. $9) in 1978-1979. The payment of such a fee has become a well-established practice in Hong Kong. The amount was not so large that it would be likely to encourage falsification, but was large enough to make it possible for the respondent to cover the expense of transportation and foregone work opportunities.[3]

I conducted interviews with thirty-one students and three teachers. Each student was interviewed in a least two sessions of three hours each; those with good memories were questioned in as many as seven three-hour sessions. The teachers were interviewed in one session apiece. I used a topic outline to conduct semi-structured interviews on all aspects of school life (copies of the interview outline are available

3. Hiniker, "Chinese Reactions to Forced Compliance," pp. 157-166.

from the author). The interviews were conducted in my office at the Universities Service Centre.

With only a few exceptions (when my research assistant conducted interviews in Cantonese), I conducted all the interviews myself in Mandarin. The Mandarin dialect is the official national language in the PRC and is taught in all schools.

The responses were not recorded verbatim with a tape recorder, because scholars experienced in the art of interviewing advised me that the presence of a tape recorder made refugee respondents nervous and reticent. Instead, my assistant and I both took notes during the interviews, my notes were in English, and my assistant's were in Chinese. Immediately following each session, my assistant and I reviewed and compared our notes, writing an interview report which was a close as possible to a verbatim account. All quotations from respondents included in this book are reconstructions based on our interview notes.

PROBLEMS OF INTERPRETATION

The scholar who attempts to study China through refugee interviews faces several serious problems in evaluating and interpreting the data. One is the problem of authenticity. Researchers who seek respondents who held specialized leadership roles in the PRC must be wary of impersonators. The word spreads in Hong Kong that a scholar is searching for a judge or a cadre in a particular ministry, and pretenders turn up at the office to collect the interview payment. Research on Chinese high schools has not been plagued by this problem of bogus respondents. Student respondents are plentiful, and I was willing to interview anyone who had attended high school during the 1960-1966 period. Nevertheless, my Chinese assistant and I were careful to check the reliability of the interview accounts, repeating questions to test internal consistency, and comparing responses with those of other respondents, with press sources, and with observations made when visiting China.

Another methodological problem is sample size. I speak of my "sample" of students, but it would be impossible to make valid inferences from interviews with only thirty-one people, even if there were no other problems of bias. Because it is difficult to obtain samples of refugee respondents large enough to make valid statistical inferences to the Mainland population, I decided to make a virtue out of necessity and do in-depth interviews with a small number of students.[4] Since research based on refugee interviews is at best not definitive but only suggestive, I opted for intensiveness rather than extensiveness. My hope was that many hours of interviews with a small number of respondents would generate rich findings which could later be tested when field research on such subjects in China becomes possible.

The major criticism of refugee interviewing as a research method does not focus on the problems of small samples or fabricated data, but on the problem of unrepresentativeness and the related problem of bias. It can be argued that refugees are not representative of the population in China—they are the people who were least successful in adapting to the system or the most alienated from it—and that therefore they have a more negative perspective on Chinese society than the "average" citizen. Although the problem of unrepresentativeness is a serious one, it did not produce a general anti-communist bias among the respondents. Except for one or two respondents who had been minor Red Guard leaders during the Cultural Revolution, all the people who were interviewed had come to Hong Kong not to escape political repression but to seek educational and occupational opportunities. Most of them had never considered leaving China until after the Cultural Revolution when they were sent down to work in the countryside and forced to abandon their hopes for college and professional jobs. When describing past experiences, most respondents expressed a positive, even sentimental view of human relations back home on the mainland, rather than a negative view of communist society. At the conclusion of each series of interviews, I asked the respondent some general questions about Chinese politics in order to gauge his or her political bias. Almost all the respondents made positive statements about Mao Zedong, the Communist Party, or communist policies. Over half of them expressed approval of Mao's policy of resettling urban youth in the countryside, even though the policy's personal impact on them had been so negative that it had caused them to leave their families, friends, and native land.

A problem more troublesome than a general negative political bias concerns the specific characteristics of the sample. The respondents were all highly ambitious people who had been academically or politi-

4. Parish and Whyte, in their study of rural society *(Village and Family in Contemporary China)* and in their forthcoming study of urban society, were able to use refugees as informants to generate much larger samples of individuals, households, and local communities.

cally successful in school. As students at full-time urban high schools, they were an elite group whose chances of being admitted to college or getting a good city job were much better that those of their rural counterparts. About half the respondents had attended key schools, which offered an even better chance for a successful future. All the respondents were so highly motivated by career ambitions that they decided to leave China to pursue them. These students had a tendency to project their own ambitions onto their classmates and to exaggerate the importance of career competition in the high school arena.

Another source of sample bias is the under-representation of political activists and worker-peasant youth. Among the 31 respondents, only 10 had applied to join the Youth League, and only 5 had become members. My analysis of avoidance relationships between activists and non-activists is therefore more heavily influenced by the non-activists' perspective, although it was corroborated by the activists as well. The class background distribution of the sample—2 of good background, 15 of middle-range background, and 14 of bad background—appears very skewed when compared with a national population which is probably 90 percent good background; it is not, however, as unrepresentative of student bodies in city high schools. In most city high schools there were few or no peasants from suburban communes, no more than 50 percent children of workers, 50 percent or more children of teachers, technicians, clerks, and other middle-range categories, and about 10 percent children of exploiting class parents. Nevertheless the high proportion of bad background youth in the sample certainly influenced my analysis of school life. The class background factor played a critical role in the analysis because of its salience to these respondents. Even those of middle-range and good class backgrounds confirmed, however, that class origin was an important consideration in the formation of social relationships for all students, not just for those stigmatized by it.

Other secondary problems of potential sample bias derive from the preponderance of Cantonese respondents and of male respondents. The city of Canton is only 70 miles from Hong Kong. The route of most young refugees took them from high schools in Canton or other towns in the surrounding Guangdong Province, to rural communes in the Guangdong countryside, and then over the border to Hong Kong. Popular Chinese regional stereotypes describe social intercourse in Guangdong as especially conflictual and pervaded by deceit and mistrust. Cantonese schools might be especially prone to social conflict, and

Cantonese respondents might have heightened perceptions of such conflict. However, comparisons of the accounts of the twenty respondents who had attended school only in Canton with the six respondents who had gone to schools in Guangdong towns, the two who had gone to schools both in other regions and in Canton, and the three who had obtained all their education outside of Guangdong in other regions of China, did not reveal any clear differences.

Only seven of the thirty-one respondents were female. Although this certainly under-represents the proportion of females in the population as a whole, there is less of a discrepancy when comparing the sample to the number of females in city high school classes. Respondents reported that many classes of approximately fifty students had only ten to twenty girls. In any case, the female respondents' descriptions of student life did not vary in any consistent way from those of their male counterparts, except that the girls were somewhat more compliant to school authorities and less ambitious than the boys.

Because of the problems of unrepresentativeness and bias in refugee interviewing, it is particularly important to cross-check interview data with data from other types of sources. All interview accounts of what from the Chinese leadership's perspective were negative phenomena—for example, political competition, opportunism, bitterness over class background issues, avoidance of activists, and unwillingness to criticize friends—were corroborated by documentary sources. One documentary source was the official Chinese press, particularly articles and short stories about student life from the youth periodicals *Zhongxuesheng* (High School Student), *Zhongguo qingnian* (Chinese Youth), and *Zhongguo qingnian bao* (Chinese Youth Journal). Another valuable source was the unofficial Red Guard press during the Cultural Revolution. My confidence in the accounts of the refugee respondents has also been strengthened by interviews I conducted in 1980 in Hong Kong with legal emigrants from China, and in China and the United States with current Chinese college students.

With all its shortcomings, refugee interviewing is still the best method for studying Chinese political life in schools, villages, neighborhoods, and work units. As Parish and Whyte point out, all methods of research on China present their own problems of bias.[5] Articles in the official media are designed to exhort rather than report. When for-

5. Parish and Whyte, *Village and Family in Contemporary China,* p. 345.

eigners visit China they are taken to schools, factories, and communes which are unusually well-equipped and which have benefited from relationships with the officials who arrange the tours. The positive bias of the official side of the tour has, since 1978, been countered by the tendency for discontented individuals to seek out informal contacts with foreigners visiting China. Because many of the ordinary people whom visitors meet are the politically persecuted who have little to lose by being seen telling their tales of woe to foreigners, the visitors may take away an overly negative impression of "real life" in China. Moreover, data obtained from documentary sources and visits to China are of limited value in studying the impact of policies on social behavior. Observations from visits are too superficial, and the press is informative about policy but not about the effects of policy at the basic level. The rich texture of human experience in China has, up to now, been revealed only through refugee interviews. I hope, however, that the findings of this study and others also based on refugee interview accounts, will soon be tested by surveys, interviews, and observations of informal relations in organizations in China.

BACKGROUND INFORMATION
ON THE RESPONDENTS

Xie Female, non-YCL, father a doctor, key senior high school graduate in Canton, admitted to key national university, illegally left China in 1969, six interviews.

Cai Male, non-YCL, father a doctor, ordinary junior high school in Canton, illegally left China in 1970, two interviews.

Lu Male, non-YCL, father bourgeois, key senior high school graduate in Canton, illegally left China in 1969, three interviews.

Zhou Male, non-YCL, father a landlord, key senior high school graduate in a Hunan town, illegally left China in 1967, four interviews.

Xu Male, non-YCL, father a middle peasant, ordinary senior high school graduate in Canton, illegally left China in 1970, seven interviews.

Liu   Male, non-YCL, father an Overseas Chinese, ordinary junior high school graduate in Canton, legally left China in 1964, four interviews.

He   Male, YCL, father a poor peasant, key senior high school graduate in a Guangdong town, admitted to university, illegally left China in 1970, three interviews.

Lin   Male, non-YCL, father a rightist professor, ordinary senior high school graduate in Nanjing, illegally left China in 1969, five interviews.

Guo   Male, non-YCL, father an Overseas Chinese, Overseas Chinese senior high school graduate in a Guangdong town, admitted to university, illegally left China in 1970, four interviews.

Wang   Male, non-YCL, father a capitalist, key senior high school graduate in Canton, illegally left China in 1967, two interviews.

Li   Male, applied to YCL, father a former Kuomintang employee, key senior high school graduate in Canton, illegally left China in 1969, two interviews.

Wei   Male, non-YCL, father a landlord, key senior high school graduate in a Guangdong town, illegally left China in 1963, two interviews.

Huang   Male, non-YCL, father a former minister, key senior high school graduate in Canton, admitted to university, illegally left China in 1970, three interviews.

Shi   Male, non-YCL, father a clerk, key senior high school graduate in Canton, illegally left China in 1970, five interviews.

Yang   Male, applied to YCL, father a doctor, ordinary senior high school graduate in Canton, illegally left China in 1971, six interviews.

Xi   Male, non-YCL, father a doctor, key senior high school graduate in Canton, illegally left China in 1969, four interviews.

Tang   Female, non-YCL, father a teacher, key senior high school graduate in Canton, illegally left China in 1969, five interviews.

Chen   Male, non-YCL, father a teacher, key senior high school graduate in Canton, illegally left China in 1970, five interviews.

Zhang   Male, non-YCL, father a capitalist, ordinary junior high school and specialized senior high school graduate in Canton, illegally left China in 1970, two interviews.

Wu   Female, non-YCL, father a former Kuomintang employee, ordinary junior high school and private senior high school graduate in Canton, illegally left China in 1970, five interviews.

Luo   Female, applied to YCL, father a capitalist, key junior high school graduate in Canton, illegally left China in 1969, four interviews.

Peng   Male, applied to YCL, father in Taiwan, Overseas Chinese senior high school graduate in a Guangdong town, illegally left China in 1968, seven interviews.

Deng   Female, non-YCL, father a landlord, ordinary senior high school graduate in a Guangdong town, illegally left China in 1971, seven interviews.

Yao   Male, non-YCL, father a landlord, ordinary senior high school graduate in Canton, legally left China in 1966, five interviews.

Gao   Male, non-YCL, father an Overseas Chinese, Overseas Chinese senior high school graduate in a Guangdong town, illegally left China in 1968, five interviews.

Kang   Male, YCL, father a poor peasant, junior high school graduate in a Jiangxi suburban commune, illegally left China in 1971, two interviews.

Jiang   Male, applied to YCL, father a former Kuomintang employee, ordinary junior high school graduate in a Jiangsu city, key senior high school graduate in Canton, left China illegally in 1970, five interviews.

An   Male, non-YCL, father a technician, attended ordinary junior high school in a Hunan city, ordinary senior high school graduate in Canton, admitted to university, left China illegally in 1971, five interviews.

Yu   Female, YCL, father a clerk, key senior high school graduate in Canton, left China illegally in 1975, four interviews.

Ding   Male, YCL, father a former Kuomintang employee, ordinary senior high school graduate in Canton, left China illegally in 1973, two interviews.

Fang   Female, YCL, father a clerk, key senior high school graduate in Canton, left China illegally in 1975, three interviews.

Bibliography

Aird, John S. "Population Growth and Distribution in Mainland China." *An Economic Profile of Mainland China.* Prepared for the Joint Economic Committee, United States Congress, February 1967. Vol. II.

Andreski, Stanislav, ed. *Reflections on Inequality.* London: Croon Helm, 1975.

Bailey, F. G. *Gifts and Poison: The Politics of Reputation.* Oxford: Basil Blackwell, 1971.

Barnett, A. Doak. *Cadres, Bureaucracy, and Political Power in China.* New York: Columbia University Press, 1967.

Barry, Brian. *Sociologists, Economists, and Democracy.* London: Collier Macmillan, 1970.

Becker, Gary S. *The Economic Approach to Human Behavior.* Chicago: University of Chicago Press, 1976.

Bendix, Reinhard. *Work and Authority in Industry: Ideologies of Management in the Course of Industrialization.* Berkeley: University of California Press, 1956.

Bennett, Gordon A. "China's Mass Campaigns and Social Control." *Deviance and Social Control in Chinese Society.* Edited by Amy Aurbacher Wilson, Sidney Leonard Greenblat, and Richard Whitingham Wilson. New York: Praeger, 1977.

——— and Ronald N. Montaperto. *Red Guard, The Biography of Dai Hsiao-ai.* Garden City: Anchor Books, 1972.

Bernstein, Thomas P. "Cadre and Peasant Behavior Under Conditions of Insecurity and Deprivation: The Grain Supply Crisis of the Spring of 1955." *Chinese Communist Politics in Action.* Edited by A. Doak Barnett. Seattle: University of Washington Press, 1969.

———. *Up to the Mountains and Down to the Villages: The Transfer of Youth from Urban to Rural China.* New Haven: Yale University Press, 1977.

Blau, Peter M. "Cooperation and Competition in a Bureaucracy." *The American Journal of Sociology,* LIX (May 1954), 530-535.

———. "Social Mobility and Interpersonal Relations." *American Sociological Review,* XXI (1956), 290-295.

Bock, John C. "Countervailing Outcomes of Malaysian Education: National Identity and Political Alienation." *Education and Urban Society* (February 1978).

————. "Education and Nation-Building in Malaysia: A Study of Institutional Effect in Thirty-Four Secondary Schools." Ph.D dissertation, Stanford University, 1970.

Bowen, James. *Soviet Education: Anton Makarenko and the Years of Experiment*. Madison: University of Wisconsin Press, 1962.

Bowles, Samuel, and Herbert Gintis. *Schooling in Capitalist America: Educational Reform and the Contradictions of Economic Life*. New York: Basic Books, 1976.

Brinton, Crane. *The Anatomy of Revolution*. New York: Vintage Books, 1965.

Bronfenbrenner, Urie. "Response to Pressure from Peers versus Adults among Soviet and American School Children." *International Journal of Psychology*, II (1967), 199-207.

————. *Two Worlds of Childhood: U.S. and U.S.S.R.*. New York: Russell Sage Foundation, 1970.

Burns, John. "The Election of Production Team Cadres in Rural China: 1958-1974." *The China Quarterly*, 74 (June 1978), 273-296.

Chang Ching-li. "CCP's Treatment of the 'Five Categories of Elements.'" *Issues and Studies*, XVI, No. 3 (March 1980), 13-27.

Ch'en, Jerome, ed. *Mao Papers*. London: Oxford University Press, 1970.

Chen Jo-hsi. *The Execution of Mayor Yin*. Bloomington: Indiana University Press, 1978.

Chen Pi-chao. "The Political Economics of Population Growth: The Case of China," *World Politics* XXIII, No. 2 (January 1971), 245-272.

Chen Yuan-tsung. *The Dragon's Village*. New York: Pantheon Books, 1980.

"Ch'en Yun's Speech at the CCP Central Committee Work Conference, April, 1979." *Issues and Studies*, XVI, No. 4 (April 1980), 80-97.

Chin Ai-li. Unpublished paper. 1972.

Clark, Burton R. "The 'Cooling-out' Function in Higher Education." *Education, Economy, and Society*. Edited by A.H. Halsey, Jean Floud, and C. Arnold Anderson. New York: Free Press, 1961.

Coleman, James S. "Academic Achievement and the Structure of Competition." *Education, Economy, and Society*. Edited by A.H. Halsey, Jean Floud, and C. Arnold Anderson. New York: Free Press, 1961.

————. *The Adolescent Society*. New York: Free Press, 1961.

Deutsch, Morton. "The Effects of Cooperation and Competition Upon Group Process." *Group Dynamics: Research and Theory*. Edited by Dorwin Cartwright and Alvin Zender. 3rd ed. New York: Harper and Row, 1968.

The Diary of Wang Jieh. Beijing: Foreign Languages Press, 1967.

Dittmer, Lowell. "Thought Reform and Cultural Revolution: An Analysis of the Symbolism of Chinese Polemics." *American Political Science Review,* Volume 71 (March 1977), 67-85.

Doolin, Dennis J. *Communist China: The Politics of Student Opposition.* Stanford: The Hoover Institution, 1964.

Dore, Ronald P. *The Diploma Disease: Education, Qualification, and Development.* Berkeley: University of California Press, 1976.

Downs, Anthony. *An Economic Theory of Democracy.* New York: Harper and Brothers, 1956.

Dreeben, Robert. *On What is Learned in School.* Reading, Massachusetts: Addison-Wesley, 1968.

Emerson, John P. "Manpower Training and Utilization of Specialized Cadres, 1949-1968." *The City in Communist China.* Edited by John W. Lewis. Stanford: Stanford University Press, 1971.

Etzioni, Amitai. *Modern Organizations.* Englewood Cliffs, New Jersey: Prentice-Hall, 1964.

Fagen, Richard. *The Transformation of Political Culture in Cuba.* Stanford: Stanford University Press, 1969.

Finifter, Ada W. "The Friendship Group as a Protective Environment for Political Deviants." Annual Meeting of the American Political Science Association, 1972.

Frolic, B. Michael. *Mao's People.* Cambridge: Harvard University Press, 1980.

Gardner, John. "Educated Youth and Urban-Rural Inequalities, 1958-1966." *The City in Communist China.* Edited by John Wilson Lewis. Stanford: Stanford University Press, 1971.

Goffman, Erving. *Asylums: Essays on the Social Situation of Mental Patients and Other Inmates.* Garden City, New York: Anchor Books, 1961.

———. *The Presentation of Self in Everyday Life.* Garden City, New York: Anchor Books, 1959.

Gordon, C. Wayne. *The Social System of the High School: A Study in the Sociology of Adolescence.* New York: Free Press, 1957.

Greeley, Andrew M. *The Making of the Popes, 1978: The Politics of Intrigue in the Vatican.* Kansas City: Andrews and McMeel, 1979.

Grichting, Wolfgang R. *The Value System in Taiwan, 1970.* Taipei, 1971.

Guo Sheng. "On Collectivism and Collective Education," *Beijing shifan daxue xuebao* (The Journal of Peking Normal University), Vol. I, 1958.

Hargreaves, David H. *Social Relations in a Secondary School.* London: Routledge and Kegan Paul, 1967.

Hiniker, Paul J. "Chinese Reactions to Forced Compliance: Dissonance Reduction or National Character," *Journal of Social Psychology,* Vol. 77 (April 1969), 157-166.

———. *Revolutionary Ideology and Chinese Reality: Dissonance Under Mao.* Beverly Hills: Sage Publications, 1977.

Hinton, William. *Fanshen: A Documentary of Revolution in a Chinese Village.* New York: Random House, 1968.

Hirschman, Albert O. *Exit, Voice, and Loyalty.* Cambridge: Harvard University Press, 1970.

Homans, George C. *The Human Group.* New York: Harcourt, Brace and World, 1950.

Inkeles, Alex, and Raymond A. Bauer. *The Soviet Citizen.* Cambridge: Harvard University Press, 1959.

Jiaoyuxue (Pedagogy). Nanjing: Renmin chuban she, First edition, 1960.

Johnson, Chalmers, ed. *Change in Communist Systems.* Stanford: Stanford University Press, 1970.

———. "The Failure of Socialism in China." *Issues and Studies,* XV, No. 7 (July 1979), 22-33.

Jowitt, Kenneth. "An Organizational Approach to the Study of Political Culture in Marxist-Leninist Systems." *American Political Science Review, LXVIII (September 1974), 1171-1191.*

Kessen, William, ed. *Childhood in China.* New Haven: Yale University Press, 1975.

Kraus, Richard. "Class Conflict and the Vocabulary of Social Analysis in China." *The China Quarterly,* No. 69 (March 1977), 54-74.

———. *Class Conflict in Chinese Socialism.* New York: Columbia University Press, forthcoming.

Kurth, Suzanne B. "Friendships and Friendly Relations." *Social Relationships.* Edited by George J. McCall and others. Chicago: Aldine Publishing Co., 1970.

Lacey, C. *Hightown Grammer: The School as a Social System.* Manchester, England: Manchester University Press, 1970.

Lane, David. *The Socialist Industrial State: Towards a Political Sociology of State Socialism.* London: George Allen and Unwin, 1976.

Lang, Olga. *Chinese Family and Society.* Hamden, Conn.: Archon Books, 1968.

Langton, Kenneth P. "Peer Group and School and the Political Socialization Process." *American Political Science Review,* LXI, No. 3 (September 1967), 751-758.

Lee, Hong Yung. *The Politics of the Chinese Cultural Revolution: A Case Study.* Berkeley: University of California Press, 1978.

"Letter from a Chinese College." *The New York Review of Books.* September 25, 1980.

Levine, Daniel. "Issues in the Study of Culture and Politics: A View from Latin America." *Publius,* IV (Spring 1974), 77-104.

Lewis, John Wilson. "Party Cadres in Communist China." *Education and Political Development*. Edited by James S. Coleman. Princeton: Princeton University Press, 1965.

Li Yizhe. "Concerning Socialist Democracy and Legal System." *Issues and Studies*, XII, No. 1 (January 1976), 110-149.

Lifton, Robert Jay. *Thought Reform and the Psychology of Totalism*. New York: Norton, 1961.

Logan, John R. "Growth, Politics, and Stratification of Places." *American Journal of Sociology*, 84, No. 2 (1978), 404-416.

Lu Xinhua and others. *The Wounded—New Stories of the Cultural Revolution*. Translated by Geremie Berme and Bennett Lee. Hong Kong: Joint Publishing Company, 1979.

Mao Zedong. "Analysis of the Classes in Chinese Society." *Selected Works of Mao Zedong*. Beijing: Foreign Languages Press, 1965. Volume I.

———. "Combat Liberalism." *Selected Works of Mao Zedong*. Beijing: Foreign Languages Press, 1965. Volume II.

———. "Speech to the Tenth Plenum of the Central Committee" (September 1962). *Chairman Mao Talks to the People*. Edited by Stuart Schram. New York: Pantheon, 1974.

Merton, Robert K. "Anticipatory Socialization." *Role Theory: Concepts and Research*. Edited by Bruce J. Biddle and Edwin J. Thomas. New York: John Wiley and Sons, 1966.

Metzger, Thomas P. *Escape from Predicament: Neo-Confucianism and China's Evolving Political Culture*. New York: Columbia University Press, 1977.

Meyer, John W. "The Charter: Conditions of Diffuse Socialization in Schools." *Social Processes and Social Stuctures*. Edited by W. Richard Scott. New York: Holt, Rinehart and Winston, 1970.

Montaperto, Ronald N. "From Revolutionary Successors to Revolutionaries: Chinese Students in the Early Stages of the Cultural Revolution." *Elites in the People's Republic of China*. Edited by Robert A. Scalapino. Seattle: University of Washington Press, 1972.

Moore, Barrington, Jr. *Injustice: The Social Bases of Obedience and Revolt*. White Plains, New York: M.E. Sharpe, 1978.

Munro, Donald J. *The Concept of Man in Contemporary China*. Ann Arbor: University of Michigan Press, 1977.

Nathan, Andrew J. *Peking Politics, 1918-1923: Factionalism and the Failure of Constitutionalism*. Berkeley: University of California Press, 1976.

Newcomb, Theodore M. *Personality and Social Change: Attitude Formation in a Student Community*. New York: Holt, Rinehart and Winston, 1943.

Novak, Joseph. *No Third Path*. Garden City, New York: Doubleday, 1962.

Nove, Alec. "The Soviet Economy: Problems and Prospects." *New Left Review,* No. 119 (January-February 1980), 3-13.

Oksenberg, Michel. "Getting Ahead and Along in Communist China: The Ladder of Success on the Eve of the Cultural Revolution." *Party Leadership and Revolutionary Power in China.* Edited by John Wilson Lewis. Cambridge: Cambridge University Press, 1970.

———, ed. *China's Developmental Experience.* New York: Praeger, 1973.

Parish, William, and Martin King Whyte. *Village and Family in Contemporary China.* Chicago: University of Chicago Press, 1978.

Parkin, Frank. *Class Inequality and Political Order.* London: MacGibbon and Kee, 1971.

Parsons, Talcott. "The School Class as a Social System: Some of its Functions in American Society." *Education, Economy, and Society.* Edited by A.H. Halsey, Jean Floud, and C. Arnold Anderson. New York: Free Press, 1961.

Pateman, Carole. "Political Culture, Political Structure, and Political Change." *British Journal of Political Science,* I (July 1971), 291-305.

Pepper, Suzanne. "Chinese Education After Mao: Two Steps Forward, Two Steps Back, and Begin Again?'. *The China Quarterly,* No. 81 (March 1980), 1-65.

Popkin, Samuel L. *The Rational Peasant.* Berkeley: University of California Press, 1979.

Prewitt, Kenneth. "Schooling, Stratification, Equality: Notes for Research." *State, School, and Politics.* Edited by Michael W. Kirst. Lexington: Lexington Books, 1972.

———. "Some Doubts about Political Socialization Research." *Comparative Education Review,* XIX (1975), 105-113.

Pye, Lucian W. *Guerrilla Communism in Malaya: Its Social and Political Meaning.* Princeton: Princeton University Press, 1956.

———. *The Spirit of Chinese Politics: A Psychocultural Study of the Authority Crisis in Political Development.* Cambridge: M.I.T. Press, 1968.

Raddock, David M. *Political Behavior of Adolescents in China: The Cultural Revolution in Kwangchow.* Tucson: The University of Arizona Press, 1977.

Richman, Barry M. *Industrial Society in Communist China.* New York: Random House, 1969.

Ridley, Charles Price, Paul H. B. Godwin, and Dennis J. Doolin. *The Making of a Model Citizen in Communist China.* Stanford: The Hoover Institution Press, 1971.

Roberts, Joan I. *Scene of the Battle: Group Behavior in Urban Classrooms.* Garden City, New York: Anchor Books, 1971.

Rosen, Stanley. "Background to Rebellion: Contradictions Dividing Middle School Students in Canton Prior to the Cultural Revolution." Paper presented at the Workshop on the Pursuit of Political Interest in the People's Republic of China, Ann Arbor, 1977.

———. "The Influence of Structure on Behavior: Recent Changes in China's Secondary School Structure in Cultural Revolution and Pre-Cultural Revolution Perspective." Paper presented at the Asian Studies on the Pacific Coast Conference, Honolulu, June 1981.

———. "The Radical Students in Kwangtung During the Cultural Revolution." *The China Quarterly,* No. 70 (June 1977), 390-399.

———. "Students, Administrators, and Mobility: Tensions in Canton Middle Schools in the 1960s." Paper presented at the California Regional Seminar on Contemporary China, Berkeley, November 1977.

Schurmann, Franz. *Ideology and Organization in Communist China.* Berkeley: University of California Press, 1968.

———. "Organization and Response in Communist China." *Annals of the American Academy of Political and Social Science,* No. 321 (January 1950), 51-61.

Schwartz, Benjamin I. "Modernization and the Maoist Vision—Some Reflections on Chinese Communist Goals." *China under Mao.* Edited by Roderick MacFarquhar. Cambridge: M.I.T. Press, 1966.

———. "The Reign of Virtue: Some Broad Perspectives on Leader and Party in the Cultural Revolution." *Party Leadership and Revolutionary Power in China.* Edited by John Wilson Lewis. Cambridge: Cambridge University Press, 1970.

Shirk, Susan L. "Dissent in China and the Soviet Union." *Studies in Comparative Communism,* XII, Nos. 2 and 3 (Summer-Autumn 1979), 263-268.

———. "Educational Reform and Political Backlash: Recent Changes in Chinese Educational Policy." *Comparative Education Review,* 23, No. 2 (June 1979), 183-217.

———. "Going Against the Tide: Political Dissent in China." *Survey,* 24, No. 1 (106) (Winter 1979), 82-114.

———. "The 1963 Temporary Work Regulations for Full-Time Middle and Primary Schools: Commentary and Translation." *The China Quarterly,* No. 55 (July-September 1973), 511-546.

———. "Work Experience in Chinese Education." *Comparative Education,* 14, No. 1 (March 1978), 5-18.

Skinner, G. William, and Edwin A. Winckler. "Compliance Succession in Rural Communist China: A Cyclical Theory." *Complex Organizations: A Sociological Reader.* Edited by A. Etzioni. New York: Holt, Rinehart and Winston, 1969.

Solomon, Richard H. "Mao's Effort to Reintegrate the Chinese Polity: Problems of Authority and Conflict in Chinese Social Processes." *Chinese Communist Politics in Action.* Edited by A. Doak Barnett. Seattle: University of Washington Press, 1969.

——. *Mao's Revolution and the Chinese Political Culture.* Berkeley: University of California Press, 1971.

Stinchcombe, Arthur L. *Rebellion in a High School.* Chicago: Quadrangle Books, 1964.

Stouffer, Samuel A., and others. *The American Soldier: Adjustment During Army Life,* Vol. I. Princeton: Princeton University Press, 1949.

Suttles, Gerald D. "Friendship as a Social Institution." *Social Relationships.* Edited by George J. McCall and others. Chicago: Aldine Publishing Co., 1970.

Taylor, Robert. *Education and University Enrollment Policies in China, 1949-1971.* Canberra: The Australian University, 1973.

Theodorson, George A. "The Relationship Between Leadership and Popularity Roles in Small Groups." *American Sociological Review,* 22, (February 1957), 58-67.

Townsend, James R. *The Revolutionization of Chinese Youth: A Study of Chung-kuo ch'ing-nien.* Berkeley: Center for Chinese Studies, 1967.

Tucker, Robert C. "Toward a Comparative Politics of Movement Regimes." *American Political Science Review,* LV, No. 2 (June 1961), 281-289.

Turner, Ralph H. "Modes of Social Ascent Through Education: Sponsored and Contest Mobility." *Education, Economy, and Society.* Edited by A.H. Halsey, Jean Floud, and D. Arnold Anderson. New York: Free Press, 1961.

Unger, Jonathan. *Education Under Mao: Class and Competition in Canton Schools, 1960–1980.* New York: Columbia University Press, forthcoming.

Unger, Roberto M. *Knowledge and Politics.* New York: Free Press, 1975.

Verba, Sidney. *Small Groups and Political Behavior: A Study of Leadership.* Princeton: Princeton University Press, 1961.

Vogel, Ezra F. "From Friendship to Comradeship: The Change in Personal Relations in Communist China." *China Under Mao: Politics Takes Command.* Edited by Roderick MacFarquhar. Cambridge: M.I.T. Press, 1966.

——. *Canton Under Communism.* Cambridge: Harvard University Press, 1969.

Walzer, Michael. "The Revolutionary Uses of Repression." *Essays in Theory and History: An Approach to the Social Sciences.* Edited by Melvin Richter. Cambridge: Harvard University Press, 1970.

Watson, Andrew J. "A Revolution to Tough Men's Souls: The Family,

Interpersonal Relations, and Daily Life." *Authority, Participation, and Cultural Change in China.* Edited by Stuart R. Schram. Cambridge: Cambridge University Press, 1973.

Weaver, Kitty D. *Lenin's Grandchildren: Preschool Education in the Soviet Union.* New York: Simon and Schuster, 1971.

Weber, Max. *From Max Weber: Essays in Sociology.* Edited by H. H. Gerth and C. Wright Mills. New York: Oxford University Press, 1958.

———. *The Theory of Social and Economic Organization.* Edited by Talcott Parsons. New York: Free Press, 1964.

Weisskopf, Thomas E. "The Relevance of the Chinese Experience for Third World Economic Development." *Theory and Society,* 9, No. 2 (March 1980), 283-318.

Wesolowski, W. "The Notions of Strata and Class in Socialist Society." *Social Inequality.* Edited by Andre Beteille. Harmondsworth: Penguin Books, 1969.

Wesson, Robert. *The Aging of Communism.* New York: Praeger, 1980.

White, [Douglas] Gordon. *The Politics of Class and Class Origin: The Case of the Cultural Revolution.* Canberra: The Australian National University, 1976.

———. "Social Inequality and Distributive Politics in China, 1949-1969." Unpublished Ph.D. dissertation, Stanford University, 1977.

White, Lynn T., III. *Careers in Shanghai.* Berkeley: University of California Press, 1978.

Whyte, Martin King. *Small Groups and Political Rituals in China.* Berkeley: University of California Press, 1974.

Wills, Morris. "Peking University." Unpublished manuscript.

Wolf, Eric R. "Kinship, Friendship, and Patron-Client Relations in Complex Societies." *The Social Anthropology of Complex Societies.* Edited by Michael Banton. London: Tavistock Publications, 1966.

Woodward, Susan Lampland. "Socialization for Self-Management in Yugoslav Schools." *Comparative Communism.* Edited by Gary K. Bertsch and Thomas W. Ganschow. San Francisco: W. H. Freeman, 1976.

World Bank. *China: Socialist Economic Development.* Annex G: Education Sector, 1981.

Yeh Sheng-tao. *Schoolmaster Ni Huan-chih.* Beijing: Foreign Languages Press, 1958.

Yen, Maria. *The Umbrella Garden.* Delhi: Naochetan Press, 1954.

Zaslavsky, Victor. "Socioeconomic Inequality and Changes in Soviet Ideology." *Theory and Society,* 9, No. 2 (March 1980), 383-407.

Zysman, John. *Political Strategies for Industrial Order, State, Market, and Industry in France.* Berkeley: University of California Press, 1977.

Index

Academic achievement: among criteria for higher education, 41, 48, 53, 65; influence of class background on, 65; methods to promote, 170–172; vs. political requirements for higher education, 42, 44–47, 65–66, 78; respect and prestige of, 106–108, 110, 172; as a strategy choice, 63–65, 70–71, 75, 98

Academic competition: compared to group cooperation, 158, 159; compared to political competition, 108, 174–178; individual contests in, 169–172, 173; and national entrance examinations, 46, 161, 189; objective criteria for, 174–175, 176; social relations influenced by, 162–163, 174–178; in the United States, 156–157

Academic cooperation, 161–165, 167; cheating, 163, 164–165; ideological inconsistency in, 163; student attitudes toward, 162–163

Activists, political. See Political activists

Adult education, 35

Adult organizations, and behavior in socialist systems, 180–181

Affirmative action, 16; and class label policies, 48, 49–50; for educational opportunity, 44, 46

Age: for formation of close friendships, 137; for university enrollment, 44,45

Agricultural work: attitudes toward, 41, 202; cooperation among students during, 158, 160, 161; education for, 33–34; urban youth

assigned to, 27, 29–30. See also Rural transfer program

Agriculture, modernization of, 28–29

Alienation, 2–3; caused by virtuocracy, 12, 14, 18, 20; of political activists, 70, 73–74, 84, 96, 112, 118–120, 122–125

American education, 156–157

Anti-competitive ethic, 154–157, 170, 173. See also Cooperation

Anti-Rightist Campaign, 188n

Army recruitment policies, 49, 69

Arts, as a strategy choice, 63. See also Cultural activities

Asch, S. E., 127n

Athletics: combined with academic achievement, 71; cooperation promoted by, 158, 159, 160; as a strategy choice, 63; student respect for achievement in, 108–109; winners of sports contests, 160–161

Athletic schools, 13n, 59

"Backbone elements," 87, 120

Bauer, Raymond, 199

Behavior in communist and socialist systems, 4–7; approaches to understanding of, 5–7; effect of variables in the incentive structure on, 180–181; impact of political educational policies on, 56–62; impact of revolutionary political policies on, xi–xii; influence of career opportunities and future expectations on, 57–62; motivations of, xii, 7. See also